The Intelligent Citizen's Guide to

THE POSTAL PROBLEM

Carleton Library Series No. 154

The Intelligent Citizen's Guide to
THE POSTAL PROBLEM

Lawrence M. Read

Carleton University Press
Ottawa, Canada
1988

ISBN 0-88629-081-3

Printed and bound in Canada

Canadian Cataloguing in Publication Data

Read, Lawrence M., 1919-
   The intelligent citizen's guide to the postal problem: A case study of industrial society in crisis, 1965-1980

(The Carleton library ; 154)
ISBN 0-88629-081-3

   1. Postal service—Canada.   I. Title.   II. Series.

HE6655.R43   1988   385′.4971   C88-090399-6

Distributed by: Oxford University Press Canada,
                70 Wynford Drive,
                Don Mills, Ontario,
                Canada. M3C 1J9
                (416) 441-2941

Cover design: Chris Jackson

ACKNOWLEDGEMENTS
Carleton University Press gratefully acknowledges the support extended to its publishing programme by the Canada Council and the Ontario Arts Council.

The publication of this book was aided by a grant given by the Dean of the Faculty of Arts of Carleton University.

Thanks are also due to the Carleton University Department of Religion — specifically the Edgar and Dorothy Davidson Fund in Religious Studies — for the grant given to assist publication. Professor Read was a founding member of the Department of Religion, and a part of it for many years.

TO
FRANCES

Contents

Acknowledgements

I wish to acknowledge my indebtedness to H. L. Griffin, who was seconded from the post office in June 1980 to the Institute of Canadian Studies, Carleton University, to do a study of the history of labour-management relations in the post office. Mr. Griffin was appointed Director of Personnel for the Ontario region of Canada Post when it was first established in 1970 and was, therefore, in a good position to observe the tensions that arose on both sides of the labour-management relationship. His advice at all points has been appreciated. I am particularly indebted to his contribution as source for the historical account of Chapter 8.

I also wish to acknowledge my deep indebtedness to T. K. Rymes of Carleton University who discussed various chapters with me at some length. Professor Rymes applied his considerable argumentative skills with force and at all times displayed a deep passion for academic excellence. However, for the follies which still remain I publicly absolve him.

The contribution made to the study by numerous past and present employees of the post office whom Mr. Griffin and I interviewed is considerable. We had lengthy discussions with many senior postal officials, from Walter Turnbull to J. C. Corkery. We also interviewed many union leaders from both national and regional levels. I especially wish to thank those postal employees who worked with me for some weeks developing consistent series spanning three decades.

To Roger Bouvier go special thanks for his highly significant story in Chapter 4.

Finally, I wish to thank those who read the whole manuscript at various stages: A. D. Dunton, D. W. Slater, D. H. Fullerton, A. Kielland, and W. A. T. White. Their suggestions have led to significant improvements in the presentation of the study.

PART 1

INTRODUCTION

CHAPTER 1

A Preliminary Word to the Intelligent Citizen

In a book that intends to say something about a crisis in motivation, it is appropriate that the author make clear what his own intentions are. In 1976–77 I spent a sabbatical year in London and, although I was not formally studying the contemporary situation, I was much impressed—indeed, depressed—by evidence of what economists were coming to call "the British disease." A primary symptom of this disease was that workers to an alarming extent were not interested in working, and managers to a disturbing extent were afraid to manage. Correlated with this symptom in the case of the workers was a generally antagonistic attitude to management. This attitude was intellectually grounded in the theory that in the competitive, free-enterprise system the workers are ruthlessly exploited in the interests of the private owners. Furthermore, the attitude was institutionally grounded in a system of labour unions set up to serve the workers' interests and arrayed adversarially against management. In this context management felt much "unloved" and morally on the defensive. Hedged about by a labyrinthian set of rules deposited by exhaustive labour-management agreements, management was unable to manage or, where able, was made hypersensitive to the perils of introducing anything new in an antagonistic, adversarially organized workplace.

A curious aspect of the course of the British disease was that when important sectors of British industry were socialized—removing these sectors from exploitation by private owners—the disease did not abate, but became even more virulent. Workers became even more indifferent to work and managers even more timid in managing. It began to appear that the socialized sector of the economy was more vulnerable to the disease than was the private, capitalist sector.

When I returned to Canada in the fall of 1977 I was struck by the idea that what was happening in Canada Post was a clear case of the British disease. The disease had jumped the Atlantic! If so, someone should study the case with great care in the hope that something could be done about it. In 1978 I accepted a transfer within Carleton University to the Institute of Canadian Studies to make such a study. The study as I envisaged it was not only an examination of an isolated public institution in crisis, but an exploration of some of the basic issues facing contemporary industrial society.

My own formal training and professional experience has been in two fields: economics and philosophy of religion. Somewhat to my own surprise I found in the postal scene matters of absorbing interest to myself both as an economist and as a philosopher of religion. What I discovered were three diverse but interrelated crises: an economic crisis, a crisis in community, and a spiritual crisis. The symptoms of the first two were all too evident: on the one hand, a disastrous fall in productivity, and on the other hand, a succession of acrimonious strikes. The spiritual crisis was somewhat less obvious, but nonetheless significant.

We mean by "spiritual" in this context that which is concerned with ultimate meaning, with "the chief end of man," with the ultimate good. The renowned sociologist Max Weber argued in his work *The Protestant Ethic and the Spirit of Capitalism* that commitment to the Christian—especially the Protestant—view of the ultimate good has contributed to the "industriousness" that was essential to the development of the modern industrial system. Protestants were industrious not only for the sake of acquiring more and more economic goods, but for the sake of the ultimate good as well. However, the 1960s and 1970s were decades in which more and more uncertainty was being expressed—especially among the youth—concerning traditional values. In the postal time of troubles the Protestant ethic was conspicuous by its absence. On the other hand, increasingly visible was a small minority committed to an alternative vision of the ultimate good. Central to this vision was the prophecy of a great struggle between the exploiters and the exploited, culminating in the liberation of the exploited and the establishment of a classless society. The new ethic for the interim period of struggle was not industrious participation in the common efforts of the productive unit, but rather persistent application to the promotion of the class war. Again, not the acquisition of economic goods but the pursuit of an ultimate good was the primary motivation. Here, however, the pursuit of the ultimate good contributed not to the upbuilding of the modern industrial order, but to its present, although intentionally only interim, breakdown. In a context of widespread uncertainty with respect to an ultimate good, a very small minority passionately committed to a new vision of the ultimate good can have a remarkable impact. For this reason the attention paid in this study to the impact of the Marxian ethic is not a digression.

The author confesses further to a predilection for a mixed economy for Canada at this point in its history. We owe a great deal to the competitive, free-enterprise system. It has promoted a remarkable improvement in productivity and real incomes. However, the dynamics of the system itself have promoted a concentration of economic power and hence a cutback in competition. In this context the intervention of government in the economy is highly desirable. On the other hand, a completely socialist alternative to a competitive, free-enterprise system also has its drawbacks. A socialized economy does not do away with the fact that different groups are differently affected by economic changes. In the socialized system response to economic changes is determined by political and bureaucratic decisions. However, at the end of the twentieth century we are far enough along the road in experience of socialist administrations to know that these political/bureaucratic decisions are not always wiser or more humane than the outcome that would have been imposed by a competitive, free-enterprise system. Also it is becoming clearer that political or bureaucratic office is as potent a medium whereby certain persons can exercise control over other persons in their own interests or those of their class as is the medium of private ownership of the means of production.

In this context the author prefers an open society with a mixed economy where politicians, bureaucrats, corporate managers, and union leaders may be praised or blamed according to their effective contribution in what is *currently* taking place. A mixed economy is untidy because no group is in complete control; but precisely because no group is in complete control it is highly desirable. If what has been happening in the post office were to spread to Canadian industry in general, our remarkably successful mixed economy would be in deep trouble.

CHAPTER 2

An Introduction to the Postal Problem

Canadians born before World War II can well remember the exceptionally good postal service that Canada enjoyed in the first two decades after the war. During the period 1945 to 1957, when Walter Turnbull as deputy postmaster general directed the flow of mail across Canada with no uncertain hand, Canada had, perhaps, the finest postal system in the world. "All up" had been introduced in 1948—that is, all first-class mail was transmitted by air whenever such transmission speeded up the service. Over the vast expanse of Canada the mail moved with surprising speed, reliability, and economic efficiency. An important factor in this excellence of service was the devotion of its thousands of employees to the common objective of transmitting the mail as quickly and efficiently as possible. In the annual reports of the department, the deputy postmaster general acknowledged this regularly. The Glassco Royal Commission on Government Organization, reporting in 1962, made some suggestions for reorganization, but noted that "the Post Office staff is conscientious, hard-working and dedicated, and morale is very high. This has enabled the service to function in a highly commendable manner."[1]

It was all the more shocking for Canadians, therefore, when after 1965 the postal service suffered a dramatic decline. The transition was signalled by an unexpected strike of postal workers in the summer of 1965. The strike was led off by Montreal, Vancouver, and Hamilton, but spread quickly to some ninety post offices across Canada. Given the postal workers' high reputation for service and the fact that they had not had a raise in three years, the Canadian public was inclined to sympathize with them. The Public Service Staff Relations Act of 1967 cleared up all uncertainty with respect to the right of federal employees to organize full-fledged unions and to take strike action if deemed necessary in support of their claims. The principal unions of the postal workers were the Canadian Union of Postal Workers (CUPW) and the Letter Carriers Union of Canada (LCUC). The relation of these unions to management became increasingly adversarial. There was a succession of national strikes: one in 1968; a rotating strike in 1970; an illegal strike in 1974; an extended forty-two-day strike in 1975; and further strikes in 1978 and 1981. Interspersed between these major national strikes were something of the order of two hundred and fifty local strikes or work-stoppages, all of which were illegal.

Correlated with these dramatic signs of labour-management tension was a drastic deterioration in postal service. A service that had been noted for its

---

[1] *The Royal Commission on Government Organization* Vol. 3. Ottawa: The Queen's Printer, 1962, p. 342.

consistent reliability and efficiency suffered an abrupt about-face. More and more frequently, mail began to arrive late, parcels arrived damaged, some mail disappeared. Postal users, businesses, and private citizens began to collect their own files of postal horror stories. In image and in fact the post office changed from a model of reliability and efficiency to one of unreliability and inefficiency.

It might have been hoped that more slovenly service would at least cost less per unit of service. The opposite, however, was the case; the poorer service was costing more, a great deal more. By the mid-1970s unit costs were 3.8 times those of 1964–65. In real terms—that is, after adjustment for inflation—unit costs in the mid-1970s were more than double those of 1964–65. This startling increase in real unit costs was the consequence of a dramatic drop of roughly 40 percent in labour productivity combined with an increase in real gross compensation of the bulk of the workers of over 40 percent. Postal workers were clearly getting a great deal more for a great deal less!

Postal rates were increased substantially during this period. By 1972–73 postal rates in general, after allowing for inflation, were 50 percent higher than in 1964–65. Postal rates were then pegged for a few years and postal deficits rose to astronomical heights. By the mid-1970s the annual deficit was over half a billion dollars. Hence the accumulated deficits of the post office over these years accounted for a substantial slice of the national debt.

In 1968 when Eric Kierans was appointed postmaster general, he decided that it was time the post office was dragged kicking and screaming into the twentieth century. An impressive set of studies, summarized as *A Blueprint for Change*, proposed a decentralization of the post office into four regions and a massive program of new plant construction and technological transformation. By 1979 the program was substantially completed. The program, costing in the vicinity of a billion dollars, put Canada at the forefront among the mechanized postal systems of the world. What it also did, however, during the period of implementation, was to accentuate further most of the basic postal problems. Since that time it has helped to hold the line more or less on productivity— whatever comfort one can draw from that after the drastic drop of the previous decade. In general, however, Canada Post's bold plan of modernization has not proved—at least not yet—an outstanding success.

It would seem clear that the postal problem has its centre in labour-management relations. But precisely what it is that is causing the problem here is more difficult to discern. Our hypothesis, or set of interrelated hypotheses, is the following:

(1) An advance in affluence, and especially a rapid advance, tends to produce apathy and hence a fall in motivation to work. The postal time of troubles coincided with the latter years of a period of remarkable advance in affluence in Canada.

(2) An insufficient challenge to human agency tends to produce alienation in the workplace. Efforts to improve efficiency in the post office in the 1950s and 1960s tended on the whole to reduce the challenge to worker agency. Moreover,

the massive technological transformation in the 1970s was planned and implemented largely without regard for the agency-sufficiency of the jobs required by the new technology. Consequently, postal workers in general have suffered agency-insufficiency.

(3) Organizations set up to promote the common good nonetheless provide opportunities for those in authority to follow the "power principle," that is, to use their powers of agency to promote their own good whether or not the interests of others are also served. Pursuit of the power principle by those in authority tends to evoke, among those working under authority, a consciousness of being exploited. The unexpected postal strike of 1965 and the poor labour-management relations thereafter were based on the consciousness of the postal workers that they were being unjustly treated by their employer, the federal government. The Public Service Staff Relations Act of 1967, in effect, recognized that workers' claims of unjust treatment by those in authority may sometimes be true even in the federal civil service.

(4) Worker organizations set up to promote the common good of the workers also provide opportunities for the leaders to follow the power principle. The activities of the postal unions in the 1970s were sometimes oriented more toward consolidating and extending the power of the unions—and hence the power of the union leaders—than to serving the fundamental interests of the postal workers.

(5) Organizations set up on an highly adversarial basis tend to transform themselves into the mirror-image of the adversary. For example, CUPW, the most adversarially minded of the postal unions, showed minimal regard for the interests of others—for other postal unions, Canada Post as a productive unit, other Canadian workers, and the Canadian public generally—and as the many illegal strikes indicate, showed minimal regard for fulfilling the letter or intent of its own contractual agreements. That is, the union was illustrating in its own activities the kind of insensitivity that it claimed made management utterly untrustworthy.

(6) Workers are motivated by their own good, but also by the common good and even an ultimate good. An unconditional commitment to an ultimate good constitutes an ethic that, if followed even by a small minority, may have remarkable consequences for any organization. The absence in the postal time of troubles of what Max Weber called the Protestant ethic, and the presence here and there of what we shall call the Marxian ethic and the Québécois ethic, have had significant consequences for the post office.

(7) Postal management in its time of troubles was weakened by division. The rapid changes on the labour side called for perceptive, unified action on the side of management. However, it was not at all easy to perceive what was producing the radical change in worker behaviour. University staffs, for example, were as bewildered as postal managers when the students behaved quited differently in this same period. Moreover, it was not at all easy to achieve unified action. That part of the overall management that was most sensitive to a particular issue did

not always have the power to do anything about it. The wage dispute in 1965, for instance, probably would not have aggravated a strike if the post office had been a crown corporation at the time, that is, if postal management, which was well aware of the problem, had had the power to decide the issue. In fact, management in this instance was dependent on the belated decisions of Treasury Board, the legal employer of the postal workers.

Management was further divided within itself by differences in basic orientation. Many of the traditional managers were inclined to be offended not only by the new mood of the workers, but also by the lack of respect for their seasoned judgment shown by the modernizing managers whom Eric Kierans brought into the post office in the early 1970s to implement *A Blueprint for Change*. They were, therefore, less eager and perhaps less able than they otherwise would have been to save the new senior management from their mistakes. The major mistake of the modernizers was that they grossly underestimated the importance of the new orientation of the workers and the ability of workers so oriented and so situated to confound the best laid plans of engineers. As the 1970s progressed they were inclined in exasperation to take more seriously the advice of more co-operative-minded managers in personnel. However, this last group suffered from support given too late and too little, and in general from suspicion seeping in from all sides.

These factors contributing to the postal problem are a matter of concern to the intelligent citizen because of what they have done to an outstanding postal service and what they have done to postal employees. However, they also have a wider significance.

(1) The enhancement of worker apathy and alienation in the 1960s and 1970s was not confined to the post office. Individual private enterprises could not give way easily to an increasing apathy and alienation among their workers because they could be so quickly run out of business by their competitors. However, as the effect of enhanced apathy and alienation gradually seeped into the private sector, individual enterprises could give way somewhat because their competitors were being similarly affected. Thus, in time, a damper on productivity began to be felt in the economy as a whole in spite of continuing improvements in technology. A declining rate of improvement in productivity, and even an absolute decline in productivity, became an overall problem for the Canadian economy.

(2) The failure of Canadian labour unions in general to *understand* their own fundamental interests is a matter of deep concern not only for labour, but for all Canadians. Alienation and productivity are correlated issues of fundamental but generally unacknowledged importance to Canadian workers. Alienation is a fundamental concern because it means that the workers are not enjoying normal, human satisfactions from their work. This, in the long run, is much more important to the enjoyment of life than the usually contentious issue of current wage rates. However, postal unions have tended to regard alienation not as a fundamental problem to be resolved through sustained and concerted effort

in co-operation with management, but rather as a symbol of the ill-will of management and a welcome spur to union solidarity and strength.

The correlated issue of productivity is a fundamental concern for labour because of what we might call the new iron law of wages. The traditional iron law of wages, introduced by the English classical economists and picked up by Marx, sought to establish that real wages tend to settle at a subsistence level, that is, at a level just sufficient to sustain the workers and their families. Since real wages in the industrial West are now a healthy multiple of a subsistence level, the law clearly no longer applies. What we are calling the new iron law of wages is the tendency in the economy as a whole for real wages to correspond with productivity in such a way that the percentage change in real wages tends to equal the percentage change in productivity. The law acts simply: a percentage change in money wages in excess of the percentage change in productivity will tend to promote inflation, thereby reducing the real value of money wages until for the economy as a whole the percentage change in real wages equals the percentage change in productivity. The iron law applies to the workers as a whole, but not to a particular group. This means that a particular union can divorce itself from the question of productivity and grab as it can a higher real wage; but workers as a whole across the nation cannot. Ignoring the interests of all other workers in Canada, the postal unions have refused to be concerned with productivity and have treated it exclusively as a management problem.

(3) If the encounter between labour and management in Canada Post becomes the model for the Canadian economy generally, then the mixed economy that has been so remarkably successful in Canada in recent decades is in deep trouble. Alienation will be accentuated, labour-management relations pushed consciously toward greater antagonism, productivity dampened, the pressure for higher wages increased, the tempo of inflation accelerated and, if a tight money policy is maintained to combat inflation, a major recession with massive unemployment and widespread business failure will be produced. This interrelated chain of consequences is basically a matter of economic arithmetic: something we cannot escape.

The above set of hypotheses represents judgments about the character of contemporary Canadian society that some, but not all, intelligent citizens will find *make sense*. This draws to our attention a basic intellectual problem that is particularly important in a study of this kind. The problem is that we typically perceive, think, and talk about a particular matter within a conceptual framework that guides and shapes but also definitely limits our perception, thinking, and talking about this matter. Although it is theoretically possible to go beyond that framework and to approach the matter from another point of view, we nevertheless find it exceedingly difficult to do so in practice. The framework in question is itself the product of experience and thought; hence, what concerns us here is how experience and thought guide and constrain further experience and thought. The framework is a set of concepts that the thinker presupposes catches the fundamental structure of the matter at hand.

For "framework" we may substitute the word "model." The thinker proceeds to think about a matter in terms of the model that he or she presupposes is appropriate to it.

The following incident illustrates the problem. In 1969 I happened to be for a few days in Kabul, Afghanistan. One morning I observed a street vendor selling his wares, which included a conserve of some sort with a striking cranberry colour. As I watched he spooned some of this onto a leaf and sold it to a passer-by. Then he paused, looked at his spoon, which had obviously got a bit sticky, and sluiced the spoon vigorously in the open sewer running at his feet. I recoiled a bit in horror; the vendor proceeded amiably with his business.

What the vendor "saw" and what I "saw" were obviously the same thing: the spoon sluiced in the open sewer. But just as obviously, what he "saw" and what I "saw" were quite different: he saw a spoon getting cleaned; I saw a spoon becoming contaminated, with the possibility that somebody would be infested with this or that terrible disease. The difference in the beholding lay in the difference in the models brought to the beholding by the street vendor and myself.

The difficulty here is emphasized if we imagine what might have happened if I had immediately tried to bridge the gap between us and remonstrated with the vendor for contaminating the spoon. Let us suppose he had the patience to respond, held up the spoon and said, "Show me!" The difficulty is that the spoon is *clean*—apparently. The process of proof is then a complex one involving at the minimum a good microscope and finally faith in the reports of a succession of scientific investigations that neither the vendor nor myself have the time or resources to repeat. That is, in order to show the vendor what I "saw" I would have to convert him to my model of seeing such things. A tough assignment in the circumstances!

T. S. Kuhn in his influential work *The Structure of Scientific Revolutions* discusses this problem in terms of "paradigms," another word meaning "models." Scientific evolution takes place within accepted paradigms. Scientific revolutions take place only through conversion to new paradigms.

The matter is relevant to the study of the postal problem because quite different models of seeing are brought to bear on it. What is at stake is important and the models are taken very seriously by the masters of the models. The models, for example, of some of the union radicals on the one side and of some of the traditional postal managers on the other side are about as far apart as that of the Kabul street vendor and myself. What is sanitizing for one is contaminating for the other. Around these mutually incompatible models many others weave in and out. It is not easy, therefore, to approach postal issues in a relaxed manner or with a no-nonsense, "let's call a spade a spade" frankness. The following three incidents illustrate the problem.

In the summer of 1980 I had an interesting interview with a leader of the Canadian Union of Postal Workers in Halifax. As we began, he said he would be glad to talk to me, but that if I said anything in my study against the union they would *clobber* me. As I started to say, "I expect that!" he interjected hurriedly, "A joke! A joke!" Although the union leader himself had recently been charged by the post office with assaulting a postal official, it *was* a joke. However, it was a joke with a point: there was to be no doubt whatsoever where he stood in the battle of postal workers against postal management.

The incident symbolizes the stance of the postal unions and in particular that of CUPW, which has been self-consciously radically adversarial since 1974. It symbolizes more: a significant segment of the academic community that is expert in Canadian labour matters—historians, economists, sociologists, political scientists—is also self-consciously radically adversarial. This latter group does not represent a random sample of Canadian academic viewpoints: those who are already committed to a position are drawn to this field. My own study also intends to be pro-labour—that is, to help workers to see where their fundamental interests lie. However, to the extent that I criticize the radically adversarial stance—as indeed I intend—I expect to be "clobbered" by radical-minded unionists and academics alike.

Sometime later I talked with an economist at postal headquarters in Ottawa who I understood had had something to do with assessing postal productivity. It turned out that he had been involved with the assessment of particular postal processes, but not with overall, global performance. However, I explained to him how I had made my global estimates and told him I would appreciate any criticism he or his colleagues might have to offer. He was shocked at my results and told me that if the productivity drop was of that order the situation was serious indeed. He promised to consider the matter over the next few days. When I called him by phone a few days later his mood had radically altered. My results were obviously wrong. The drop that I indicated in productivity had not occurred. Did I for a moment think that an enterprise of the size of Canada Post did not know what was happening to its productivity? My trouble clearly was that I was another of these blankety-blank university professors who thought he knew it all. If I published results like that they would make mincemeat out of me!

The attitude was oddly out of keeping with the co-operation I normally received from postal headquarters. However, one can appreciate the sort of tension that accumulates over time for staff on the management side as they are beset by chronically hostile unions on the one hand and an increasingly critical public on the other. This study intends to be pro-management in the same sense as it is pro-labour—that is, to say something relevant about management's basic concerns. However, a management that presides over a 40 percent drop in productivity in one decade can scarcely expect to be praised. The economist's reaction perhaps symbolizes the response I can expect from a significant segment of management as "yet another" critical study of the postal problem appears.

A third incident is amusing in the light of the two just mentioned. Earlier I had an interesting exchange with a federal government department that sometimes gave grants for private research of the type I was proposing. They indicated some interest in the project, but said, "We would want to be assured that the study we support would not be an aggravation to either party," that is, to either management or unions. One reading of this—my own—was that it was a prescription for innocuousness. My inclination was to expect that the "truth"— whatever that might be—would in the circumstance be an aggravation to *both* parties. However, one can also understand that a federal department would not want to finance a critical study that might inflame the already highly adversarial labour-management relationship within another federal department.

One might, nonetheless, take the incident to symbolize something more far-reaching: the tendency for Canadians to sweep under the political mat what we do not want to face up to. After some decades of political evolution it is now generally politic to criticize corporate management individually or collectively. If we are to promote and sustain our successful mixed economy it is very important that it be equally politic to criticize unions individually or collectively. But where among our political parties is there exercised an equal freedom to criticize both management and unions? The New Democratic Party freely criticizes corporations, but as the unions' party it has sold its right to criticize the unions openly. Since most workers still vote for the Liberals or Conservatives, these parties are loath to "be an aggravation" to either management or unions. The consequence is that the unions in particular are lacking that kind of open political criticism that would help them to assume a mature, responsible role in a modern mixed economy.

A general assumption of this study is that labour unions are older than they think: they are *mature* partners in the mixed economy and therefore must expect serious criticism from time to time, as must all senior partners. Neither labour unions, nor corporate management, nor government officials, nor their academic critics have a corner on the social truth. We must all learn to take our knocks, unions included, and to learn from them.

The problem, however, remains: each of us typically perceives, thinks, and talks about the postal problem within a framework or model that we presuppose is appropriate to it. To the extent that our models are incompatible with each other, our perceptions and our thinking and talking about what has been happening in Canada Post will tend to be incompatible. We will not make much sense to each other. However, one of the dimensions of intelligence is its capacity to go beyond, to transcend, previously established limits. Indeed, to grasp any limit with our intelligence we must in some sense grasp what goes beyond that limit, what is on the other side of that limit, as well. To know what something *is* we must know something about what it *is not*. The models of which we have been speaking constitute a set of limits that give our seeing, thinking, and speaking a certain character. It is not a mark of human intelligence to be without character; but it is a mark of human intelligence to understand something of its own character. For such understanding it is essential that intelligence also explore beyond its characteristic limits; to understand our own model well we must also understand what it would mean to have some different model. It may be for some that this study will serve as an opportunity to explore beyond characteristic model-limits.

A further characteristic of this study may be noted: the discussion jumps the boundaries of many disciplines. Part 2 is concerned with the economic performance of Canada Post and the significance of this performance in relation to that of the Canadian economy as a whole. Part 3 is concerned with the crisis in motivation in the post office and with matters as diverse as the nature of human nature in general, the cause of apathy and alienation, the adoption of adversarial and antipathetic attitudes by the new public service unions, and the impact of the ethics of Marxism and of the Quiet Revolution in Quebec. We are involved, therefore, with matters that concern economists, sociologists, political scientists, psychologists, philosophers, and philosophers of religion.

The defence of this approach is a simple one: in human relations problems do not stop conveniently at disciplinary boundaries. If as specialists we analyze a problem and then, as the discussion begins to become really interesting, we label it a "political question," or a "psychological question," or a "philosophical question"—implying that our intellectual pursuit stops short at that point—it may be that we have so hedged ourselves in that we are prevented from ever engaging the problem in its essential wholeness. Our contention is that a good generalist purview is essential in order to put the specialist's analysis in appropriate perspective. Otherwise the specialist does not know the real significance of his or her limits and is apt at crucial points to be led astray.

Part 4 of this study dares to make alternative proposals concerning the organization of the post office. Like most proposals the strength of these alternatives depends on the appropriateness of the analyses on which they are based. Long ago, Plato pointed out that there are two groups of people who might be expected to have some critical judgment concerning houses: one, those who build them; and, two, those who live in them. It is not ruled out, therefore, that postal users may make relevant proposals for the reform of the postal system. It follows, of course, that either one of our proposals is easier said than done. Although the many will benefit, a few both in management and in union leadership will lose something by it. Hence, as simple as the proposals may be, it will take a unique combination of intelligence and social courage to put either one in place.

PART 2

AN ECONOMIC ANALYSIS

CHAPTER 3

The Economic Performance of Canada Post

3.1 A Preview

This chapter will assess the economic performance of Canada Post in the post-war period. The focus is on the fifteen-year period 1964–65 to 1979–80 in which performance deteriorated badly and continued low in spite of the massive technological revolution introduced in the 1970s. The previous fifteen-year period, 1949–50 to 1964–65, is assessed in order to put Canada Post's "time of troubles" in perspective.

Two things may be noted about the statistical analyses of this chapter. First, a great deal of use is made of indexes. For example, since productivity has to do with output per unit of input, productivity indexes are derived by first calculating output indexes and input indexes (using the same base year) and then dividing the former by the latter. (We may note that since an index is a ratio multiplied by 100, the arithmetical value of an index is always the index divided by 100.) Second, two pairs of input and productivity indexes are calculated. The one pair is the labour input and the labour productivity indexes; the other pair is the total input and the total-input productivity indexes.

Frequently, when the term productivity is used, what is meant is labour productivity, that is, output per unit of labour input. However, for most economic comparisons what is needed is total-input productivity, that is, input per unit of total input. This becomes evident: (1) when the relative contributions of secondary inputs differ, that is, when the relative contributions of raw materials and intermediate products purchased from other producers differ; and (2) when the relative contributions of labour and non-labour primary inputs differ, that is, when the relative contributions of real capital used differ. For example, in the 1970s Canada Post took over certain urban trucking services previously contracted out (thereby lowering the relative contribution of secondary inputs) and also implemented a technological transformation (thereby increasing the relative contribution of non-labour inputs). Consequently, only the total-input productivity indexes are relevant here for long-term comparisons. Similarly, in comparing the performances of Canada Post and the U.S. Postal Service, only the total-input productivity indexes are relevant since there are significant differences between the two systems in contracting-out practices and in the relative contributions of non-labour inputs.

The difficulty with moving to a total-input approach to productivity is that economists are not yet in agreement on how non-labour inputs may be made commensurate with labour inputs. Professor T. K. Rymes has been showing us for years how this may be done,[1] but in economics, as in other disciplines,

---

[1]See Alexandra Cas and Thomas K. Rymes, *On Concept and Measures of Multifactor Productivity in Canada* (Cambridge: Cambridge University Press, forthcoming.)

19

practitioners are slow to adopt new paradigms. The attempt is made in this study to approximate the Rymes measure of total-input productivity. Appendix A discusses in some detail both this approach and the approximations made for this study.

The total-input approach is important not only in assessing productivity changes in Canada Post (see section 3.2) and in making a rather unflattering comparison with the U.S. Postal Service (section 3.5), but also in setting forth Canada Post's links with the Canadian economy (sections 3.3 and 3.4). The *real* wages that Canada Post was called upon to pay were closely tied to productivity: not, however, to the productivity of Canada Post, but rather to the productivity of the Canadian economy as a whole. Hence, in the post-1964 period constant-dollar unit costs in Canada Post were shoved upward by *improvements* in the productivity of the Canadian economy (bringing in their wake corresponding increases in real wages throughout the economy) and pushed further upward by the *fall* in Canada Post's own productivity. That is, constant-dollar unit costs for Canada Post tended to vary directly with productivity in the Canadian economy and inversely with its own productivity. Hence, the index of Canada Post's constant-dollar unit costs varied with

$$\frac{\text{the index of productivity of the Canadian economy}}{\text{the index of productivity of Canada Post}}$$

which is the reciprocal of what we might call Canada Post's comparative productivity index. The relevant comparison here, it may be noted, is of total-input productivities.

It is important that intelligent citizens, whether working in the post office or merely using its services, should comprehend the strong links that bind Canada Post and the Canadian economy together. For example, however militant the postal unions may become in pushing for higher *real* wages, their long-term prospects are poor indeed *unless* the Canadian economy as a whole improves its productivity. The other side of the coin is that productivity in Canada Post is a part determinant of productivity in the Canadian economy and, therefore, a part determinant of the real wages of all Canadians. If all enterprises had followed the lead of Canada Post, the impact on real incomes throughout the economy would have been disastrous. Reflections on this point should be equally disturbing to intelligent managers and unionists both inside and outside the post office.

3.2 Output, Input, and Productivity in Canada Post

Table 3.2A summarizes changes in the output of Canada Post together with changes in population and number of households in Canada for the fifteen years before and the fifteen years after 1964–65 (the year before the turning-point in postal performance). In the earlier fifteen-year period the population rose impressively by more than 40 percent, reflecting especially the post-war baby boom. At the same time, the number of households and the volume of mail handled by Canada Post both rose by over 50 percent. In the later fifteen-year

Table 3.2A Population, Number of Households, and Volume of Postal Services, Canada, 1949–50 to 1979–80

	Population	Number of Households	Volume of Mail	Volume of Mail plus Other Postal Services
	(1)	(2)	(3)	(4)
1949–50 = 100				
1949–50	100	100	100	100
1954–55	114	114	111	112
1959–60	130	132	134	134
1964–65	143	151	151	151
1964–65 = 100				
1964–65	100	100	100	100
1969–70	109	116	104	104
1974–75	116	136	111	108
1979–80	123	159	121	117

Source: Columns (1) and (2), *Canada Year Book*; columns (3) and (4), based on data provided by Canada Post.

period the population explosion subsided to roughly half its earlier rate of expansion, the number of households again rose by over 50 percent, but the volume of mail rose only modestly and in fact less proportionately than population.

Table 3.2B summarizes changes in the volume of mail and other postal services by major classes. The index numbers shown are "peculiar" in the sense that the base for *all* figures is "total mail, 1964–65." The advantage of this form is that the indexes may be compared in magnitude class by class as well as year by year. The underlying figures before transformation into index numbers are numbers of pieces handled multiplied by average cost per piece in 1971–72. Calculations were made for twelve to sixteen sub-classes of mail.

First-class mail includes "letters, postcards and other articles, paid at first class rates and receiving preferred handling throughout the service."[2] The post office enjoys a statutory monopoly of the transmission of letters. As the table indicates, this is clearly the most important and dynamic category of mail. The rate of expansion of first-class mail has been much higher than that of other mail: in the earlier fifteen-year period the expansion was over 80 percent and in the later fifteen-year period over 60 percent. Indeed, in the later period first-class mail accounted for what expansion there was since the weighted total of all mail other than first class fell by over 10 percent. By 1979–80 first-class mail constituted almost 60 percent of total weighted mail.

Second-class mail covers newspapers and periodicals mailed by publishers and newsdealers. As the table indicates, this class has constituted a relatively static component of postal operations.

---

[2]Definition supplied by Canada Post.

Table 3.2B Volume of Postal Services, Weighted, by Classes, 1949–50 to 1979–80

	First	Second	Third	Fourth	Special Mail Services	Total Mail	Non-Mail Services
				Total Mail 1964–65 = 100			
1949–50	24	10	14	12	7	66	4
1954–55	30	10	15	13	6	74	5
1959–60	37	10	19	16	6	89	5
1964–65	44	12	20	18	7	100	6
1969–70	52	10	19	16	7	104	6
1974–75	63	8	16	15	9	111	4
1979–80	71	9	20	11	9	121	3

Note: Index numbers shown are unique in form in that the base for *all* figures is "total mail, 1964–65."
Source: Based on data provided by Canada Post.

Third-class mail includes printed matter of various sorts, e.g., advertising materials, books mailed by distributors, etc. As a class it has frequently been disparaged as junk mail. There was a steady increase in this category of mail in the earlier fifteen-year period, a substantial falling off in the first decade of the later period, and some recovery in the late 1970s.

Fourth-class mail is parcel post. Parcel post expanded along with other mail in the earlier period, but declined by over one-third in the later period. There is little doubt that poor service, i.e., unreliability and higher risk of damage, affected parcel volumes. Mail order retail business, for example, was adversely affected. Parcel post, which constituted 18 percent of weighted volume of mail in 1964–65, fell to less than 10 percent fifteen years later.

Special mail services include C.O.D., registered mail, special delivery, etc. Also included in the figures here is a small amount of mail carried "free" for members of Parliament. Special mail services have constituted a relatively small but steady category of mail service in both periods.

"Non-mail" services of the post office include among other things money orders and savings bank services. The phasing out of savings bank operations after 1968 contributed to the decline in this category of services in the 1970s.

Table 3.2C summarizes changes in labour, transportation, and other inputs for Canada Post over the two fifteen-year periods. The index numbers shown are again "peculiar" in the sense that the base for all figures is "total input, 1964–65." Hence, the inputs may be compared in magnitude category by category as well as year by year. "Labour input" includes the input of all employees working directly for Canada Post. "Transportation input" represents the input of enterprises with which Canada Post has contracted for the transport of mail by rail, land, air, or water (see, however, the note to the table respecting urban trucking services taken over by Canada Post early in the 1970s). "Other input" reflects outlays on machinery, equipment, supplies, and foreign settle-

Table 3.2C Volume of Inputs, Weighted, Canada Post, 1949–50 to 1979–80

| | | Total Input 1964–65 = 100 | | | |
	Labour Input	Transportation Input	Other Input	Total Input	Total Output 1964–65 = 100
1949–50	47	26	6	79	66
1954–55	54	27	5	85	74
1959–60	61	28	5	94	89
1964–65	68	28	5	100	100
1969–70	86	28	6	121	104
1974–75	115	25	12	152	108
1979–80	130	28	16	174	117

Notes: 1. Input index numbers shown are unique in that the base year for *all* figures is "total input, 1964–65."
2. In the early 1970s Canada Post took over urban trucking services earlier contracted out. To ensure comparability, labour input in urban trucking in the 1970s is included under transportation input rather than labour input.

Source: Based on data provided by Canada Post.

ments. The underlying figures before transformation into index numbers are, in the case of labour input, categories of salaries paid deflated by appropriate indexes of salary rates. Calculations were made for four or five categories of employees. The underlying figures for transportation and other inputs are expenditures by Canada Post in these categories deflated by the index of average compensation per person in the Canadian economy. (Adjustments were made respecting expenditures on machinery and equipment in order to approximate "current account" as distinct from "capital account" outlays.)

A remarkable feature of the table is the surprising stability of transportation input over both periods, that is, in spite of the substantial increase in mail carried in the earlier period and the modest increase in the later period. The substantial increase in other (non-labour) input in the 1970s reflects in large part the technological transformation of the postal system in that decade. The second remarkable feature is the great jump in labour input in the later period correlated with the modest increase in postal services of that period. This contrasts sharply with the relatively modest increase in labour input in the earlier period correlated with a much greater expansion in postal services (and, as we shall see, a substantial reduction in hours worked per week). In terms of our measurement of total inputs, labour input increased from less than 60 percent of the total in 1949–50 to roughly 75 percent thirty years later. This rise in share of total inputs means that the improvement in labour productivity in the earlier period is less and the fall in the later period is greater than that of total-input productivity.

Table 3.2D indicates that labour inputs have expanded rapidly in almost all major categories in this later period. The exception is what we have called "revenue offices." This term is used here to represent the small postal offices that have been called, according to arrangements reflecting amounts and kinds of

Table 3.2D Indexes of Volume of Labour Inputs, Weighted, Canada Post, 1964–65 to 1979–80

| | | | Total Input (including non-labour input) 1964–65 = 100 | | | |
	Revenue Offices	Mail Processing	Letter Carriers	Admin. & Other (excl. transp.)	Total Labour (excl. transp.)	Labour in Transportation
1964–65	12.0	29.2	19.6	6.7	67.5	0.2
1965–66	12.2	30.4	20.2	8.1	70.9	0.1
67	12.9	33.0	22.2	8.3	76.3	0.1
68	13.2	34.1	24.2	9.9	81.4	0.2
69	13.0	35.1	24.7	10.6	83.4	0.1
70	13.2	38.4	25.3	9.4	86.4	0.1
1970–71	13.0	38.0	23.9	12.8	87.8	0.1
72	12.7	40.9	25.9	12.6	92.0	1.3
73	12.8	45.1	26.7	15.1	99.6	5.0
74	14.0	46.6	27.2	14.5	102.2	4.4
75	14.8	53.0	30.4	16.7	115.0	4.2
1975–76	15.0	52.1	30.9	17.1	115.1	4.1
77	13.2	60.0	33.1	19.5	125.8	6.4
78	14.7	62.6	34.7	19.9	131.9	6.6
79	14.6	59.9	35.3	19.6	129.4	6.5
80	14.9	58.4	37.1	19.2	129.7	6.8

Source: Based on data provided by Canada Post.

postal business handled, semi-staff post offices, revenue post offices, and sub post offices. The increase in the labour input of such offices was modest in this period. Elsewhere, however, the increases have been far from modest: labour in mail processing doubled; labour in letter carrying almost doubled; and other labour, mostly administration at local, district, regional, and head-office levels, almost tripled.

Table 3.2E and Figure 3.2F present the year-by-year consequences for labour productivity and total-input productivity of the changes in outputs and inputs we have been examining. In general, total-input productivity improved slowly but steadily in the pre-1964–65 period, the rate of growth being slightly over 1 percent per year. Labour productivity improved only slightly in this period.

The occasional dips in productivity in this period are attributable to the following causes: (1) The drop in labour productivity in 1949–50 reflects the reduction in the work week to forty-four hours (presumably from forty-eight hours) for 10,760 revenue offices. Since we assess labor inputs here in terms of person-years or their equivalent, any reduction in the work week tends to reduce accounted productivity. (In this year it also happens that the Newfoundland figures are incorporated for the first time.) (2) The dip in total-input productivity in 1950–51 reflects the impact of the extended rail strike in the summer of 1950

Table 3.2E Outputs, Inputs, and Productivity, Canada Post, 1947–48 to 1979–80

	Total Output	Labour Input	Total Input	Labour Prod. (1) ÷ (2)	Total-Input Prod. (1) ÷ (3)
	1964–65 = 100				
	(1)	(2)	(3)	(4)	(5)
1947–48	58	60	74	96	79
49	63	65	76	98	83
50	66	69	79	96	83
1950–51	69	71	82	96	83
52	69	68	78	101	88
53	70	71	79	99	89
54	72	73	81	99	88
55	74	79	86	93	86
1955–56	75	82	87	92	87
57	79	83	87	96	91
58	84	85	90	98	93
59	85	87	91	97	93
60	89	90	94	99	94
1960–61	92	91	95	101	97
62	91	94	96	97	95
63	94	96	97	98	97
64	98	98	99	101	100
65	100	100	100	100	100
1965–66	101	105	104	97	98
67	107	113	110	95	98
68	110	121	116	91	95
69	107	123	116	86	92
70	104	128	120	81	87
1970–71	97	130	118	75	82
72	101	136	122	74	82
73	101	147	132	69	77
74	105	151	136	69	77
75	108	170	150	64	72
1975–76	99	171	151	58	66
77	113	186	165	61	69
78	113	195	173	58	65
79	114	192	171	59	67
80	117	192	161	61	68

Notes: 1. After 1964–65 the labour input excludes labour in transportation in order to avoid the impact of the takeover of urban transport services by Canada Post in the early 1970s.
2. Total input, for practical not theoretical reasons, excludes "accommodation," that is, the rental service of postal buildings.
Sources: Based on data provided by Canada Post.

and the use by the post office of less economical transport alternatives. (3) The more substantial drop in productivity in 1954–55 and 1955–56 reflects the introduction of the five-day, forty-hour work week in the post office generally, cutting the work week presumably by four hours, that is, 9 percent. (The dip in

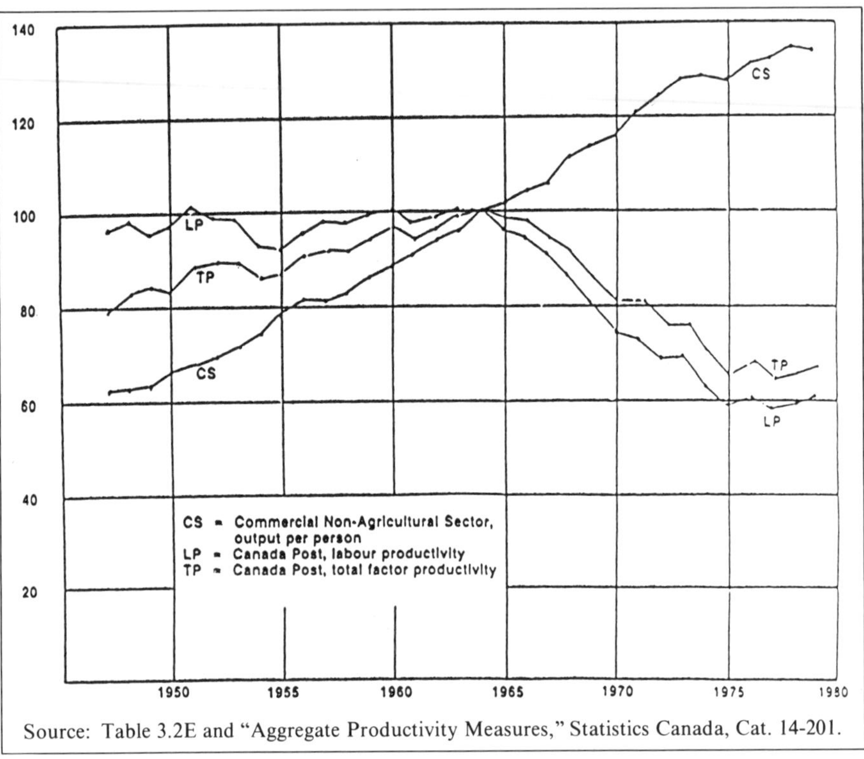

Source: Table 3.2E and "Aggregate Productivity Measures," Statistics Canada, Cat. 14-201.

productivity in the early 1960s, however, probably reflects an error in the estimates of mail volumes.) Given the recovery from reductions in the work week in this period, it would appear that if person-hours rather than person-years had been used in assessing labour inputs, labour productivity would have registered an overall improvement of about 15 percent and total-input productivity of about 30 percent.

The post-1964 period was calamitous for productivity. National strikes in 1965, 1968, 1970, 1974, and 1975 and a plethora of local work-stoppages reflected a tumultuous labour-management situation, and productivity fell precipitously. By 1975–76 the indexes of total-input and labour productivity (1964–65 = 100) had fallen to 66 and 58 percent respectively. A major response of postal management to this critical problem was a technological transformation of the postal system beginning in the early 1970s. However, this tended to exacerbate rather than relieve the strains in human relationships that were at the heart of the problem. In the latter half of the 1970s the technological transformation was completed, new approaches to the resolution of labour-

Table 3.2G Number of Households, Letter-Carrier Points of Call, and Letter-Carrier Input

	Number of Households	1964–65 = 100 Letter-Carrier Points of Call	Letter-Carrier Input
	(1)	(2)	(3)
1959–60	87	80	-
1964–65	100	100	100
1969–70	116	125	130
1974–75	136	158	156
1979–80	159	185	190

Source: Column (1), *Canada Year Book*; columns (2) and (3), based on data provided by Canada Post.

management tensions were explored with mixed results, the CUPW strikers in 1978 were quickly ordered by Parliament back to work, and productivity more or less levelled off at the historical low point reached in mid-decade.

An important "external" factor contributing to the reduction in productivity (given the method of assessment) relates to the letter carriers. For a number of demographic reasons the proportionate rise in number of households in Canada substantially exceeded that of the population, particularly in the later of our two periods (see Table 3.2A). At the same time Canada became more urban. The number of Canadians living on farms fell from 20 percent of the population in 1951 to less than 5 percent twenty-five years later. The number of *urban* households thus increased proportionately even more than households in general. Consequently, letter-carrier points of call (which are urban) expanded quite rapidly—including in the later period, when mail volumes were rising only modestly. Table 3.2G compares changes in number of households (including rural households), letter-carrier points of call, and an estimate of letter-carrier inputs. Although in the post-1964 period letter-carrier productivity clearly fell in relation to the amount of mail delivered, it fell only modestly in relation to the number of points of call. However, it is to be noted that service to an expanding number of points of call was partly offset by the cutback in delivery from six days a week to five days a week in 1970–71. Hence, even in terms of service calculated in terms of aggregate calls made, there was a decrease of some significance in letter-carrier productivity in the post-1964 period.

As Tables 3.2C and 3.2D indicate, of the 74-point increment in total inputs in 1979–80 as compared with fifteen years earlier, 18 points were contributed by the letter carrier. Of the remainder, 29 points were contributed by mail processing, 15 points by other employees (mainly administrative), and 12 points by non-labour inputs (mainly inputs of machinery, equipment, and supplies). Given that there was some reason for a substantial increase in letter-carrier input, the main focus of Canada Post's productivity problem has been in the mail processing area. The substantial increases in administration were perhaps to be expected given the difficulty of the problems to be faced; and the substantial increases in inputs of machinery, equipment, and supplies reflected the technological transformation that was itself an attempt to cope with the productivity problem.

In general, therefore, the collapse in productivity after 1964–65 was due to internal rather than external factors. The story of the 1970s, when Canada Post launched its massive program of technological renovations in an attempt to resolve its problems, is one of further sharp declines in productivity in the first half, partly accepted in order to facilitate the rapid technological transformation, and of virtual stalemate in the second half when a recovery in productivity had been anticipated. It is *as if* postal employees had made good the promise made by the Canada Union of Postal Workers and adopted as a national policy in 1977:

> We therefore declare that unless the above reasonable and just conditions are met by our Employer, we shall ensure that the enormously expensive and complex mechanization program in the Post Office WILL NOT SUCCEED.[3]

3.3 Productivity and Real Wage Rates in the Post Office

Labour productivity and total-input productivity are measures of the effectiveness of employees in fulfilling the purpose for which they have been hired. Real wage rates are a measure of what the employees receive in return. How have postal employees fared in this latter respect?

Table 3.3A presents indexes of implicit real salary rates paid for the period 1949–50 to 1964–65 and the period 1964–65 to 1979–80.[4] Also presented are indexes of real salaries paid and real salaries accrued for postal clerks, the most populous classification of postal employees. Salaries accrued include income finally accounted as arising from work done during the year in question. Salaries paid differ from salaries accrued in that retroactive salary settlements sometimes mean that part of the salary eventually accounted as accrued in a particular year is actually paid in a later year, tending to make the amount paid in the earlier year lower than the amount accrued and the amount paid in the later year higher than the amount accrued. It may be suggested that worker satisfaction or dissatisfaction with salary tends to be linked more with salary paid than with salary accrued, particularly, of course, in periods when the latter is still under negotiation.

In the earlier period, total-input productivity rose modestly by 20 percent while real annual salaries rose by about 40 percent. In the later period, total input productivity fell disastrously by over 30 percent while real annual salaries rose by well over 50 percent. In the first period, workers produced more and got

---

[3]See "National Policies Adopted at the National Convention," p. 5, included with *National Constitution, Adopted, July 1977*. Emphasis in the original.

[4]The indexes are based on salaries and allowances paid, including superannuation and other employee benefits in the later period, but excluding superannuation and other employee benefits in the earlier period.

Table 3.3A Indexes of Real Salary Rates, Canada Post and the Canadian Economy, 1949–50 to 1979–80

	Canadian Economy Weighted Average[1]	Canada Post Implicit Average Salary Paid	Postal Clerks[2] Amount Paid	Postal Clerks[2] Amount Accruing
	(1)	(2)	(3)	(4)
1949–50 = 100				
1949–50	100	100	100	100
51	102	98	97	101
52	102	104	105	102
53	108	105	107	107
54	116	110	113	113
1954–55	119	113	112	112
56	123	113	112	112
57	129	123	120	120
58	132	127	123	123
59	134	125	121	121
1959–60	136	123	119	119
61	140	132	128	128
62	143	134	130	130
63	146	133	128	133
64	148	146	142	136
1964–65	151	139	134	139
1964–65 = 100				
1964–65	100	100	96[3]	100[3]
66	103	109	107	104
67	107	111	106	106
68	112	113	107	113
69	115	130	125	120
1969–70	119	126	118	124
71	123	138	133	128
72	128	136	131	131
73	132	132	126	134
74	136	139	137	129
1974–75	141	138	130	135
76	143	148	146	141
77	152	157	152	154
78	152	158	150	156
79	150	156	145	154
1979–80	148	159	163	155

[1]Calculated by using fixed (1964–65) weights according to employment by major industrial sectors and deflating by the Consumer Price Index.
[2]P.O.4 or equivalent maximum salary.
[3]Amount accruing 1964–65 = 100.
Source: Column (1), based on data provided by Input-Output Division, Statistics Canada; columns (2), (3), and (4), based on data provided by Canada Post.

even more proportionately in return. In the second period, they produced substantially less and, notwithstanding, got substantially more.

Table 3.3A also presents indexes of weighted average real compensation per person for the total economy. This calculation assesses average compensation by weighting the compensation per person by major industrial sectors according to employment in 1964. The application of fixed weights for all the years eliminates the impact, reflected in the unweighted overall average, of substantial inter-industry shifts in employment, e.g., from the low-paid agricultural sector to other, higher-paid sectors. The data indicates that in the earlier period the increase of postal real salaries was about 8 percent *less* than that of the average compensation per person in the Canadian economy. In the later period, in contrast, the increase in postal real salaries was about 8 percent *more* than the Canadian average. However, it may be noted that the comparative gains in postal real salaries in this later period were made in the first half-decade and last half-decade; in the early 1970s, a more forceful holding of the line on postal real salaries meant that for a few years postal salaries again fell off relative to the Canadian average. In general, it may be said that by 1979 postal real salaries had regained their 1949 position relative to weighted average real salaries for the Canadian economy.

The comparative improvement in postal real salaries in the post-1964–65 period was not shared equally by all classes of employees. Table 3.3B displays the salaries of nine classes of postal employees expressed as a percentage of current postal clerk salaries for the quinquennial years 1964–65, 1969–70, 1974–75, and 1979–80. In general, it can be said that the more distant the employees were from the scene of the militant action of the postal clerk and letter carrier unions, the less well did they fare in the struggle to maintain relative

Table 3.3B Salaries of Classes of Postal Employees as a Percentage of Postal Clerk (PO4) Salaries

	1964–65	1969–70	1974–75	1979–80
Postal Clark (PO4)	100	100	100	100
Letter Carrier (PO3)	94	96	97	99
Postal Supervisor (PO-SUP-2)	112	118	116	114
Postmaster (PL2)	152	144	141	137
Administrative Services (AS3)	159	154	150	125
(AS8)		308	296	223
Clerical Services (CR3)	90	88	89	76
Revenue Postmaster Grade 1	79	80	77	78
Semi-Staff Postmaster Grade 4	99	102	93	91

Source: Based on data provided by Canada Post.

salary status. Postal supervisors, the immediate supervisors of the great body of postal clerks, of course had to maintain at least the modest differential that they enjoyed in 1964–65. To a lesser extent the same was true of postmasters who, although they suffered some loss in relative status, did better in this respect than the administrative service categories. Even the lower-paid clerical group suffered a drop in relative salary status. This group is represented by the Public Service Alliance of Canada. However, it must be admitted that a strike of the clerical staff scarcely carries the wallop of a strike by CUPW or LCUC, which immediately and dramatically brings the transmission of mail to a halt.

3.4 Canada Post and Its Links with the Canadian Economy

Canada Post and the Canadian economy are closely interlinked. What happens in the Canadian economy has significant implications for Canada Post. It is important, therefore, that we understand these "happenings" and their implications. What happens in Canada Post also has significant implications for the Canadian economy. It is equally important, therefore, that we also understand this interrelation and its implications. In this section six propositions will be made to assist in elucidating the interlinkage of Canada Post and the Canadian economy. (See also Appendix A for a more detailed, technical discussion of certain of these propositions.)

Proposition 1. For the economy as a whole, real wage rate indexes follow total-input productivity indexes very closely; that is, there is no increase in real wage rates without a comparable increase in productivity. This might be called the new iron law of wages. Table 3.4A demonstrates for the thirty-year period 1949 to 1979 how closely real wage rates have followed productivity for the Canadian economy as a whole. Although real wages increased more than 100 percent, the real wage and productivity indexes approximated each other throughout, the maximum deviation being 6 percent. (The productivity indexes here are *labour* and not *total-input* productivity indexes. However, it is our claim that the two sets of indexes approximate each other at the level of the national economy. (See Appendix A for more detailed discussion of this point.)

If "real compensation per person" and "real output per person" (Table 3.4A) vary together, then "total labour compensation" and "total national output" must vary together. Stated another way, "total labour compensation" must constitute a relatively constant percentage of "total national output," i.e., of national product or domestic product. This is demonstrated in Table 3.4B. In the period 1949 to 1979 labour compensation averaged 67.7 percent of domestic product, the maximum deviation being 2.7 points. Thus, again, the operation of the iron law of wages is confirmed.

This finding, which is no surprise to the statistically minded economic historian, runs directly counter to the belief of many, perhaps most, workers who assume that in wage-bargaining they are determining the wage-share in output price. Given the overall remarkable constancy of wage-share, what is determined in wage-bargaining is not the wage-share in output price, but the

Table 3.4A Indexes of Real Labour Compensation per Person and Output per Person, Canada, 1949 to 1979

	Real Labour Compensation per Person[1]	(1964 = 100) Output per Person	Column (1) ÷ Column (2)
	(1)	(2)	(3)
1949	64	63	101
1950	67	67	101
1	69	70	99
2	71	74	96
3	76	76	99
4	76	75	101
1955	79	82	97
6	83	85	97
7	86	84	102
8	88	87	101
9	89	89	100
1960	91	90	102
1	94	90	104
2	96	94	102
3	98	97	101
4	100	100	100
1965	103	103	100
6	107	106	101
7	112	107	104
8	115	112	103
9	119	114	104
1970	122	116	105
1	128	121	106
2	131	124	106
3	132	128	103
4	131	128	102
1975	132	127	104
6	137	131	104
7	138	132	105
8	137	133	104
9	134	133	101

[1]The unweighted average compensation per person employed for the total economy was divided by the implicit *GNP* price index excluding the impact of indirect taxes less subsidies.
Source: Based on data provided by Input-Output Division, Statistics Canada.

output price itself. That is, given the state of productivity, when an increase in wages is negotiated what is determined is not an increase in wage-share, but an increase in output price. However, price is significant only in relation to other prices. Hence, given the state of productivity throughout the economy, what wage-bargaining does affect is relative output price and relative wage rates.

Table 3.4B Total Labour Compensation and Gross Domestic Product at Factor Cost, Canada, 1949 to 1970 ($ million)

	Total Labour Compensation	GDP at Factor Cost	Labour Compensation as a % of GDP
1949	10,281	15,322	67.1
1950	11,219	15,854	66.6
1	13,107	19,688	66.6
2	14,374	22,125	65.0
3	15,447	23,060	67.0
4	15,773	23,267	67.8
1955	16,820	25,630	65.6
6	18,835	28,658	65.7
7	20,381	30,078	67.8
8	20,837	31,096	67.0
9	22,023	32,827	67.1
1960	23,222	34,192	67.9
1	24,229	35,388	68.5
2	25,690	38,377	66.9
3	27,282	41,150	66.3
4	29,542	44,696	66.1
1965	32,621	48,894	66.7
6	36,705	54,764	67.0
7	40,635	58,793	69.1
8	43,921	61,165	68.4
9	49,087	70,778	69.4
1970	52,990	75,427	70.2
1	58,305	82,867	70.4
2	64,846	92,719	69.9
3	75,093	109,830	68.4
4	89,710	132,255	67.8
1975	104,352	150,726	69.2
6	119,576	172,584	69.3
7	131,831	188,624	69.9
8	144,059	210,632	68.4
9	160,622	241,104	66.6

Notes: 1. Total labour compensation includes salaries and wages plus all supplementary income such as employers' contributions to superannuation and social insurance schemes for the benefit of the employees.
2. Gross Domestic Product is the value of all economic goods and services produced within Canada. (Gross National Product includes in addition net investment income of Canadian residents received from abroad.) *GDP* at factor cost equals *GDP* at market prices less (a) allowances for depreciations, etc. on capital and (b) indirect taxes (less subsidies).
Source: "National Income and Expenditure Accounts," Statistics Canada, Cat. 13-201.

Consequently, although overall improvements in real wage rates are determined by overall productivity, the distribution of these improvements among workers in different sectors of the economy is significantly affected by wage-bargaining. The importance of this for transsectoral worker solidarity is discussed below (proposition 6).

Proposition 2. Input price indexes (including wage rate indexes) tend to be the same for different sectors of the economy. Whenever there is a degree of competition and a degree of mobility of inputs, then we may expect that a relative improvement in input prices in one sector of the economy will encourage a migration of inputs to that sector from other sectors, with a tendency to increase input prices in the emigrating sectors and to reduce input prices in the immigrating sector. That is, there will be a tendency for input price indexes in different sectors to converge. Hence wage rate indexes for different sectors of the economy will tend to converge toward the overall wage rate index for the economy. Consequently, sectors with high productivity performance and sectors with low productivity performance will tend to have the same real wage rate index—that is, the index determined by the productivity performance of the economy as a whole. Hence the iron law of wages applies to the economy as a whole, but *not* to particular sectors of it.

This is illustrated in Table 3.3A. Although the productivity performance of Canada Post in the period 1949 to 1979 differed sharply from that of the economy as a whole, postal workers for the period as a whole enjoyed real wage increases comparable to those of the economy as a whole. (The "falling behind" in the first half of this period and the "catching up" in the second half are explicable in terms of proposition 3.)

Proposition 3. Structural developments affecting the degree of competition and mobility, such as that accompanying the agricultural revolution in the early post-war years and the introduction of unionization in the public service in the later post-war years, cause deviations from the tendency for input price indexes to be the same for different sectors of the economy. In periods when such institutional factors are in process of being developed, the deviations are particularly pronounced.

Traditionally the agricultural sector in Canada has been sufficiently different institutionally that the migration of workers out of that sector in response to higher wages elsewhere has not been sufficient to bring agricultural wages up to non-agricultural levels. In 1964, after a decade and a half of rapid improvement, wage rates in agriculture were still only 47 percent of the average Canadian wage (see Table 3.4C, column 2). The period 1949 to 1964 witnessed a revolution in mechanization on Canadian farms that reduced employment in agriculture from 22 percent of the national total to only 10 percent (see Table 3.4C, column 1). In percentage, however, agricultural wage rates increased 30 percent *more* than the national average, while agricultural labour productivity increased 91 percent *more* than the national average (see Table 3.4C, columns 3 and 4).

Another important institutional factor affecting competition and mobility is labour organization. Particularly during a period in which unions are being introduced into a sector, wage rates in the sector will tend to increase more than the national average. A vivid illustration of this is given by a comparison for the period of 1964 to 1979 of, first, the non-commercial sector and, second, the trade, finance, and other commercial services sector. The former is dominated

Table 3.4C Canada: Comparative Sectoral Data

	1964 Persons Employed (Total Economy = 100)	1964 Labour Compensation Per Person (Total Economy = 100)	1964 1949 = 100		1979 1964 = 100	
			CLC Index[2]	CLP Index[3]	CLC Index[2]	CLP Index[3]
	(1)	(2)	(3)	(4)	(5)	(6)
Agriculture	10	47	130	191	99	114
Other Primary Industries	3	120	98	199	125	94
Manufacturing	23	113	104	137	99	123
Construction	6	130	99	122	102	81
Transportation, communication, electric power, and gas	9	120	95	143	103	140
Trade, finance other commercial services	29	97	94	83	81	86
Non-commercial sector	21	94	101	70	120	80
TOTAL ECONOMY	100	100	100[1]	100[1]	100[1]	100[1]
Canada Post		(115)[4]	92	80	108	47

[1]Averages for the Total Economy were calculated after weighting sectoral figures in all years according to employment in 1964.

[2]Comparative Labour Compensation (*CLC*) indexes equal the labour compensation per person for the sector divided by the *weighted* labour compensation per person for the Total Economy divided further by the comparable quotient for the base year.

[3]Comparative Labour Productivity (*CLP*) indexes equal the labour productivity index for the sector divided by the *weighted* labour productivity index for the Total Economy.

[4]The compensation of a postal clerk PO4 maximum is introduced here as representative.

Source: Based on data provided by Input-Output Division, Statistics Canada.

by the public service, which was becoming unionized in this period; the latter is less unionized than other sectors of the economy (apart from agriculture). The non-commercial sector enjoyed wage increases 20 percent *more* than the national average, while the trade, finance, and other commercial services sector enjoyed increases 19 percent *less* than the national average (see Table 3.4C, columns 5 and 6). The comparable figure for Canada Post, which was also being unionized in this period, was 8 percent more than the national average.

We conclude, therefore, that apart from its productivity performance, the introduction of unionization into a sector brings in its train greater than average wage increases; and these greater than average wage increases are paid for by less than average wage increases in little-unionized sectors. There is some danger, it would seem, that a dual system of privileged unionized sectors and underprivileged non-unionized sectors might become entrenched. The trade, finance, and other commercial services sector, for example, which is a large sector, has been at the bottom in terms of wage rate increases throughout the post-war period. We might ask what would happen if all sectors were unionized. Possibly, then, the premium rates would fall to the more adversarially minded.

Proposition 4. Apart from the impact of structural developments, *relative* output price indexes tend to vary inversely with *relative* total-input productivity indexes. That is, if OP'x, OP'y, and OP'n represent the output price index of output X, output Y, and the output of the national economy respectively, and D'x, D'y, and D'n represent the related total-input productivity indexes, then

$$\frac{OP'x}{OP'y} \text{ tends to equal } \frac{D'y}{D'x}$$

$$\frac{OP'x}{OP'n} \text{ tends to equal } \frac{D'n}{D'x}$$

OP'x/OP'n we may call the comparative output price index of X, or since OP'n represents output price changes in general, the constant-dollar output price index of X. D'n/D'x we may call the reciprocal of the comparative productivity index of X (i.e., the reciprocal of D'x/D'n).

If, as in the case of Canada Post, subsidies (or indirect taxes) substantially affect output prices, then unit cost indexes (including in unit costs all factor costs) may be substituted for output price indexes. Table 3.4D displays the high correlation between Canada Post's comparative unit cost indexes and the reciprocal of its comparative productivity. In the decade and a half after 1964–65 productivity in Canada Post *relative* to the productivity of the Canadian economy as a whole fell to one-half—that is, the reciprocal of its comparative productivity doubled. The consequence of this was a doubling of unit costs in the post office *relative* to the Canadian economy as a whole. That is, after allowing for a substantial general inflation, unit costs in the post office doubled.

As Table 3.4E indicates, increases in postal rates after 1964–65 failed to keep up with sky-rocketing unit costs. In little more than a decade, deficits rose from relatively insignificant amounts to a staggering half-billion dollars, constituting over 40 percent of total postal expenditures. After 1977–78, the postal deficits tended to subside somewhat as postal rates were radically scaled upward.

Proposition 5. As between workers in different sectors of the economy, there is mutual interest in striving for higher and higher productivity.

Proposition 6. As between workers in different sectors of the economy, there is adversarial interest in bargaining for higher and higher wage settlements. Propositions 5 and 6 are essentially corollaries of the iron law of wages and related matters set forth in propositions 1 to 4.

It is in the interest of workers in retail trade that productivity improve in the automobile industry because that tends to reduce the price that retail workers have to pay for new automobiles. At the same time, it is in the interest of automobile workers that productivity improve in retail trade because that tends to reduce the price that automobile workers have to pay for consumer goods generally. However, it is not in the interest of workers in retail trade that

Table 3.4D Comparative Unit Costs and the Reciprocal of Productivity, Canada Post, 1949–50 to 1979–80

	(1964–65 = 100)	
	Comparative Unit Costs	Reciprocal of Comparative Productivity
1949–50	87	75
1950–51	88	81
52	85	79
53	85	83
54	90	86
55	94	87
1955–56	94	94
57	94	94
58	96	90
59	96	94
60	94	94
1960–61	97	93
62	102	96
63	100	97
64	103	97
65	100	100
1965–66	108	105
67	110	109
68	118	112
69	134	121
70	141	132
1970–71	158	141
72	159	146
73	168	161
74	169	165
75	172	178
1975–76	196	192
77	196	190
78	209	201
79	207	199
80	202	195

Notes: 1. The index of unit costs for Canada Post is calculated as equal to the index of total current costs divided by the index of total output. The index of unit costs for the Canadian economy is calculated as varying with GNP in current dollars minus indirect taxes less subsidies divided by GNE in constant dollars.

2. The index of productivity for Canada Post is the total–input productivity index. The index of productivity for the total economy is based on unweighted average output per person. The unweighted comparison is used here to correspond with the unweighted comparison of unit costs, sufficient data to make weighted comparisons not being available.

Source: Data provided by Canada Post; "National Income and Expenditure Accounts," Statistics Canada, Cat. 13-201; and "Aggregate Productivity Measures," Statistics Canada, Cat. 14-201.

automobile workers get high wage settlements because that tends to put up the price of automobiles; and it is not in the interest of automobile workers that workers in retail trade get high wage settlements because that tends to put up retail prices.

Table 3.4E Canada Post's Deficits, 1964–65 to 1979–80

	Deficit $(000)	Deficit as % of Total Expenditure
1964–65	11,980	4.3
1965–66	30,668	9.7
67	47,763	13.5
68	66,183	16.4
69	86,341	18.7
70	45,456	9.3
1970–71	108,170	20.0
72	73,165	12.7
73	84,876	13.1
74	153,981	20.7
75	285,979	31.6
1975–76	495,837	46.6
77	546,455	41.4
78	563,207	37.3
79	493,944	30.8
80	429,197	24.2

Note: In estimating the deficits the figures are adjusted (a) to eliminate expenditures on capital account and to substitute current capital cost allowances and (b) to put salaries on an "amounts paid" basis in 1969–70 to 1971–72 as in other years.

Source: Based on data provided by Canada Post.

Indeed, it may be argued that the parties whose interests may be most adversely affected are not typically represented at the wage-bargaining table. Management may not be too excited by relatively high wage requirements so long as all competitors in the sector are subject to the same requirements. For example, if productivity improvements are relatively good, then relatively high wage settlements may be met without increasing relative output prices. Workers in other sectors, however, are definitely affected adversely by overly favourable settlements in this sector—even if all it means is that prices of that sector's output will not be reduced as much as they otherwise would have been.

With respect to the post office the situation is clear: in the post-1964 period both the radical drop in productivity and the more modest rise in comparative labour compensation tended to reduce the real income of workers in other sectors. The modest rise in comparative labour compensation might be justified on the ground that it redressed the fall in comparative compensation that the post office suffered in the pre-1964 period. The drop of productivity, on the other hand, was not only drastic, but without any apparent redeeming feature. Within an unfortunate thirteen-year period Canadians had to pay twice as much in constant dollars for a unit of postal service. On top of this the units of postal service sadly deteriorated in quality, as any Canadian who lived through the period can testify. That is, the rate and reliability of mail transmission fell off seriously—a matter that irritated the Canadian public perhaps more than the rise in unit costs.

Unfortunately, the iron law of wages and its corollaries are not well understood within Canadian labour ranks. The practical unionist finds it hard to abstract from a gut feeling that improvements in productivity contribute mainly to the swelling of profits, which are typically already unconscionably high. For those who are willing to look, however, the statistical evidence is overwhelming: productivity improvements *are* passed on to employees as a class. The percentage increase in real wages in general equals the percentage increase in productivity in general. No matter how high money wages are pushed by vigorous wage negotiations, average real wages in the economy are tied in fact to average productivity. Increases in money wages that exceed productivity simply inflate output prices and thereby reduce the real value of money wages. If some labour unions are more vigorous or more successful than others in pressing wage increases, they may indeed win increases in real wages in excess of average productivity, but they do so only at the expense of less than average increases in real wages for workers in other sectors of the economy.

What the iron law and its corollaries tell us, therefore, is not what many faithful unionists want to hear. That various unions have a common interest in promoting productivity everywhere is perhaps a palatable truth; but it will be a surprise to some that this is demonstrably the case outside a socialist economy. What will set some unionists' teeth on edge is that with respect to productivity it is now apparent that workers share a common interest, not only with each other, but with management as well. For labour lambs to collaborate with management wolves has not been their paradigm of labour-management relations. More shocking, however, is that with respect to wage negotiations it now appears that a union has adversarial interests, not only as over against management, but also as over against other unions as well. This threatens to undermine the ethic of labour solidarity that is so close to the heart of faithful unionists.

The iron law and its corollaries may, however, throw some light on worker voting behaviour. It has puzzled some observers that so many workers, when given the opportunity, do not vote for a party that has declared itself a labour party. Acrimonious wage negotiations are news and are reported with gusto by the media. However, given that increases in wages *elsewhere* are *not* in the worker's commercial interest, it should not be assumed that a worker naturally sympathizes with another's militant fight for higher and yet higher wages. One can understand, for example, how workers in the trade, finance, and other commercial services sector (now constituting almost 40 percent of workers in Canada) might feel that they have more to fear from militant unionism than from exorbitant corporate profits.

3.5 An Unflattering Comparison: The U.S. Postal Service

A current comparison of the economic performance of Canada Post with the U.S. Postal Service is unflattering; and especially so since in the pre-1964 period such comparisons tended to be flattering to the Canadian service. The breakdown in the *quality* of service in the post-1964 period seems to have been of the same general order on both sides of the border. The flood of customer complaints about the service in general, the substantial loss of the parcel post trade due to the falling quality of the service, and the general state of worker unrest and alienation was experienced by the U.S. Postal Service as well as the Canadian service. However, on the quantitative side, whereas Canada Post had higher productivity than the U.S. Postal Service in 1964, fifteen years later its productivity was roughly 40 percent lower.

The investigator has to be rather cautious in making international comparisons. Things that appear to be the same turn out not to be. However, what we have attempted is to compare U.S. Postal Service productivity, compensation per employee, and unit cost estimates employing methods roughly comparable to those used in the case of Canada Post. The main difference in method arises from the fact that the U.S. Postal Service has well-developed total person-year data that can be used in developing productivity estimates. That this difference in method of calculating productivity does not vitiate comparison between the two postal services is supported by a comparison of the diverse movements in constant-dollar unit costs in the two systems. The latter appear to be consistent with the radical difference in the movement of productivity that emerges in the two estimates.

An attempt is also made to compare the productivity of the two systems directly—and not simply to compare their rates of change in productivity. This is done by reducing the pieces handled in each country in 1976–77 to first-class mail equivalence (on the basis of assessment of comparative costs of different classes of mail in each country). These aggregates were divided by total person-year data for that year to obtain estimates, which were assumed to be comparable, of output per person-year. This calculation indicated that the labour productivity of the U.S. Postal Service was 35.6 percent higher in that year than Canada Post. A similar calculation for total-input productivity indicated that the U.S. Postal Service was 47.7 percent more efficient than Canada Post in that year. With these links between the systems for 1976–77, the figures in columns 1 and 4 of Table 3.5A could be easily translated into the figures of columns 3 and 6, which express U.S. Postal Service productivity indexes in terms of Canada Post (1964 as equal to 100). The results should be treated as approximations only.

The results are at first sight rather startling. The labour productivity of the U.S. Postal Service is far below that of the Canadian service in 1964–65; and far above it fifteen years later (although still below the Canadian attainment in 1964–65). However, a large part of the poor showing of the U.S. service in 1964–65 is accounted for by the fact that in the Canadian service there is much more "contracting out," particularly of transportation services. That is, the labour involved in these services appears in non-labour expenditures in the Canadian case (other enterprises having paid for the labour required here).

Table 3.5A Canada Post and U.S. Postal Service: Productivity Compared

	Labour Productivity			Total-input Productivity		
	U.S. Postal Service (1964–65 = 100)	Canada Post (1964–65 = 100)	U.S. Postal Service (Canada Post 1964–65 = 100)	U.S. Postal Service (1964–65 = 100)	Canada Post (1964–65 = 100)	U.S. Postal Service (Canada Post 1964–65 = 100)
	(1)	(2)	(3)	(4)	(5)	(6)
1949–50	89	96	64	82	83	76
1954–55	98	93	70	96	86	89
1959–60	97	99	69	94	94	87
1964–65	100	100	72	100	100	92
1965–66	100	97	72	100	98	93
67	98	95	71	99	98	92
68	98	92	70	99	95	91
69	99	86	71	100	92	93
70	100	81	71	101	87	93
1970–71	102	75	73	102	82	95
72	103	73	74	105	82	97
73	109	66	78	111	77	103
74	106	67	76	108	77	100
75	106	62	76	107	72	99
1975–76	105	56	76	107	66	99
77	110	58	79	110	69	102
78	115	55	83	117	65	108
79	116	57	83	118	67	109
80	122	58	87	122	68	113

Notes: 1. U.S. Postal Service outputs are weighted by attributable cost per piece for 1975 for different classes of mail. (Estimates made by U.S.A. Postal Rates Commission. See, Postal Rate and Fee Increases, 1973, Docket No. R74-1, Appendices to Opinion and Recommended Decision, August 28, 1975. Vol. 2, Appendix G, Schedule 2.)
2. U.S. Postal Service labour inputs are total person-years as accounted by the service. The Canada Post labour inputs here *include* labour in transportation.
3. Other than labour, inputs for the U.S. Postal Service are based on expenditures deflated by the U.S. index of compensation per person in the non-farm business sector.
Source: Annual Reports of the Postmaster General U.S.A.; *Monthly Labour Review*, U.S. Department of Labor; and data provided by Canada Post.

The relevant comparison, therefore, is that of total-input productivity. In column 6, U.S. Postal Service total-input productivity appears as 8 percent below that of Canada Post in 1964–65 and as 13 percent above that level by 1979–80, placing the U.S. service in that year roughly 65 percent higher than its Canadian counterpart.

This depressing comparison is supported by a comparison of constant-dollar unit costs (see Table 3.5B). In both services constant-dollar unit costs tended to be pushed upward in the post-1964 period by substantial increases in real compensation per employee—the increases being apparently somewhat higher in Canada than in the United States. However, whereas the increase in real

Table 3.5B Canada Post and U.S. Postal Service: Real Compensation per Employee and Constant-Dollar Unit Costs

| | 1964–65 = 100 | | | |
| | Real Compensation per Employee[1] | | Constant-Dollar Real Unit Costs[2] | |
	Canada Post	U.S. Postal Service	Canada Post	U.S. Postal Service
1949–50	72	62	84	80
1954–55	81	70	93	74
1959–60	89	81	95	89
1964–65	100	100	100	100
1965–66	109	101	109	101
67	111	102	111	103
68	113	102	119	105
69	130	106	135	106
70	126	109	141	108
1970–71	138	119	161	114
72	136	128	161	119
73	132	131	171	115
74	139	133	177	120
75	138	138	188	124
1975–76	148	145	217	130
77	157	150	220	131
78	158	151	233	124
79	156	145	226	119
80	159	139	224	110

[1]The index of real compensation per employee for Canada Post equals the index of the implicit average salary paid (see Table 3.3A) divided by the consumer price index; and for the U.S. Postal Service equals the index of salaries and other personnel costs per person-year divided by the consumer price index.

[2]The index of constant-dollar unit costs equals the index of total current costs divided by the index of weighted total output deflated by the consumer price index.

Source: Annual Reports of the Postmaster General, U.S.A.; *Monthly Labor Review*, U.S. Department of Labor; and data provided by Canada Post.

wages was offset to some extent in the U.S. service by an increase in total-input productivity, in the Canadian case the cost-inflating impact of rising real wages was supplemented by the cost-inflating impact of the dramatic fall in productivity. The consequence was that whereas by the end of the 1970s constant-dollar *unit* costs were some 10 percent higher than in 1964–65 for the U.S. Postal Service, they were over 120 percent higher for Canada Post.

It may be noted that, to the extent that changes in constant-dollar unit costs of the U.S. Postal Service are not accounted for by changes in comparative productivity, they are largely accounted for by changes in comparative labour compensation (salaries and other personnel costs constituting 85 percent of total costs by the end of the 1970s). Table 3.5C indicates that the constant-dollar unit cost index follows closely the product of the indexes of the reciprocal of comparative productivity and the comparative total labour compensation.

Table 3.5C The U.S. Postal Service: Indexes of the Reciprocal of Comparative Total-Input Productivity (1/CTP), Comparative Labour Compensation (CLC), and Constant-Dollar Unit Costs

	1/CTP	CLC	1/CTP X CLC	Constant-Dollar Unit Costs
1949–50	87	95	82	80
1954–55	82	89	73	74
1959–60	92	92	84	89
1964–65	100	100	100	100
1965–66	102	99	102	101
67	105	98	103	103
68	107	97	104	105
69	107	98	105	106
70	105	101	106	108
1970–71	104	110	114	114
72	104	115	120	119
73	102	115	117	115
74	104	119	123	120
75	103	125	128	124
1975–76	106	129	137	130
77	106	132	140	131
78	100	132	133	124
79	98	129	127	119
80	93	128	120	110

Notes: 1. 1/CTP equals the index of output per person in the non-farm business sector divided by the U.S. Postal Service total-input productivity index.

2. CLC equals the index of salaries and other personnel costs per person-year in the U.S. Postal Service divided by the index of non-farm business compensation per person-year.

Source: Annual Reports of the Postmaster General, U.S.A.; and *Monthly Labor Review,* U.S. Department of Labor.

3.6 What Happened to Canada Post's Technological Revolution?

The response of Canada Post's management to the problems that surfaced after 1964 was in many respects bold and decisive. Eric Kierans, appointed postmaster general in 1968, decided in his usual energetic way to modernize the post office. He authorized fifteen studies by experts from both inside and outside the post office. These culminated in *A Blueprint for Change,* tabled in the House of Commons in December 1969. The *Blueprint* recommended among other things: (1) the reorganization of the post office as a Crown corporation; (2) a decentralization with respect to certain headquarters functions, with the formation of Ontario, Quebec, Western Canada, and Atlantic regions; and (3) the introduction of automated mail processing.

In accordance with the third of these recommendations a coding system for all addresses in Canada was worked out (1971–73); and between 1972 and 1979 major processing plants in Toronto and Montreal and new mechanized plants in the principal urban centres across Canada were constructed. The most efficient processing machines that could be found anywhere in the world were installed in these plants. The typical equipment installed included: coding desk suites, consisting of a set of coding desks that operators use to bar code mail bearing the postal code; letter sorting machines, which read the bar code on letters, convert this to switching information, and sort the letters accordingly; optical character readers, consisting of equipment that scans and reads most typewritten and all printed postal codes on letters and bar codes them accordingly (without the intervention of a coding operator); culler facer cancellers, consisting of equipment that combines the operations of culling, facing, and cancelling letters; and flat sorting machines that sort flats (that is, mail in large envelopes).

It is not as easy as one would expect to get an accurate accounting of the total cost of this technological transformation. However, total cost of new plant, machinery, and equipment between 1972, when the transformation began in earnest, and 1979, when the transformation was basically completed, was probably in the vicinity of one billion dollars. The 1977 annual report of Canada Post states:

> Major capital costs have been in two categories: mechanization and modernization. The mechanization program, which should be completed by early 1980, has represented an increase in capital expenditures of approximately $200 million over the past five years. Modernization, a program of replacing overburdened and outdated facilities with modern mail-processing plants, will cost approximately $700 million to complete.

It seems clear in retrospect that much more was expected from the technological transformation than was actually achieved. In the early 1970s nominal postal rates were held firm, and it seems probable that it was anticipated that the new technology would soon deliver Canada Post from its embarrassing escalation of unit costs. However, what happened was that constant-dollar unit costs, which at the time of the tabling of the *Blueprint* were already 40 percent higher than in 1964–65, rose another 60 percent while the new technology was being put in place. Thereafter, constant-dollar unit costs levelled off, but the substantial drop in unit costs that might have been expected did not materialize.

What was needed in the period of transition, while the new technology was being put into place, were the following steps. *Step 1:* A retraining of as many as possible of present staff to fill the new jobs, e.g., as coding desk operators, electro-mechanic maintenance technicians, and computer program maintenance experts. *Step 2:* A hiring of new staff to fill new jobs to the extent that step 1 could not provide the staff with the requisite training, e.g., jobs requiring intensive computer or sortation equipment knowledge. *Step 3:* A moratorium (for a period, say, of two years before the mechanized system was expected to be fully operative) on hiring regular, permanent-track staff, other than outlined in step 2, in order to reduce significantly the number of staff including those of step 2 in this class. *Step 4:* The appointment of temporary, casual workers only when new staff, other than those in step 2, were required to cope with double staffing needs (during the period when both the old manual system and the new mechanized system have to some extent to be kept operative). *Step 5:* A relatively quick reduction of staff as the new mechanized system becomes fully operative.

Steps 1 to 4 prepare the way for step 5 when the technological revolution actually realizes its objective of reducing staff relative to output. If great care is not taken with respect to steps 1 to 4, then the enterprise may reach step 5 and find that it has contractual commitments to an increased staff, which mean that step 5 simply cannot be carried out. The enterprise may now find that instead of a reduced work force, the technological revolution has bloated its work force so that productivity has fallen rather than risen. In the meanwhile, the overstaffing of the new system encourages bad work habits, which tend to become standard and hence to justify the perpetuation of substantial overstaffing. This in general would seem to be the unhappy cul-de-sac in which Canada Post found itself, by the end of the 1970s. Just how bloated Canada Post's work force had become by the late 1970s may be judged from the following. If with the massive technological transformation Canada Post's labour productivity had by the end of the 1970s improved a modest 16 percent as compared with 1964–65 (as actually happened in the case of the U.S. Postal Service), then this would have been accomplished by *one-half* of Canada Post's actual workforce. That is, one reasonable method of calculation suggests that about half of Canada Post's total work force was redundant by the end of the 1970s.

The U.S. Postal Service can by no stretch of the imagination be taken as a model of modern technical efficiency. However, one reason that service was much more successful with technological innovation than Canada Post was that it paid careful attention to step 3. Many months before installing new equipment in a given locality, the U.S. Postal Service began to cut regular staff for that locality by refusing to replace workers who retired or quit. This meant in some cases a considerable increase in overtime work; but it meant also that the mechanized system was introduced with a work force that was already much leaner than normal.

Canada Post was ill-starred with respect to almost all of these steps. *A Blueprint for Change* had stressed the importance of the understanding and co-operation of the postal workers in the process of technological change. In fact, misunderstanding and lack of co-operation seemed to mount as the process of technological change advanced. CUPW accused the post office of proceeding without appropriate consultation with the union and without regard for the workers' welfare. Step 1, the retraining of present staff, received a sharp setback by a squabble between the post office and CUPW over the classification of coding desk operators. The typical classification of postal clerks was P.O.4; the post office proposed giving the coders a lower classification with lower pay. The promise of current P.O.4 wages for postal clerks accepting retraining as coders was scarcely adequate to compensate the postal clerks for the insult of a lowered classification and dampened future prospects. To pacify the furore the post office finally accepted the P.O.4 classification for coders; but unfortunately a great deal of damage to the retraining program had already been done, and in addition, Canada Post was now locked into salary levels for coders far in excess of those elsewhere in the civil service or in the private sector.

Steps 3 and 4 were fatally undermined when CUPW, after agreeing to a liberal policy respecting casuals in 1972, made the hiring of casuals a main thrust in its militant struggle against management. For example, the hiring of casuals was the reason cited for many of the illegal, local strikes that mushroomed in the 1970s. Here again Canada Post, or we might say, a timid civil service—not fully aware of the dire consequences—gave way, and the hiring of casuals by Canada Post was maintained at roughly historically standard, relative levels.

A Blueprint for Change optimistically predicted that "the introduction of mechanization into a single terminal normally requires in excess of two years, and the Post Office should by means of natural turnover be able to accommodate any imbalance in employment opportunity that may exist at the end of this period."[5] However, the failure in steps 1, 3, and 4 meant that step 5, the objective of mechanization, was impossible for Canada Post. Thus an impressive engineering achievement became an economic disaster. The post office completed its technological revolution with a regular staff bloated by the special requirements of the transition itself. To confirm the disaster, the post office contracted with CUPW, ensuring that none of the redundant staff would lose his or her job beause of technological innovation. Workers having obtained their jobs to facilitate technological innovation, so that labour input might be economized, were now assured that they would not lose their jobs on account of technological innovation. Canada Post became, in effect, a huge labour welfare institution—certainly bad economics and probably even worse welfare.

---

[5] *A Blueprint for Change*, Canada Post Office, November 1969, p. 132.

PART 3

THE CRISIS IN MOTIVATION

CHAPTER 4

The Depressed, Confused State of Motivation in Canada Post

Our study of productivity in Canada Post in the post-war years makes clear that the problem was not that insufficient resources, human and material, were applied to the objective of providing mail service to the nation. Nor was there insufficient knowledge concerning how these services could be efficiently and cheaply provided. The problem, rather, was that overall there was a serious deficiency of will. It was noted earlier that the Glassco Royal Commission on Government Organization, reporting in 1962, commented very favourably on postal staff: "The Post Office staff is conscientious, hard-working and dedicated, and morale is very high. This has enabled the service to function in a highly commendable manner." What happened to this high morale, this industry and dedication? One short decade later these virtues were conspicuous by their absence.

The depressed, confused state of motivation in the post office is illustrated by two eye-witness accounts of the state of affairs in the 1970s. One account, "Working in the Post Office," is that of Peter Taylor, a postal worker in Toronto in the early 1970s. The other account, "Supervising in the Post Office," is that of Roger Bouvier, a young supervisor in Ottawa in the mid-1970s.

4.1 Peter Taylor's "Working in the Post Office"[1]
Peter Taylor begins his account by stating his alienation from work in the post office: "I really didn't like working at the Post Office. In fact, I hated it." He ends by admitting that quitting after nine months is only a temporary escape: "But at best it's only a temporary reprieve. My next job will probably put me back in much the same kind of situation." The account reflects what appears to be a deep-seated alienation against the system of work in the post office in particular, but also against the system of work in modern industry generally. Various reasons for the alienation are stated: the post office is like a prison and the supervisors are like prison guards; the work itself is lacking in challenge, is repetitious, monotonous, boring; the work is organized according to the presumed need for quick processing of the mail and not according to the needs of the workers, e.g., the night shift in particular seriously interferes in day-to-day relations with friends. He is forced to work because he needs money to live; but he resents a system that gobbles up so unpleasantly such a large part of his living time.

---

[1]Walter Johnson, ed. *Working in Canada.* Montreal: Black Rose Books, 1975, Chapter 1.

49

Out of resentment Taylor and his fellow workers strike back. "Every night I worked was a night lost forever. If they were to try to take my life away from me, then they weren't going to get away with it without a fight that would cost them as much as possible." The alienated workers engaged therefore in a concerted "struggle against work." The aim of this struggle was "more money for less work." Taylor describes a number of the tactics employed. For example: workers call in sick when they want to take a night off; they punch out sick after six and a half hours, taking advantage of the contract provision that grants full eight-hours' pay in such a case; they take a day off during the week and then work a day's overtime at time and a half on weekends, thereby increasing the week's pay by 10 percent without increasing the hours worked; they extend the practice of unofficial breaks—a great variety of games are played here; they sort carelessly or intermittently; and they participate happily in illegal strikes—when union officials usually tried to take over. Taylor displays some ambivalence concerning the union: it certainly strengthened the worker's hand, but it too could become bossy and officious. Taylor takes pride in the signs of success in this struggle against work. He cites the postmaster general's public confession that productivity has fallen 12 percent. Taylor wagers that the workers will be able to outwit the incoming new technology as well.

Taylor recognizes the deficiency in mutuality of working in the post office. The us–them battle of workers against management gave him his only relief from alienation. Here he found some mutuality and whole-hearted engagement, some self-determination and a sustaining common purpose.

> Our struggle against work provided a much better basis for relationships. First, because they were enjoyable . . . . Second, because we had to do it ourselves . . . . Third, because all of us were engaged to some extent, there was a real feeling of being together against management . . . . Hating work, and feeling the need to fight back, I found this support expressed in both actions and words to be the best thing in the whole Post Office.

What is remarkable about the picture Taylor paints is the contradiction of workers struggling against work. The workers are not in spirit behind their own work. Hence, they work as little as they can manage to get away with and sometimes even sabotage their own product, for example, through mis-sortation. The famed Protestant ethic, which Max Weber taught us to see motivated dedicated, efficient work, is absent. It is replaced by the contradictory ethic of alienation. The raison d'être of the post office is the transmission of mail as quickly, reliably, and efficiently as possible. Management and workers are hired to accomplish this purpose. It would appear that management and workers are invited to assume a common purpose, the fulfillment of which is a contribution to the welfare of the citizens of Canada. In return for this contribution, management and workers are offered salaries of greater or lesser adequacy, which the citizenry in one way or another pays. However, as Taylor's account illustrates, things are not working that way in reality: management may be committed to the quick, reliable, and efficient transmission of the mail, but the workers are not.

4.2 Roger Bouvier's "Supervising in the Post Office"

In 1975 Roger Bouvier, a young French Canadian postal worker, was promoted to the rank of first-line supervisor. As a rookie first-line supervisor in the Alta Vista post office in Ottawa, Bouvier found himself confronted with the awesome problem of an alienated, adversarial work force such as the one Peter Taylor had so graphically described in the Toronto post office a few years earlier. Amazingly, within a few months, Bouvier found a solution to the postal problem. Unfortunately, however, his solution involved local modifications of the system of controls engraved in the contractual agreement between CUPW and the post office. For some months, lower management and CUPW tolerated this infringement of the rules. Finally, however, the system could stand it no longer, and Bouvier was ordered to desist. A remarkable experiment vanished from the scene. Roger Bouvier wrote the following report of his experiences for inclusion in this study.

"Early in 1975 I was promoted to the position of first-line supervisor and assigned by the Ottawa Alta Vista post office to the government section in the city mail division. Before my assignment to this section, the post office had had difficulty keeping supervisors because of lack of co-operation on the part of the postal clerks. Productivity was very low, absenteeism very high, and a lot of grievances originated in the section.

"In this section, there were twenty PO4s and one PO2 (mail handler). The section was about evenly divided between French and English, but there was only one woman. The one woman was over fifty years of age, but 80 percent of the men were under twenty-five.

"For the first two weeks in the section, I observed the staff at work, noted their strong and weak points, and gathered data on their productivity and absenteeism. The PO4s were sorting an average of one tray of mail (600 pieces) per hour — less than average. Employee absenteeism for the previous year was 552 days lost. Motivation was obviously lacking; the workers were frequently away from their work area, chatting with each other, visiting the washrooms, taking long coffee breaks.

"I was determined to try everything possible within my own jurisdiction as a supervisor to change the situation. I decided first to meet with the shop steward to discuss my findings and to get his reactions to some of my ideas for improvement. The shop steward was an employee with a lot of experience dealing with workers' problems and also a militant unionist. At our meeting, held outside the work area, he was very apprehensive. He said that over the years he had seen too many supervisors taking advantage of employees just to prove themselves to higher management. However, he promised not to interfere with my proposal but would keep an eye on me to see that I did not step outside my jurisdiction.

"I spent the first week of March talking to the employees one by one about their own interests and noting their responses. Most of them when approached began to produce more because they were talking about something they cared very much about as human beings. Some of them enjoyed art, music, lectures, sports, family, and not least, sex.

"After talking to my immediate supervisor, I decided to meet the staff during the second week of March to discuss the situation. The meeting was held during working hours, but at a different location than the work area. I was very nervous because I did not know what their reactions might be. However, prior to the meeting, the shop steward guaranteed that nobody would walk out of the meeting and promised to help me if I had any problems.

"I explained to the staff that their production was too low, their absenteeism too high, and their work habits poor. However, I promised them that I would be sensitive to their problems and receptive to any suggestions they might make. Furthermore, I said that if they could produce more, then I would permit early finishing time. This last point created an uproar: they did not believe what I was saying. Most of them laughed at my suggestion. However, the shop steward took over the meeting and told them to give me a chance.

"During the following week, the staff argued among themselves about my suggestion. In the end, they were ready to try it. There was more discussion back and forth among them about how to improve productivity, and they began actually to produce more.

"I had promised also to hold regular meetings to discuss the work and other things on their minds. At these meetings, each employee had a chance to be the leader of the group. The employee was in charge, and I was frequently only a silent participant.

"At the beginning of the shift, each employee had a role to play: taking inventory of the mail; gathering all the oversize mail; getting mail from other sections. After half an hour on duty, the group knew how much mail they had, and employees were making decisions about its processing. As I listened, they were deciding to cut their coffee breaks in half, or not to take any, or to have coffee in their work area, in order to finish early. Quite often they even refused to take their lunch break.

"The regular shift was from 11:00 p.m. to 7:30 a.m. By April, the staff started to go home early—two to two and a half hours early. I could not believe my own eyes: they were running; they had smiles on their faces; they had *motivation*. By the time they went home, the section had been cleared of all mail. Even the second-, third-, and fourth-class mail was cleared every twenty-four hours.

"Most of the younger staff were cancelling their annual leave because they could get home early in the morning, have a few hours' sleep, and then enjoy a free afternoon and evening. For a period from April 1975 to January 1976 (given the forty-two-day strike in the fall of 1975), I never had to apply discipline, nor did I receive a grievance. The staff were disciplining themselves by discussing and resolving matters among themselves. During this period, productivity went up 300 percent: the PO4s were sorting an average of four to five trays an hour. Absenteeism went down from 552 days to 102 days. There was almost no sick leave, and no overtime was registered. Employees from other sections were requesting transfers to my section in order to have the same incentive program.

"Finally, however, upon arrival at work one evening in February 1976, there was a note in my office from the superintendent advising me to stop my program. I couldn't believe my eyes. I talked with the superintendent, but his only comment was that he had orders from higher management to cancel it. In the section things quickly reverted: lacking motivation, the employees reported sick more often, absenteeism rose steeply, productivity fell, and again lots of overtime was required."

CHAPTER 5

A General Hypothesis Concerning Human Motivation

It is appropriate that we pursue our investigation of what happened to motivation in the post office within the context of a general theory of human motivation. We may assume in advance that the subject matter is sufficiently difficult that one is well advised to proceed with care step by step.

(1) First, a word about intellectual hardship. In a generation that is more science-oriented than any before it, there is a tendency to shove to the side any kind of being which is not amenable to the application of the methods of science. However, our hypothesis is that if we are to understand human motivation we must understand both being which is amenable to the application of the methods of science and being which is *not* amenable to the application of the methods of science. Because we take the former kind of being seriously, we are willing to put up with the intellectual hardship of learning the sophisticated mathematical language that it is necessary to use in talking about it. Because we are uncertain how seriously we should take the latter kind of being, we are inclined to defend our uncertainty by assuming that sophisticated language designed for talking about it reflects a tedious academic addiction to esoteric language. We thereby avoid the intellectual hardship of struggling with this language and its meaning. However, without a struggle with the language designed to express it, there can be little insight into new meaning.

We may recall the account of my encounter with the Kabul street vendor who "sanitized" his spoon by sluicing it in the open sewer; I saw things differently. It might be surmised that if we were to propose a model of human motivation that departed significantly from that currently accepted, we might face intellectual difficulties surpassing those dividing the scientific-minded Westerner and the Kabul street vendor. Moreover, the significance of the issue might far surpass that of the Kabul encounter.

In any case, the reader is forewarned: although what follows has been designed with care to make the essential points as clearly as possible, it will doubtlessly communicate little without a considerable intellectual input on the part of the reader.

(2) We begin our investigation of the subject matter itself by considering human consciousness. We discover in human consciousness two radically different kinds of being: the being which is conscious, and the being of which consciousness is conscious. The first we may call subjective being or the subject; the latter we may call objective being or the object. Consciousness looks both ways: to subjective being on the one side and to objective being on the other. Consciousness is the interrelationship between the two.

We shall use two verbs to characterize these two kinds of being: "immanate," which we derive from the Latin verb "immanere" meaning "to remain within;" and "transcend," which is derived from the Latin verb "transcendere" meaning "to climb beyond." Objective being is characterized by its immanating of limits. Immanating limits, an object immanates a constant form, or insofar as there is change, immanates a constant order—order in the interrelation of its component parts and order in its interrelation with other objects.

Subjective being, on the other hand, is characterized by its immanating *and* transcending of limits. The subject of consciousness in being conscious of an object *immanates* a specific form. However, the subject *transcends* that specific form and passes on to consciousness of another object. Furthermore, the subject of consciousness in its passage from one form of immanence to another retains a consciousness of its own unity. The unity of the subject *transcends* the diversity of its form of immanence. Thus subjective transcendence is to be discovered not only in the alternation of conformity to specific forms and escape from these forms, but also in the transcendent unity of the subject that is present along with the immanence of each and every specific form.

One may object to this characterization of the subject on the grounds that it is contradictory. Nothing, it may be argued, can simultaneously immanate and transcend given limits. The answer is that, indeed, no *object* can: it would be contradictory to claim for an object that it immanates *and transcends* given limits. However, we must not confuse the logic of objective being and the logic of subjective being. What is contradictory and impossible for an object is the characteristic way of being of the subject. We must not attempt to reduce a subject to an object: transcendence is as essential to the subject of consciousness as is immanence.

(3) We discover through human consciousness not only subjective being and objective being, but also two kinds of objective being: objective being dependent on the subject, and objective being independent of the subject.

Objective being dependent on the subject consists of what we may call imaginal objects.[1] The images of the image-making consciousness are the creatures of the image-making subject. Insofar as consciousness confines itself to imaginal objects, we may speak of the imaginal world. In the imaginal world the subject is the sovereign lord of all the world. What "is" or "is not" is by decree of the subject. The subject is one without a second; the objects of this world are simply the creations of this subject.

Our first hypothesis concerning human nature, therefore, is that insofar as the human being is a conscious subject, immanating and transcending all possible limits, it is free, creative, autonomous.

(4) The consciousness of objective being which is independent of the subject opens up for the human being its existence as a dynamic interplay of subjective

---

[1] We introduce the term "imaginal" to escape the implication of unreality usually associated with the term "imaginary." Imaginal objects have their own kind of reality.

being with being other than itself. This existence assumes three forms: first, a perceptual world in which a subjective being incarnate as a complex perceptual object exists in dynamic interplay with other perceptual objects; second, a communal world in which incarnate subjective beings exist in dynamic interplay with each other; and, third, a spiritual world in which incarnate subjective beings in community with each other encounter an ultimate good. As the perceptual world is dimensionally richer than the imaginal world so is the communal world dimensionally richer than the perceptual world and the spiritual world dimensionally richer than the communal world.

The transitions of consciousness from the imaginal to the perceptual world, from the perceptual to the communal world, and from the communal to the spiritual world, are effected by processes of symbolization. A symbol is something which is accepted as pointing beyond itself to something else. The "something else" we shall call the "symbolandum" (plural "symbolanda"). The symbol symbolizes the symbolandum. The subject's power of transcendence makes possible the process of symbolization whereby consciousness leaps from something in one world to something in another.

(5) In the perceptual world independent objects *in* consciousness, i.e., sensations, are accepted as pointing beyond themselves to independent objects *outside* consciousness, i.e., perceptual objects. Through the symbolization that constitutes perception, the leap is made from consciousness of objects *within* consciousness to consciousness of objects *outside* consciousness. In practice the leap from symbol to symbolandum is made so quickly that consciousness typically accepts the perceptual object as its object and pushes to the side consciousness of the correlated sensations.

In perceptual consciousness the human being discovers its self as a subjective being incarnate in a complex perceptual object. Hence, the self is an intricate interrelationship of subjective and perceptual being. Moreover, the perceptual being of the self mediates for the self its dynamic interplay with perceptual objects in general.

The interplay of self and perceptual objects runs both ways. (a) The sensory organs of the perceptual self mediate sensations to consciousness. On the foundation of these sensations as symbols, a perceptual world is perceived. In this aspect of the interplay with perceptual objects the self is primarily passive. In this context the self is a "patient" (in contrast to "agent") and is to be characterized by "patiency" (in contrast to "agency").

(b) Other organs of the perceptual self mediate the will of the subject to the perceptual world. My hand, for example, is a complex perceptual object; but I, the subjective being, will the movement of the hand, and it moves. Through the movement of the hand other perceptual objects (which are not a part of the perceptual self) may also be moved. In this aspect of the interplay with perceptual objects, the self is primarily active. In this context the self is an agent and is to be characterized by agency.

There is no role for agency so long as the will of the subject is effected without obstacle, as is the case in the free play of the imagination. Agency implies the proposing of certain ends and the marshalling of certain means to attain these ends. The requirement of means reflects the fact that some obstacles stand between mere willing and the realization of what is willed. Hence, the exercise of agency implies a limited, not an absolute, autonomy of subjective being. The limitation on autonomy in the perceptual world is provided by the fact that perceptual objects immanate limits not imposed by the subject. Over against the absolute autonomy of the subject in the imaginal world, there is only a limited autonomy of the subject in the perceptual world.

Our second hypothesis concerning human nature, therefore, is that insofar as the human being is also a complex perceptual object in a world of perceptual objects, it is an incarnate subject with limited autonomy.

(6) The limited autonomy of the self provides the self with its primary motivation in the perceptual world: the motivation to marshal means to attain its own ends. The ability of the self to marshal means we may call its powers of agency. In the perceptual world the self is motivated to exercise its powers of agency to serve its own good. We shall refer to this primary motivation of the self in the perceptual world as the egocentricity principle. The perceptual world, we may note, is inherently egocentric: I and I alone perceive with my perception. The perceptual world is inherently monological: there are many objects, but only one subject.

The good which the self discovers in the marshalling of means to attain ends is either (a) in the marshalling of means, or (b) in the ends attained, or (c) in both. That is, the self may find that the marshalling of means is itself a creative, challenging activity and that it is good. Here, the encounter of the subject with perceptual obstacles is found to be good in itself. Or, the self may find that the end attained, the outcome achieved, is good. The encounter in itself is discounted or treated negatively: the good is the outcome achieved. Or, the self may find both the encounter and the outcome to be good.

Insofar as we focus on the encounter as good, we shall speak of encounter motivation and encounter agency. Insofar as we focus in on the outcome as good, we shall speak of outcome motivation and outcome agency. The word "encounter", it may be noted, is derived from the Latin "in contra" meaning "to bring into condition of being against." All agency involves encounter, but outcome agency is encounter for the sake of something else.

Our third hypothesis concerning human nature, therefore, is that insofar as the human being is an incarnate subject with limited autonomy, it is motivated to use its powers of agency for its own good, that is, the good of the encounter with perceptual objects as a creative activity and end in itself and the good of some outcome for which the encounter serves merely as means.

In the context of outcome motivation the system of obstacles provided by the fact that perceptual objects immanate limits not set by the subject appears to be of negative worth only. The system of obstacles prevent direct fulfillment of the subject's will. However, in the context of encounter motivation the system of obstacles provided by perceptual objects assumes a positive worth. Perceptual objects are of worth in this context precisely in their being *over against* subjective being. Here finitude assumes positive worth. Without the limitations provided by perceptual being there would be no human agency, no challenge for the creativity which characterizes subjective being.

The playing of games offers a ready illustration of these two kinds of motivation and agency. The formal end of the game is set forth in the rules (e.g., to kick the ball into the net as frequently as possible). Motivated to attain this formal outcome, we play to win. However, there is another motivation for play: the enjoyment of exercising agency under challenging conditions. Motivated by the enjoyment of an appropriately challenging encounter, we play "for the fun of it," win or lose. In playing games, we may note, encounter motivation is primary: if the challenge in encounter is consistently insufficient, the enjoyment of winning withers away.

The distinction of encounter and outcome agency is important in that while the former is inherently self-sustaining, the latter is inherently self-terminating. In English usage the word "end" has the double meaning of "goal" and "terminus." In encounter agency the "end" is the goal, but not the terminus. Because the goal is the creative activity itself, attainment of the goal sustains the activity, the motivation, and the agency. In outcome agency, on the other hand, the "end" is the end in both senses: with the achievement of the goal the agency is terminated.

For example, let us take the marshalling of means to get food as a model of outcome agency. My perceptual being immanates limits not set by myself as subject, and I find that I must ingest food in order to sustain my perceptual being. I chronically lack, need, want, food. Hence, I exercise agency to obtain food for consumption. Not surprisingly, the ingesting of food, the satisfaction of want, is usually accounted as worthwhile. However, the level of satisfaction enjoyed is dependent on the level of want suffered. That is, if there is no want, then there is no satisfaction. The activity of ingesting food when there is no want is no longer accounted a worthwhile human activity. Hence, if we ingest food at a continuous rate just sufficient to keep want at zero, we thereby keep satisfaction at zero also. If no agency were required to ingest food at this rate, then food would be ingested at this rate, a rate where neither want nor satisfaction would be experienced.[2] We shall call this absence of positive and negative experience apathy.

We may assess the success of outcome agency in terms of efficiency, that is, in terms of the minimization of means relative to ends. The theoretical limit of efficiency is the point where means are reduced to zero, that is, where human agency is no longer required. In this limit-case food would be ingested at that continuous rate where neither want nor satisfaction is experienced. The optimal "outcome," therefore, is one where outcome motivation and agency, want and satisfaction, are all zero.

---

[2]See Appendix B for a discussion using the traditional economic terms of marginal and total utility. When marginal utility is zero there can also be zero total utility if positive marginal utility arises from a reduction of a negative, i.e., a reduction in want.

The practical significance of these observations is that greater efficiency in outcome agency leads to greater affluence in consumption and a reduction in both want and satisfaction. That is, efficiency leads toward a state of apathy. This approach to apathy means a reduction in outcome motivation, e.g., in motivation to work.

There is an analogy to be drawn here with the second law of thermodynamics dealing with entropy. This law finds that thermal energy tends to move toward states of higher and higher entropy. This means an ever-increasing *unavailability* of thermal energy for doing work. Human want/satisfaction tends to move toward a state of apathy and hence toward zero motivation. This also means an ever-increasing unavailability of energy (here human energy) for doing work.

The correlation of affluence and apathy has relevance for an understanding of the postal problem in that the postal time of troubles coincided with the latter years of a remarkable general advance in affluence in Canada. This theme is pursued further in Chapter 6 (section 6.1).

A practical corollary to what we have been saying is that in a time of advancing affluence motivation to work will be undercut unless: (a) the horizon of wants is continually extended to motivate new outcome agency; or (b) attention is paid to strengthening encounter agency, i.e., making the work itself a creative, challenging activity for the workers. There is little doubt that the horizon of wants does tend to be extended with the advance of affluence. Wants that previously could not be considered emerge to make demands on agency. However, it seems probable that in a time of *rapid* advance in affluence the extension of the horizon of wants does not provide new motivation sufficient to compensate for the reduction accompanying the rise in affluence. To offset a decline in outcome agency, therefore, a strengthening of encounter agency is required.

Outcome agency may be assessed in terms of efficiency; encounter agency may be assessed in terms of what we shall call "sufficiency." Agency is sufficient when in the marshalling of means the creative powers of the agent are appropriately challenged. Agency is over-sufficient when in the marshalling of means the creative powers of the agent tend to be overwhelmed. Agency is under-sufficient or insufficient when in the marshalling of means the creative powers of the agent are not adequately challenged.

A difficulty in modern industrial development is that improvements in agency-efficiency may be attained at the expense of agency-sufficiency. Or, put somewhat differently, agency-efficiency has sometimes been attained at the expense of a more unequal distribution of agency-sufficiency. That is, scientists, technologists, industrial planners, and managers have enjoyed agency-sufficiency (even over-sufficiency), whereas many general workers have suffered agency-insufficiency. One might offer the opinion that the unequal distribution of agency-sufficiency is fundamentally a greater problem in the industrial world today than the unequal distribution of incomes.

A consequence of agency-insufficiency is that workers are not subjectively invested in their work: they are alienated from their work. This alienation means a lowered motivation to work and even a "struggle against work," as examined in Chapter 4 (section 4.1). This is a matter of considerable importance in understanding the postal time of troubles. In the 1950s and 1960s efforts to improve efficiency in the post office tended on the whole to produce agency insufficiency. Moreover, the massive technological transformation in the 1970s was planned and implemented (against the advice of some lone voices in personnel) largely without regard for the agency-sufficiency of the jobs created by the transformation. It would appear that the technologists assumed that the lower the demands on the powers of agency of the workers the better. If workers were only complex perceptual *objects* the assumption would have been safe enough. But since workers are also subjective beings seeking creative activity the consequences of the assumption are serious. This theme is pursued further in Chapter 6 (section 6.2).

(7) The communal world is one in which incarnate subjective beings exist in dynamic interplay with each other. The incarnate subject discovers that it is not alone: it encounters others in its own image. The leap to the recognition of other incarnate subjects is effected by means of a process of symbolization— but not by perception. One *perceives* another as incarnate, that is, as a perceptual object, but not as a subjective being. The subjective being of the other is disclosed by another process of symbolization, namely, language. We encounter the perceptual world through perception; we encounter the communal world through language. With respect to the communal world, therefore, it may be said: "In the beginning was the word."

In speech certain perceptual objects, i.e., sounds, which are easily produced by human agency, are accepted as symbols of certain subjective states; and these are used to communicate subjective states from one incarnate subject to another. As in perception certain subjective states, i.e., sensations, are accepted as symbols of objective beings, so, in speaking, certain objective beings, i.e., sounds, are accepted as symbols of subjective states. Hence, language involves a double symbolization: the symbolization whereby we leap from sensations to recognition of sounds and the symbolization whereby we leap from sounds to the thoughts intended.

It is interesting to note that it is as incarnate that subjective beings are able to communicate their subjectivity to each other. It is through their perceptual objectivity that human beings achieve intersubjectivity. Monologue can carry on in imagination without perceptual objectivity; but dialogue uses perceptual objectivity as its medium.

Essential to community is mutuality. The one and the other participating in communication must share the symbol/symbolandum connections. The leap from a specific set of symbols to a specific set of symbolanda must be the same for all participants in intercommunication. Moreover, there must be trust that when the speaker utters sounds that symbolize the shared meaning, the speaker "means what he says." That is, there must be trust and a basis for trust that speakers will use their utterances to disclose and not to hide their subjective states. The limits of community are the limits of trustworthiness. One is trustworthy insofar as one wills the good of the other as one wills the good of the self.

Our fourth hypothesis concerning human nature, therefore, is that insofar as human beings are also communal beings they are motivated to use their powers of agency for the common good. This we may call the mutuality principle.

We shall examine the pursuit of mutuality in a number of contexts. Common to these contexts, we shall find, is the possibility of reversion to a perceptual orientation or, what amounts to the same thing, the possibility of subversion of the mutuality principle by the egocentricity principle. Powers of agency may be used to serve one's own good or to serve the common good. However, we shall also call the egocentricity principle simply the power principle, thereby emphasizing the importance of the use of power with an egocentric orientation. Lord Acton spoke effectively and succinctly of the tendency to subversion of the mutuality principle by the power principle in his famous maxim, "Power tends to corrupt and absolute power corrupts absolutely."

(a) Mutuality is given a more or less favourable environment through the organization of human relationships. In the pursuit of mutuality human beings organize themselves. If each and every one freely expresses his or her autonomy and seeks his or her own good without acknowledging any restraint, the result is anarchy (from the Greek "an arko" meaning "no rule"). This is a kind of rulelessness that cannot be sustained. As Thomas Hobbes envisaged in his *Leviathan*, it is a war of all against all in which life is "solitary, poor, nasty, brutish and short." Human beings, therefore, turn from anarchy to the acceptance of some form of rule, some form of organization.

The acceptance of organization places certain restraints on human beings using their powers of agency to promote their own good. That is, organization places certain restraints on the operation of the power principle. This system of restraints provides an environment within which the mutuality principle may operate. However, in practice organizations provide more or less favourable environments for the expression of mutuality.

Within an organization authority to exercise power may be distributed among persons for the common good. For example, some are authorized to formulate the "rule," some to interpret the "rule," some to enforce the "rule." These persons thereby exercise control over others within the organization. This authority is granted for the common good. However, in submitting to authority the members of the organization conform to rule and in conforming to rule are immanating limits and assuming a form analogous to that of perceptual objects. In this context those in authority are tempted to revert to a perceptual orientation and to exercise their powers accordingly. That is, those who exercise control over others within the organization are tempted to use that control to treat others as objects to be manipulated for their own advantage (whether or not the interests of others are also served thereby). Hence, within any organization those granted authority for the common good are tempted to let the power principle subvert the mutuality principle.

A subversion in thought, in ideology, tends to accompany this subversion in practice. The treatment of others as objects to be manipulated for one's own good is offensive to both one's own and others' sense of community. Hence, this treatment of others tends to be camouflaged by consistent protestations that the control is exercised for the common good.

(b) Mutuality is fully expressed only in an all-inclusive or non-discriminating way. However, in practice mutuality falls short of this and is expressed in a partially exclusive or discriminating way. Discriminating community is limiting in two respects: (i) it cuts out of community those who are excluded; and (ii) the exclusions affect the quality of the community among those who are doing the excluding.

The more intense the exclusions, the more serious are the limitations of discriminating communities. Let us take, for example, a morally discriminating community, that is, one that identifies itself as the good and arrays itself against others as adversaries of the good and hence evil. The relation of the in-group to the out-group in this case is fundamentally adversarial. There is no possibility of community with the out-group, no possibility of establishing an acceptable common good. Thus, the adversarial attitude of the morally discriminating community becomes itself a major obstacle to the establishment of a wider community.

Further, the nature of the exclusion affects the quality of the discriminating community's own mutuality. We offer the following model of the kind of deterioration that tends to occur in the morally discriminating community's mutuality. (i) Since the morally discriminating community is arrayed against an evil adversary, the morally discriminating community must protect itself from the evil practices of the adversary. It needs, therefore, to be free to use whatever tactics or strategies the adversary uses against it. Consequently, the morally discriminating community comes to use the same practices as its adversary. (ii) A non-discriminating observer now sees little difference in the ethics practised by the morally discriminating community and its adversary. The morally discriminating community, however, objects to this non-discriminating assessment on the grounds that it gives comfort to the adversary. Hence, the non-discriminating observer is also accused of serving the adversary, i.e., of serving evil. "Truth" is now held to be that which serves the interest of the "good" in-group; falsehood is that which serves the interest of the "evil" out-group. Non-discriminating truth is pushed aside. (iii) What is in the interest of the in-group is not always easy to decide. If one advocates what is not in the interest of the in-group, one will be cast out of the community as serving the interest of the adversary. However, if there have been differences of opinion within the in-group as to what is in the interest of the in-group and the differences are settled, then those on the losing side are either allowed to repent or are cast out of the community. Under these conditions authority within the in-group gravitates toward autocracy with orthodoxy effectively established as being what the autocrat wills. The autocrat falls an easy prey to the power principle, and the subjective autonomy of the members of the in-group is seriously suppressed.

(c) Mutuality is fully expressed only as an end and not as a means to an end. However, the exercise of mutuality also frequently serves egocentric interests as well. For example, the introduction of division of labour and exchange, which requires some exercise of mutuality, also serves egocentric interests by increasing productivity so that in general all enjoy a greater harvest of goods. This leads persons to use mutuality as a means to serve their own ends. The weakness of the mutuality principle as a means is that whenever circumstances arise in which the mutuality principle does not serve egocentric ends, or some other approach better serves egocentric ends, the mutuality principle is abandoned. Hence, the mutuality principle as a means is unstable.

The use of the mutuality principle to serve the power principle may assume a blatantly corrupt form. It is clear that one's powers are severely circumscribed unless one can also control other people. Our control of perceptual objects is based on: (i) the immanation of limits by perceptual objects; and (ii) our knowledge of the limits which perceptual objects immanate. Analogously, our control of persons may be based on: (i) the conformity to rule of persons and in particular their conformity to rule in the service of the common good; and (ii) our knowledge of this conformity to rule. Hence, as individuals use their knowledge of the limits perceptual objects immanate to manipulate objects for their own ends, so individuals may use their knowledge of the conformity to rule of persons serving the common good to manipulate persons for their own advantage.

In the context of community it is always possible for the power principle to subvert the mutuality principle. This is a matter of considerable importance in understanding what happened in the postal time of troubles. The beginning of the time of troubles was marked by a sense of outrage on the part of the postal workers that those in authority in the postal organization were using their authority in ways contrary to the common good, or at least the good of the postal workers. The 1965 strike reflected this outrage; and the Public Service Staff Relations Act of 1967 in effect reflected some recognition that subversion by the power principle might appear even within the civil service. However, neither the government nor the civil service unions recognized the limitations of discriminating communities. The postal unions organized as discriminating communities and arrayed themselves adversarially against postal management. This had important consequences: the possibility of creating a united postal community to serve the public good faded, and the quality of mutuality within the discriminating communities themselves was seriously affected. This theme is pursued further in Chapter 6 (sections 6.4 and 6.5).

(8) The spiritual world is one in which incarnate subjective beings in community with each other encounter an ultimate good. We may make a first

approach to this world through its negative symbol. As loneliness is a negative symbol of a communal world where loneliness is appeased, so a sense of meaninglessness is a negative symbol of the spiritual world where meaninglessness is appeased. A fundamental characteristic of the spiritiual being is the need for a good that fulfils the void of meaninglessness.

As the subjective being needs conformity-to-order with respect to its objects, so it needs fulfillment-of-meaning with respect to itself. The being of an object is not sustained unless it immanates its order. The being of a subject is not sustained unless there is a reason, a meaning, a good, which is fulfilled through its being. Hence, subjective being presupposes both *order* sufficient to sustain its objects and *good* sufficient to sustain itself.

Our fifth hypothesis concerning human nature, therefore, is that insofar as human beings are also spiritual beings, they are motivated to use their powers of agency for the ultimate good.

The modern age, which has excelled in objective science, grasps very firmly the need of *order* sufficient to sustain its objects. However, the modern age is rather uncertain about the need of a *good* sufficient to sustain its subjects. Hence, the contemporary age is one of strong faith in the sense of confidently presupposing the order which sustains objective being, but an age of uncertainty in the sense of presupposing the good which sustains subjective being. As a consequence, great steps forward have been made in objective terms while human beings themselves grope about uncertainly searching for meaning but lacking even the confidence that this quest itself is a legitimate one. The psychotherapist Viktor E. Frankl in his work *The Unheard Cry for Meaning* asserts that "the feeling of meaninglessness" constitutes "the mass neurosis of today." The problem that brings people "crowding into our clinics and offices now is existential frustration, their 'existential vacuum.'"[3]

The strength of the scientific faith in sufficient order and the apparent weakness of the spiritual faith in sufficient good is partly explicable in terms of a distinction we might make between an open and a closed faith. An open faith is one that is embodied in a set of beliefs, but that remains open to a modification of beliefs insofar as continuing experience warrants it. A closed faith is one that is embodied in a set of beliefs, but is not open to a modification of these beliefs. Hence, when for whatever reason a scientific belief becomes questionable the response of the open faith is: "If the specific form of order in this case is not that which we postulated, then let us look for the specific form of order which does obtain." The response of the closed faith is: "If the specific order which we postulated does not obtain, then chaos reigns in this case." Similarly, when for whatever reason a spiritual belief becomes questionable the response of open faith is: "If the specific form of the good in this case is not that which we postulated, let us seek the form of the good which does obtain." And the

---

[3]Viktor E. Frankl. *The Unheard Cry for Meaning.* New York: Simon and Shuster, p. 23.

response of the closed faith is: "If the specific form of the good is not that which we postulated, then there is no good sufficient to sustain subjective being."

Modern science has tended to espouse an open faith. Western spirituality, on the other hand, has frequently leaned in the direction of a closed faith. At the same time, certain traditional spiritual beliefs have included propositions concerning the nature of the perceptual world. Therefore, when advances in science rendered some of these propositions questionable, the response of closed faith was: "If the specific form of the good is not that which we postulated, then there is no good sufficient to sustain subjective being." That is, the debate now radically called in question the reality of the spiritual world itself. In these terms, granted the advance of science as itself good, the chief cause of spiritual uncertainty in the contemporary world is the choice of a closed faith by advocates of the spiritual world.

The question arises as to whether there is sufficient good in the perceptual and communal world to obviate the need of a leap to a dimensionally more-comprehensive spiritual world. There is good to be found in the perceptual-communal world, indeed there are many goods, but these are all conditional, that is, they are dependent on the presence of favourable conditions. These goods are not sufficient to sustain meaning for the subject. For example, in the perceptual world an abundance of economic goods brings us not sustained euphoria, but rather chronic apathy. Furthermore, although we may find the challenge of coping with perceptual obstacles to be itself good, we may suffer from time to time from agency under-sufficiency or over-sufficiency. In any case, old age, sickness, and death (what the Buddhists call the three enemies of mankind) confront us with obstacles that eventually and inevitably overwhelm us in our perceptual existence. In the communal world various forms of mutuality are found to be good. However, communities large and small depend on the good will and wisdom of all, and when the good will and wisdom of some for whatever reason falter, the community may break up, leaving the individual bruised and broken. What is needed, therefore, to sustain subjective being is an unconditional or ultimate good that transcends the conditional goods of the perceptual and communal worlds.

The leap from the perceptual-communal world to the spiritual world is made by a process of symbolization. A great variety of elements from the perceptual-communal world may symbolize something of the dimensionally more-comprehensive spiritual reality. For example, in worship, words, chants, singing, instrumental music, vestments, sculptures, architecture, incense, lights, colours, processions, dancing, rituals, water, bread, wine, all may serve as symbols pointing beyond themselves to spiritual symbolanda. Symbols, of course, may for one reason or another cease to symbolize, in which case they simply revert to their perceptual-communal setting and to whatever significance they have there.

Pursuit of the ultimate good may take a religious form explicitly recognizing that dimension of spirituality which transcends perceptual-communal reality.

Worshipping communities are formed that give expression to an unconditional commitment to the transcendent source. However, the pursuit of the ultimate good can also take a secular form with the transcendent dimension of its spirituality muted in conception although not in practice. An important contemporary example of a secular form of spirituality is Marxism. The ultimate good is here conceived to be a classless society, an end to be achieved by means of a class struggle. In the fullness of time the oppressed classes will be liberated from their oppressors. What is explicitly spiritual about Marxism is its unconditional commitment to the attainment of a classless society as an unconditional good. We may note that in practice Marxism also has tended to be a closed faith.

We may note three consequences which spiritual faith, expressed as an unconditional commitment to an ultimate good, has for human existence. First, it gives meaning sufficient to sustain subjective being in spite of the instability of the goods of the perceptual-communal world. This is the point we have emphasized above.

Second, it gives extraordinary powers to the faithful. To give a dramatic example from religious history: In the seventh century a nondescript group of tribesmen from the fringe of the Arabian desert committed themselves unconditionally to Allah as revealed by Muhammad, erupted into the Mediterranean world, and in one generation became its political-cultural masters. Or, to give an equally dramatic example from a contemporary secular faith: In the second quarter of the twentieth century an unimpressive group of Chinese Marxists committed themselves unconditionally to the class struggle for a classless society, thrust themselves into the turbulent Chinese scene, and in a single generation acquired undisputed mastery of the most highly populated nation of the world.

Third, an unconditional commitment to the ultimate good is embodied in beliefs and practices that are more or less adequate expressions of the ultimate good. As we have noted, we may respond to our experience of the greater or lesser adequacy of beliefs and practices either with open or closed faith.

Some of the implications of this for human existence may be illustrated with reference to the analogue provided by the pursuit of science. Science is embodied in various theories that are more or less adequate expressions of the nature of the perceptual world. Insofar as continuing scientific experience discloses the inadequacy of theories, scientists are motivated to seek out theories that are more adequate expressions of the nature of the perceptual world. Hence, precisely because they are unconditionally committed to the pursuit of truth, scientists are prepared to surrender theories that were intended to express this faith, but that are now found to be inadequate. That is, the unconditional commitment that applies to the truth is not extended to the theories that intentionally express the truth; rather, commitment to theories is conditional in nature. The scientist remains committed to a theory only so long as among alternative possibilities it appears to be the most adequate representation of perceptual reality. The truth to which the scientist is unconditionally committed is, therefore, something that is known only in part and in part is only promise, invitation, or challenge. However, it is the truth as "promise, invitation, or challenge" that gives modern science its dynamic vitality.

Analogously, insofar as continuing spiritual experience discloses the inadequacy of beliefs and practices intended to express the ultimate good, persons of spiritual faith are motivated to seek out more adequate beliefs and practices. Hence, precisely because they are unconditionally committed to the ultimate good, they are prepared to surrender beliefs and practices intended to express this good, but which are now found to be inadequate. The unconditional commitment to the ultimate good does not imply an unconditional commitment to beliefs and practices, but rather a conditional commitment to beliefs and practices. The person of faith remains committed to a belief or practice only so long as among alternative possibilities it appears to be the most adequate expression of the ultimate good. The ultimate good to which the person of faith is unconditionally committed is, therefore, something that is known only in part and in part is only "promise, invitation, or challenge." Nonetheless, it is the ultimate good's "promise, invitation, or challenge" that gives faith its dynamic vitality.

We describe here what we called above open faith. The error of a closed faith is that it stops short with an image of the ultimate good that is too small, and that in its stopping it cuts off the dynamic pursuit of the ultimate good.

The set of beliefs and practices that embody spiritual faith have important implications for the forms of community life. It is important, therefore, to discover what communal forms modern expressions of spirituality foster. Max Weber, in his influential work *The Protestant Ethic and the Spirit of Capitalism*, has argued that the Christian, and in particular the Protestant, vision of the ultimate good has fostered the kind of industriousness important in the development of the modern industrial system. Protestants have been industrious not simply for the sake of a greater acquisition of economic goods, but for the sake of the ultimate good as well. A non-economic motivation has had a profound economic impact. Similarly, the unconditional commitment of contemporary Marxists to the pursuit of the class struggle is a non-economic motivation that can have a profound economic impact. In this case the impact presses toward a breakdown of the modern industrial system (at least in the pre-revolutionary phases of the historical movement).

Consideration of commitment to an ultimate good seems far removed from a crisis in the postal service. However, as we have noted, spiritual commitment may have a profound impact on the secular community. In the postal time of troubles, the Protestant ethic was conspicuous by its absence. Many of the contemporary youth, on the contrary, carried on a "struggle against work." Moreover, a small but effective minority of Marxists and like-minded radicals waged a class war within Canada Post, making co-operative effort to provide a unified and efficient mail service more and more remote. At the same time the Quiet Revolution in Quebec produced its own "ethic" with some disquieting consequences for Canada Post. These themes are pursued further in Chapters 7 and 8.

CHAPTER 6

Contemporary Developments Affecting Motivation in Canada Post

This chapter is concerned with certain contemporary developments and the kind of responses to them that have seriously affected the motivation of postal workers. The following are discussed: (1) the advance of affluence and apathy; (2) the spread of agency-deficiency and worker alienation; (3) the youth movement and the thrust toward unconditional freedom; (4) unionization, the Public Service Staff Relations Act, and the problems of an adversarial attitude; (5) unionization and the problems of an antipathetic attitude; and (6) the monopoly and government-owned structure of Canada Post as enabling extreme responses to these developments.

6.1 The Advance of Affluence and Apathy

During the first three decades following World War II there was a remarkable development in Canada in the ability of the economy to satisfy perceptual needs—to satisfy what Abraham H. Maslow in his hierarchy of human needs would call the physiological and safety needs.

(1) In the twenty-five-year period 1950 to 1975 output per person in Canada doubled, and in accordance with this improvement in labour productivity real compensation per person doubled (see Table 3.4A).

(2) In the same twenty-five-year period the participation of women in the labour force increased decisively from 24 to 44 percent. Relative to the participation rate of men, that of women doubled in this period from 28 to 57 percent. The figures suggest that already by 1975 both spouses were working in the typical family. It is to be noted that points (1) and (2) together mean that Canadian families were enjoying real family incomes two to four times that of twenty-five years earlier. This is a remarkable advance in general affluence within a single generation.

(3) Sexual reinforcement of the economic drive was also greatly weakened by the revolution in sexual mores taking place in this period. Discovery of the pill accelerated the growing acceptance of extramarital sexual relations among the youth. For young men, a strong motivation for disciplined devotion to work has traditionally been the acquiring and holding of good jobs so that they can afford to get married. This marriage reinforcement of the work mores was significantly weakened in this period: sexual drives could now more easily than before be satisfied outside of marriage, and even within marriage the working spouse eased the financial pressure.

(4) A relatively high level of economic security was achieved in this period. Most important, a relatively low rate of unemployment was sustained in spite of

the influx of women into the labour force and, later in the period, the flood of youth from the post-war baby boom. This meant that generally there were job alternatives and that attachment to whatever job one happened to have was not crucial to economic security. Moreover, there was a considerable expansion in the period in collective arrangements, either through government social security provision or through employer-employee contracts, to meet the crises of the individual's existence, e.g., unemployment insurance, medical and hospital insurance, life insurance, pension and retirement plans.

The benefit of these economic security arrangements, it may be noted, is *not* to be added to the doubling of real incomes mentioned above. Costs were met by income taxes and other deductions from gross pay. However, the rapid expansion in these arrangements does indicate something about how the remarkable increase in real income was spent. More went to ensuring that income-earners would remain economically viable, as Maslow's theory (see below) would lead us to expect. (This is not to say that the security needs of Canadians were wholly satisfied in this period. The threat of a nuclear holocaust and a decline in the stability of the family unit were important new concerns.)

We have argued that the end result of satisfying perceptual needs is not the maximization of satisfaction, but rather apathy, that is, the maximization of "human entropy" whereby energy becomes unavailable for work. Abraham Maslow, the noted psychologist, argues in a parallel way that there is a hierarchy of human needs, and the satisfaction of the lower, initially more demanding of these eliminates them as motivators of human activity.[1] Maslow's theory of motivation has attracted the attention of a number of prominent industrial management specialists, particularly through the writings of Douglas McGregor of the Massachusetts Institute of Technology.[2] The theory is simple enough in outline. Certain basic needs take precedence over others and are the prime motivators until they are, at least in some degree, satisfied. However, once they are satisfied, they cease to motivate and the other basic needs come to the fore and become the prime, effective motivators. Maslow classifies basic needs in the following order of precedence or prepotency. First, physiological needs. These include the need for food and drink, shelter and clothing, sexual gratification, etc. Second, safety needs. These include "security; stability; dependency; protection; freedom from fear, from anxiety and chaos; need for structure, order, law, limits; strength in the protector; and so on."[3] Third, togetherness needs. These include the need for love, affection, and belonging in a community. Fourth, esteem needs. These include the need for self-esteem and for the esteem of others. And, fifth, the need for self-actualization. This is "the desire to become more and more what one idiosyncratically is, to become everything that one is capable of becoming."[4]

---

[1]Abraham H. Maslow, *Motivation and Personality*. New York: Harper & Row, 1954; second edition, 1970.

[2]See especially, Douglas McGregor. *The Human Side of Enterprise*. New York: McGraw-Hill, 1960.

[3]Maslow, *Motivation and Personality*, p. 39.

[4]Maslow, *Motivation and Personality*, p. 46.

It is to be noted that the needs that we would generally class as higher needs—togetherness, esteem, self-actualization—have a lesser prepotency. The higher man does not live by bread alone—but he will be tempted to do so if he has no bread. The higher need (in tendency though not always in fact) is dependent on a sufficient satisfaction of the lower needs with their higher prepotency.

In our own theory of motivation we distinguish the outcome motive for working, that is, wages and the satisfaction of the diverse wants that wages make possible, from the encounter motive for working, that is, the challenge of creative encounter in working. Wage-motivation is related primarily to the satisfaction of Maslow's physiological and safety needs. Challenge-motivation, on the other hand, is related in one way or another to self-actualization, although it may at the same time involve any of Maslow's five levels of need.

Wages provide means relevant to the satisfaction of physiological and safety needs. The higher the wages the more adequately, presumably, physiological and safety needs can be satisfied. As wages rise, we reach a level where physiological and safety needs, insofar as that which can satisfy them can be bought, will be effectively satisfied; hence these needs will tend to fade as prime motivators. According to Maslow's theory, attention will then shift to needs of belonging, esteem, and self-actualization; and these will become the prime motivators.

The problem at this point for work motivation is that wages provide means that have no definite relation to the satisfaction of these higher needs. It might be thought that a higher wage might be relevant to the satisfaction of the need for esteem; but if one's fellow workers are all getting the higher wage, one's self-esteem and the esteem of others is scarcely affected. It follows, therefore, that if work motivation is to be sustained, then work itself must have a sufficiently high agency-content and provide sufficient creative challenge to compensate for the weakening wage-motivation.

In terms of individual careers it is not uncommon that as the individual's wages rise with successive promotions to the level where physiological and safety needs are effectively satisfied, the kinds of jobs assumed are those with higher agency-content. That is, promotions introduce the worker to more highly skilled, more responsible jobs, jobs in general with more agency and less patiency. In this way increasing apathy with respect to perceptual needs is offset by greater creative challenge in the job itself. Typically promotions bring both improved wages and improved challenges. However, what happens when workers *generally* get levels of real wages that earlier were achieved only by highly skilled or managerial types? Apathy will tend to appear, wage-motivation will tend to weaken, and unless the challenge of the work itself is upgraded overall work motivation will tend to fall.

6.2 The Spread of Agency-Insufficiency and Alienation

Given the rapid advance in affluence in the early post-war decades, what was needed in the workplace to offset the correlated advance in apathy was a general upgrading of jobs to improve their agency-content and to make them more challenging in a diversity of ways. Unfortunately, in search of higher productivity, Canada Post moved slowly in the opposite direction in the earlier part of the period, and then, faced with the plummeting productivity of the "time of troubles," designed and introduced a technological transformation in the post office without regard for the agency-insufficiency of many of the new jobs.

After the Woods Gordon report on postal organization in 1952, the post office moved toward a more scientific management of its operations. The primary tool of this new management was a more careful measurement and comparison of inputs and outputs of various work processes. The initial results were encouraging: improvements in productivity took place. However, in the long run certain adverse effects began to emerge.

Concentration on the number of pieces of mail passing through a particular process per worker per hour awakened in the workers fears of indefinite speed-up. These fears began to vie with the workers' traditional pride in their acquired skills. Furthermore, concentration on the number of pieces passing through particular processes tended to undermine the traditional focus of a whole shift: supervisors and postal clerks working together as a team on the overall objective of getting the mail processed and sent out. In the "old days" the reward for a good team performance in clearing all the mail off the floor quickly might be that the whole shift could go home early. (It is interesting to note in Chapter 4 that Roger Bouvier's experiment in "Supervising in the Post Office" was able, temporarily, to revive this practice for his shift.) Now a wedge was driven between the supervisor and the postal workers: the latter did not want the former pitching in to work with them if that was apt to increase the work-load quotas in the future.

Moreover, yielding to the simplicity of the ABC sortation method, whereby mail was sorted alphabetically according to address and which temporary workers could pick up quickly, the traditional memory sortation method, which required considerable knowledge, training, and experience, was gradually supplanted as the major sortation method. To maintain the level of efficiency in memory sortation, annual national tests both in practical sortation skill and in knowledge of postal regulations had been required. Postal workers took pride in maintaining their proficiency and in the proof of this as given in the annual tests. In 1963 these tests were abolished as national requirements. The consequence was that the postal workers' sense of having a high skill which one had to be alert to retain tended to be undermined.

Inadvertently the unions contributed to this undermining process by pressing for the same classification of postal workers whatever the sortation skill required of them. This extended to the postal coders when the new sortation technology was introduced in the 1970s. The unions were driven by fear of the downgrading of their jobs. However, the common pay classification suggested that the postal clerk had a kind of job that almost anyone could do.

Hence, the move toward more scientific management culminating in the technological transformation in the 1970s in fact had two important long-term effects: it drove a wedge between the first-line supervisors and the postal workers and thereby undercut the team spirit of a shift; and it undermined the postal workers' sense that they had a highly skilled, quasi-professional occupation in which they could take pride.

After the technological transformation of the 1970s, Canada Post was a model of engineering efficiency that observers from all over the world came to study. However, the engineering efficiency masked very serious agency-insufficiencies. Note, for example, what is now required of the postal coders. Coders sit on chairs facing consoles where a mechanism confronts them with a succession of envelopes with the written or typed address code displayed. Their work is to type the code—letter, number, letter, number, letter, number—whereupon the mechanism imprints the requisite colour code. This is easily and quickly done. The mechanism takes the envelope away and replaces it with the next. The operation is repeated . . . and repeated . . . over and over again. The minutes pass, the hours pass, the days pass . . . the operation is repeated. There are, of course, humane ten-minute breaks every hour. Nonetheless, it is difficult to imagine workers rising from their coding desks at the end of a typical day and exclaiming, "It is good!"

The problem of agency-deficiency depicted here springs not so much from the servant role of the worker as from the highly specialized, simplified, and repeatable form of the work operation. The workers' degree of discretion is minimal. The operation is machine-like: indeed, if it were not for this or that complication, the operation would be done by machine. One cannot be surprised, therefore, if the workers feel that they are being used simply as complicated machines. In Canada Post, in fact, there is a machine substitute for the postal coders. If the address codes are typed by postal users on standard-size envelopes in the appropriate place with appropriate clarity, then the Optical Character Reader (OCR)—a machine developed in Japan—can read the typed code and imprint the colour code at the remarkable rate of 30,000 per hour. The OCR is a machine; the postal coders are actual persons. In the early years of its trial the OCR frequently broke down; but as machines they are perfectible in their specialized operation, and they are now working more effectively. In any case, we may assume that they never broke down because they were being treated merely as objects. The same cannot be assumed concerning the postal coders—treated like objects, they may break down not because they cannot do the work, but because they are basically offended, estranged, alienated.

The peculiar, alienating character of many modern, technology-controlled jobs may be emphasized by contrasting the temporary postal coder with, say, a hired hand on a small, non-mechanized Canadian farm of a generation ago. The servant role of both is clear—perhaps somewhat more pervasive in the case of the farm hand. The real wages of the postal coder are several times that of the farm hand, and the physical comfort of the coder's work situation far surpasses that of the farm hand. However, in the variety of the work operations performed, in the variety of skills needed to be developed, and in the wide discretion that must necessarily be used in various situations, the farm hand completely outstrips the postal coder. The farm hand plows, harrows, and plants seed; cuts, rakes, and loads hay; harnesses, drives, and tends horses; herds, milks, and feeds cows; cuts, hauls, and splits wood; and is a farmer, woodsman, mechanic, and builder. Moreover, the work changes with the seasons, with the time of day, and with the vagaries of the weather. In spite of a clearly subordinate role, the hired hand exercises responsible agency in a variety of ways, and as strenuous as the work may be, we can still imagine the farm hand saying at the end of a hard day, "It is good!" In contrast, technology-controlled jobs, such as that of the postal coders, involve an orderly, consistent, and sustained suppression of the creative capacities of the workers. One consequence is the alienation of workers from their work.

6.3 The Youth Movement and the Thrust Toward Unconditional Freedom

The first decade of Canada Post's "time of troubles" coincided with the heyday of a remarkable youth movement that passed like a great tidal wave across the Western world. The main thrust of the movement was toward unconditional freedom. Restrictions of all kinds were to be swept aside. All established authority was suspect. All discipline—including the discipline of work—was viewed as suppression.

A typical expression of this youth movement was the so-called New Left, which climaxed as a social force toward the end of the 1960s. The movement adopted the revolutionary terminology of Marxism and adapted it to promote its anarchistic vision of freedom. Kolakowski describes the New Left vision as follows:

> At the present time students were the most oppressed members of society, and therefore the most revolutionary. All were oppressed, however: the bourgeoisie had introduced the cult of labour, and the first duty was therefore to stop work—the necessities of life would be forthcoming in some way or another. One disgraceful form of oppression was the prohibition of drugs, and this too must be fought against. Sexual liberation, freedom from work, from academic discipline and restrictions of all kinds, universal and total liberation— all this was the essence of Communism.[5]

Peter Taylor wrote "Working in the Post Office" in the early 1970s. The affinity of his position with that of the New Left is apparent.

One way of viewing this youth movement is as a revolt against the all-pervasive patiency promoted by modern science, technology, and industry—a revolt, however, that displayed dimensional deficiencies as serious as those against which it revolted. Modern science, technology, and industry concentrate

---

[5]Leszek Kolakowski. *Main Currents of Marxism*, Vol. III, *The Breakdown.* Oxford: Clarendon Press, 1978, p. 489.

on the perceptual world. Here we have the complementary engagement of (1) objects conforming to limits and (2) the subject immanating and transcending limits. Overlooking the latter partner in the engagement, many proponents of modernization have focused on the first and have treated human beings as also simply objects conforming to limits. Against this extreme ascription of patiency to themselves, the youth of this period revolted. However, in this revolt the youth turned with open arms to the other partner to the perceptual engagement—the hitherto disparaged limit-transcending subject—and rejected patiency with light-hearted abandon. That is, the revolt stayed within the perceptual sphere and merely jumped from one one-sided extreme to the other. In a kind of collective ecstasy the youth of the time spurned the objective dimensions of human existence and went all out for liberation from all kinds of restrictions.

The outcome of the youth movement, predictably, was not a release from alienation, but rather a slump into an even more deeply set alienation—an alienation from the nature of human existence itself. There is no revolution in the structure of society that could possibly offer in practice the absence of restrictions that the movement demanded. (And if there were such a society, we may argue, it would be undesirable because there also would be a deficiency of creative challenge.) Jean-Paul Sartre demanded absolute freedom for his subject and discovered that this brought only an unhappy consciousness from which there was no possible deliverance. The youth movement, also demanding unconditional freedom, found only an unhappy consciousness.

For a number of reasons, what was happening to youth in the 1960s and 1970s tended to have a serious impact on Canada Post. The proportion of youth in the Canadian population increased very rapidly in this period. This resulted from the post-war baby boom. In 1951 slightly more than 15 percent of the population were in the fifteen to twenty-four age bracket; twenty-five years later this same age group constituted almost 20 percent of a population roughly two-thirds larger. Consequently, that part of the citizenry that was most sensitive to the social transformation taking place—the youth—became demographically much more important in this period.

The youth who were beginning to flood the labour force by the mid-1960s were especially favoured in a number of ways: they were born to parents who now enjoyed an affluence and economic security unique in history; they were born to a generation of parents who had been particularly sensitized to the long-term psychological damage that might result from frustrating their children; and they received more education than any generation before them. However, it would appear that there are no pluses in human affairs without minuses. Education heightens the critical faculties—the capacity to transcend one's situation—and hence probably tends to raise sensitivity to alienation. Lack of practical hardships and too much protection from frustration in one's early life may turn out to be poor preparation for the inevitable frustrations of later life. It is worth noting that according to the Buddhist tradition Gautama Buddha lived an early life of exceptional affluence, protected from the knowledge of those ultimate frustrators of human existence, old age, sickness, and death. The dramatic discovery of these fundamental frustrations was the immediate occasion for his renunciation. Carefully protected from frustrations in childhood, contemporary youth were unusually sensitive to alienation as they emerged into the adult world. Moreover, for the modern youth the situation was fraught with contradiction, for over all there hung the new and terrible threat of nuclear holocaust. It is perhaps not surprising, therefore, that as this generation grew into adulthood many found themselves peculiarly susceptible to alienation.

It appears probable that at the beginning of its "time of troubles" the post office was taking on a higher than normal proportion of alienation-sensitive youth. In the first two decades after World War II postal workers had enjoyed increases in pay, but relative to the commercial sector in general, had fallen back by about 20 percent. On the eve of the 1965 strike it looked as if they were continuing to lose out and the workers were understandably upset. In the large urban centres turnover had become high, and offering as it was relatively low wages, the post office had to scrape the bottom of the barrel to get replacements. The "bottom of the barrel" here meant younger, less experienced, less well-adjusted workers.

6.4 Unionization, the Public Service Staff Relations Act, and the Problems of an Adversarial Attitude

Modern industrialization developed in the West in the context of a competitive, free-enterprise system. The system gave great play to the egocentric drives of the human actors, but contained them nonetheless within the boundaries imposed by contractual agreements with others and within the rules established by a democratic state. The overall result was a remarkable improvement in productivity.

However, the rules of ownership within this system enabled individuals, families, and corporations to accumulate economic resources, and in particular the reproducible means of production, i.e., capital, and on the basis of this accumulation to acquire even more capital. The system was receptive, therefore, to concentration of ownership of capital. With the accumulation of capital came the ability to hire workers and, hence, to exercise control over others. As the power principle would lead us to anticipate, capital-owners tended to use this power to promote their own interests (whether or not this also promoted the interests of the workers).

The larger the accumulation of capital and the larger the collection of workers for a single corporation, the more important became the decisions of the corporation's owners/managers for a whole community. If the decisions affect the whole community but are made by the owners only, the community as a whole lacks self-determination. Where it appears that the interests of the community as a whole are not being served, this lack of self-determination tends to generate within the community a call for reform.

The experience of the Great Depression of the 1930s undermined public confidence in the adequacy of a completely laissez-faire competitive system. The interests of the community as a whole were not being adequately served. Moreover, the experience of World War II in the 1940s strengthened public confidence in the potentially favourable consequences of government intervention in the economic system. Hence, by the post–World War II period, the climate of public opinion in Canada had, in general, become favourable to interposing some power to counterbalance that of the industrial owners/managers. This counterbalancing power was exercised partly by government and partly by labour unions functioning under appropriate legislation. Both forms of counterbalancing power modified the competitive, free-enterprise system.

In the post–World War II period unionization in the private sector came of age. Unions came to be generally accepted as a standard part of the industrial set-up. Concerning unions in the public sector, there continued to be more uncertainty. If industrial managers bent on making profits cannot be trusted to promote the welfare of the workers, need the same be assumed of senior public servants pledged to serve the public good? Does the power principle prevail in spite of the presence of countervailing motivation? On the other hand, should public sector workers be denied rights that have already been granted to private sector workers?

In 1963 the Liberal government under Lester Pearson took the plunge and set up a Preparatory Committee on Collective Bargaining in the Public Service "to make preparations for the introduction into the Public Service of an appropriate form of collective bargaining and arbitration." The committee reported in 1965 and the Public Service Staff Relations Act was passed in 1967.

As the preparatory committee was planning collective bargaining in the public service, trouble was brewing in the post office. Shortly after the committee reported in 1965, recommending collective bargaining with recourse if necessary to compulsory arbitration (but not permitting strike action), the postal trouble erupted in a strike by the letter carriers and postal clerks. The wage settlement of 1963 had been back-dated to 1962, so by 1965 the postal workers had been without a raise for three years. In the meanwhile, the Canadian economy was expanding dynamically. Senior postal management were well aware of the impending storm, but the Treasury Board, representing the legal employer, continued to procrastinate. Ironically, it would seem, the Pearson government was resolved to demonstrate, in its own inattention to the interests of its employees, the necessity of granting them the right to organize as unions to defend these interests. Given the fact that the postal workers actually went on strike in 1965 and instead of being disciplined were rewarded with a favourable settlement, and, moreover, given representations by the NDP and the labour unions, the Public Service Staff Relations Act, when it was enacted in 1967, contained two options for the public service bargaining units: bargaining with recourse to arbitration, and bargaining with recourse to strike. The letter carriers and the postal clerks quickly chose the latter option—an option that they could claim they had won for the public service as a whole.

From the beginning the newly organized postal unions adopted a strongly adversarial attitude to management. This was a natural sequel to the dramatic success of the 1965 strike. A strongly adversarial approach had paid off—in fact, it seemed in the context that *only* that approach would pay off. However, the adversarial attitude of the postal workers in 1965 was adopted partly in imitation of Canadian private sector unions.

Canadian labour legislation in general adopts a very negative stance toward company-dominated unions. Associations of workers applying for union recognition must prove their independence of company management. "Independence of management" tends to be translated into "adversary of management," and all concerned—management, union leaders, labour relations boards, and the courts—look upon unions and managements as being adversarially related. In consequence, it is very much easier for a union to adopt a fighting stance than a co-operative stance with respect to management. People elected as leaders of unions in Canada are not apt to think of themselves as elected to lead the labour side in promoting the success of the company. Rather, they see themselves as elected to represent the interests of the workers *against the company*—the company now being regarded as belonging to those whose interests management represents and in no way "belonging" to the workers.

The consequences, therefore, of the typically adversarial attitude of a private sector union are: (1) The union does not look upon itself as an organ of the company working for the welfare of the company, but rather as an adversary of the company. And (2) union leaders adopt a lawyer-like role with respect to serving the interests of their membership. Just as lawyers represent the interests of their clients as best they can, irrespective of the intrinsic merits of their clients' case, so the labour leader represents the presumed interests of the union irrespective of the intrinsic merit of its case.

In analogy to the encounter of adversarial parties in a courtroom situation, it may be argued that as unions take care of their interests, others will take of their interests, and from this interplay of adversarial interest the best possible accommodation of all to all and for all will take place. However, we may note that if in this context each party is seeking to maximize its own interests (even when the intrinsic merit of its case is weak), then there is little to distinguish the parties on ethical grounds.

The question remains: How much counterbalancing of powers within itself can a single productive enterprise undergo without a serious loss of productive efficiency? What are the prospects for survival of an organism with two heads— two heads of somewhat comparable power and related to each other as adversaries and not as partners? One might imagine that if the one head, the production-control head, was much stronger than the other, the labour-control head, then efficient production might proceed while the lesser power operates to keep production-control aware of workers' concerns in the process. However, if the power of the labour-control head is enhanced to something akin to parity with the production-control head, then two adverse tendencies will tend to appear: (1) The power of the production-control head to insure efficient production will falter and productivity will fall. And (2) with its enhanced power the labour-control head will have its own problems with the power principle, and consequently, genuine worker interests will be lost in the no-man's land between the contending parties.

These tendencies emerged within Canada Post with the development of strongly adversarial labour-management relations in the period 1965 to 1975. As CUPW and LCUC waxed in adversarial power, the power of Canada Post's management to control production waned, so that productivity fell disastrously; and at the same time, the unions turned from serving the interests of workers to enhancing their own power. An important illustration of the working out of the latter tendency is CUPW's reaction to the technological transformation of the post office in the 1970s.

If technological innovation is to improve labour productivity, then the output ratio (i.e., the rate of change in output) over the labour input ratio (i.e., the rate of change in employment) must rise, or put otherwise, the labour input ratio over the output ratio must fall. In this context if the output is relatively stable, employment must fall. It is this threat to employment that makes technological innovation a matter of vital concern to a union. However, if the employer guarantees to the workers that the reduction of the labour input will be effected through natural attrition, and if the workers are further assured that there will be no downward revision of pay rates for those presently on staff, then the fears of present workers are adequately met. If the union nevertheless continues to push the job-loss matter and seeks to maintain the number of jobs, then the union is going beyond the interests of its present membership and is seeking to serve the interests of the union itself. That is, it is seeking to maintain the size of the union and all that goes with union size, in particular the financial strength of the union and the power of the union leadership. This shift in focus from the interests of the present members to the interests of the union itself—that is, essentially, to the power-interests of the union leaders—is fraught with very serious consequences. If it is successful then the labour input ratio over the output ratio does not fall and labour productivity does not improve; that is, the impact of technological innovation is completely neutralized. The significance of this neutralization may be emphasized by pointing out that if there had been this kind of neutralization of technological innovation throughout the Canadian economy in the period 1950 to 1975, then the doubling of real incomes Canadians enjoyed during that period would have been replaced by no change in real incomes.

In 1970 Eric Kierans promised CUPW that no regular employee would lose his or her job as a consequence of the forthcoming technological transformation. After some false starts, the workers were eventually also assured that there would be no downward reclassification of pay rates for those presently employed. To facilitate the anticipated relative drop in labour input that would come with technological transformation, it was essential that Canada Post should begin to cut the relative number of its regular employees by means of attrition. At the same time, in order to provide the work force needed in the period of transition (when the need might be higher than usual), a flexible policy on the employment of casuals was required. In the 1970 negotiations CUPW accepted Kierans's assurance of job security and initially agreed to a flexible policy respecting casuals (it being agreed further that the pay for casuals was to be raised to the starting rate for corresponding regular employees). Shortly thereafter, CUPW reneged on the flexible casuals policy and made the number of casuals being appointed by Canada Post the major issue in scores of bitter local disputes, culminating frequently in illegal local strikes. For example, in the period 1971 to 1974 there were 116 days in which CUPW was on strike in one or more post offices across Canada. The declared issue in a large number of the cases was the number of casuals being appointed.

The issue was of the highest significance. It did not directly affect the interests of present regular members of staff. However, insofar as union strategy meant that new regular staff were appointed rather than casuals, the number of regular staff was increased and union size, union dues, etc., affected. Also affected was Canada Post's ability to reduce the number of employees quickly once the new technology was installed. Hence, the union's strategy concerning casuals tended to block the overall productivity objectives of the program of technological transformation. By the late 1970s when the technological transformation was complete, Canada Post had an inflated complement of regular employees whose work habits were now abysmal and whose productivity was 25 percent lower than in 1969 when the technological change was conceived. Productivity was roughly one-half what it could have been and the work force roughly double.

If union power is viewed as varying with the labour-input ratio and management power with the output ratio, then union power relative to management will be viewed as varying inversely with productivity. CUPW acted as if this was its way of viewing labour-management power relations. In January 1975, the Public Service Staff Relations Board dissolved the Council of Postal Unions, which had combined CUPW and LCUC in a single bargaining unit, and recognized CUPW as an independent bargaining unit. The year 1975 was filled with acrimony—for 112 days CUPW was on strike at one or more post offices across Canada. By December 12, when CUPW's first independent collective agreement was signed, the union had nailed down a number of written concessions with important productivity implications:

(1) A Canada Post commitment "to minimize as much as possible the hiring of casuals" (Article 39.02). The dire consequences of this in a period of technological innovation have been pointed out above.

(2) The reservation of CUPW functions to CUPW members only, that is, members of other postal unions and management are excluded from such functions (Article 39.01). In consequence it is a common thing to see a trained

mechanic sitting beside one of the new machines reading a technical magazine (or surreptitiously something more interesting) while the mechanic's CUPW cousins feed the machine. The mechanic can work "legally" only when the machine breaks down. Similarly when all is going well the first-line supervisors have little that they can "legally" do. While India has legally abolished the caste system, we have legally introduced it in our most prominent public corporation.

(3) A provision to prevent easy fraternizing with the adversary whereby any CUPW member who is assigned in an acting capacity to a managerial position loses his or her seniority (Artical 11.05). That is, when such persons return to normal CUPW functions, they start again at the bottom of the seniority list.

(4) The provision that "there shall be no group measurement of employees for a homogeneous group of ten employees or less" (Article 39.10). It is difficult to see what control management can exert over productivity if it is legally prevented from assessing individual performance. When the federal government legislated the striking CUPW back to work in 1968 and imposed compulsory arbitration, the arbitrator, Lucien Tremblay, excised this remarkable article from the collective agreement. However, in the next freely negotiated agreement it was again conceded that "there shall be no individual work measurement" (Article 41.01).

(5) The provision that "in carrying out technological changes, the Employer agrees to eliminate all injustices to or adverse effects on employees" (Article 29). To give effect to this provision employees are "guaranteed employment," "guaranteed classification," and "guaranteed pay."

One may well ask why any management should be as profligate as Canada Post in negotiating away its powers to control productivity. In retrospect Canada Post management appears exceedingly obtuse. However, we must recall the context and, in particular, the intensity and complexity of pressures to which management was subjected. The U.S. Postal Service was confronted with the same problems and the same pressures as Canada Post, but with the one important exception: the U.S. postal workers were not allowed to strike. In 1975, as we have noted, CUPW was on strike at one or more post offices on 112 days. The numerous illegal strikes and the long forty-two-day legal strike that ended the year were not only extremely harassing for the postal management striving to maintain postal services, but also politically embarrassing for the postmaster general and his Cabinet and party colleagues. "Peace in our time" was a great temptation for the politicians involved. Postal management was thus severely squeezed between a turbulent body of postal workers on the one side and embarrassed and anxious members of Parliament on the other side.

One may also ask what the Public Service Staff Relations Board was doing during this postal mix-up. Certainly part of the answer was that it was kept very busy adjudicating the formal grievances related to the collective agreements. The number of grievances lodged against Canada Post and the number of these cases carried to the stage of adjudication by the board in the mid-1970s were as follows:

Grievances

	Lodged	Adjudications
1974	1338	96
1975	1676	227
1976	3408	457
1977	9732	384

The high number of grievances lodged in 1976 and 1977 reflects not only a high level of dissatisfaction on the part of the postal workers, but also an intensification of effort on the part of CUPW to harass management.

The collective agreements of Canada Post read as lengthy lists of obligations owed by Canada Post to its employees. The grievances emerge from claims that these obligations have not all been fulfilled. One looks largely in vain for counterbalancing obligations owed by the employees to Canada Post. What does the employer get out of this elaborate structure set up under the Public Service Staff Relations Act? Very little it would seem apart from the stipulation that there will be no strikes during the lifetime of a collective agreement, and subsequently only after due process of formal negotiations and conciliation. However, given the great proliferation of illegal strikes on the postal landscape, this stipulation also, it would seem, was of little value to the employer. Where then was the Public Service Staff Relations Board in all this?

In this context, we may say, the board was reasonably effective in compelling management to fulfil its numerous contractual obligations, but a paper-tiger in preventing illegal strikes. In general, Canada Post was held to the legal implications of the words of the contractual agreement whether or not these implications made administrative sense. This would appear to be the case, for example, in the O'Toole adjudication of 1977. Article 39.07 provides: "When high mail volumes necessitate the working of extra hours, the Employer agrees that such work will be offered first to regular employees available to perform additional hours and/or overtime." O'Toole claimed that he was overlooked when he was available for such additional hours, although he was on his official day of rest. About 2,700 O'Toole-type grievances were lodged with an average of ten grievors per grievance. The employer argued that to rule that regular employees on their official day of rest were "available" under this article would mean: (1) that costly administrative procedures would have to be set up because "thousands of employees on their days of rest would have to be contacted, new lists would have to be compiled and permanent records kept to prove which employees were available"; and (2) that settlement of these grievances would cost over two million dollars. Canada Post lost the case before the board and subsequently in the courts. It was agreed, irrespective of the sense or nonsense of the administrative procedures required, that the words gave the postal workers claim to hundreds of thousands of dollars' compensation for work they had not done, and had not done, moreover, on their official days of rest.

The board's paper-tiger role is illustrated in the Vancouver strike case taken by Canada Post to the board in 1973 with the intent of obtaining compensation for an illegal strike and with the hope that some precedent could be set with respect to illegal strikes in general. With respect to the strike at the Vancouver post office on June 25 and 26, 1973, Canada Post claimed that the constituent unions of the Council of Postal Unions had not taken reasonable steps to prevent and stop the strike as required by article 43 of the collective agreement, that damages were sustained, and that compensation, consequently, should be paid. The adjudicator, E.B. Jolliffe, decided that the evidence was insufficient to support Canada Post's claim. However, the adjudication was remarkable for two features. First, although hearings were held promptly, the decision was not handed down until October 1981—*eight years* later. Second, a whimsical argument was advanced concerning the accounting of damages: that since Canada's postal service was a deficit operation, Canada Post might actually make a net savings from a strike.

The intelligent citizen may manage to match the paper-tiger's grin with respect to the latter matter. However, the first matter needs a bit of explaining. Jolliffe himself gives the following astounding explanation in the body of his decision.

> It may well be asked why a decision should issue after such a long delay. Rightly or wrongly, I had the view during the years 1974 to 1981 that the unhappy relations of the parties, before and after the dissolution of C.P.U., would not be improved and indeed would probably be exacerbated by a decision, whatever the result of this case might be. Nevertheless, there are indications that a new era may be dawning with the dissolution of the Post Office Department itself and the imminent transfer of its responsibilities to a Crown Corporation.

Jolliffe uses the pronoun "I." Does he literally mean "I," or does he intend the board? Is it the case then that one adjudicator or the board is free to decide whether or not one party in labour-management relations is to be denied legal recourse in a matter which is of the highest importance to it? Given that management at Canada Post got virtually nothing out of the Public Service Staff Relations Act except some insurance against illegal strikes, it sounds somewhat hollow to say that "the unhappy relations of the parties . . . would probably be exacerbated by a decision" on this illegal strike.

Partially excusing the Public Service Staff Relations Board, it may be said that throughout the 1970s Canada Post also seemed to lack the will to press its claims with respect to illegal strikes either through the board or through the civil courts. The chief explanation again, no doubt, is the political sensitivities of members of Parliament, the Cabinet, and the postmaster general. However, if in a democratic party system such as exists in Canada it is not possible for political reasons to take advantage of the provisions protecting the public service from the illicit collective actions of public service unions, then the government must be very cautious indeed in establishing the legal collective rights of public service unions. Otherwise, the adversarial parties end up with everything being very legal on the one side, and things being legal or illegal as the power struggle warrants on the other side. An unequal contest—as indeed was the case throughout most of the 1970s.

This attitude of appeasement in management, the Public Service Staff Relations Board, and the government contributed to the development of a practice that gave absolution for a great variety of illicit acts by union members and, hence, in effect, granted indulgences for future illicit acts. The practice of forced-absolution was this: when the post office objected to the illicit activities of some union members, then the union broadened and escalated the issue and refused to agree to a settlement of what was now a major dispute unless all charges concerning illicit activities of its members were withdrawn.

A king-size illustration of this practice was the illegal strike of April 1974. A number of postal clerks in Montreal began to wear boycott-the-postal-code T-shirts at work. Management suspended the workers and CUPW closed down the Peel Street post office with an illegal strike. The CUPW national president, Jim McCall, began negotiating with the postmaster general and his deputy; but the Montreal local refused to co-operate with McCall. McCall resigned and his replacement as national president, Joe Davidson, immediately escalated the illegal Montreal strike into an illegal national strike. The Public Service Staff Relations Board appointed Eric Taylor as a special mediator in the dispute. CUPW refused to settle until a non-reprisals clause was inserted in the agreement. Local illegal activity was swallowed up in nation-wide illegal activity until finally all illegality was washed away in what was, in effect, a political settlement.

If a union takes a strongly adversarial stance and has sufficient fortitude and group loyalty to pursue this practice of forced-absolution, then the union has little to fear from the illegality of strikes or, indeed, from the illegality of any activity with respect to which it is prepared to invoke the practice. In this context management treads very softly on issues lest the practice be invoked; and, consequently, its power as production-head to control productivity is seriously undermined.

6.5 Unionization and the Problems of an Antipathetic Attitude
After 1974, when McCall was forced out of office as national president and was replaced by Davidson, CUPW adopted a consistently antipathetic attitude to Canada Post. LCUC, in contrast, continued to display a cooler, more pragmatic attitude, manipulating management positions, and even the more extreme attitude of CUPW, to its own advantage. The CUPW stance was not only strongly adversarial, but morally discriminating as well: the union was arrayed against management as "good" against "evil." Flaunting the motto, "La lutte des postiers continue!" CUPW waged war on management.

A number of factors contributed to this adoption of a morally discriminating attitude:

(1) The attitude fits to some extent the mood of alienated workers. If one is

suffering alienation, then there is some satisfaction in finding that there is a specific evil source of this suffering, and in joining with others in an active struggle against this source.

(2) The attitude fits well the theory and practice of the various groups that are Marxist in orientation. According to Marx, the industrial West is in the throes of a class war. The struggle of postal workers against management and government reflect this war (see Chapter 7).

(3) The attitude fits well that faction of the Quiet Revolution in Quebec who sought to become "maîtres chez nous" by fighting the dominance both of English Canadians and the capitalist class (see Chapter 8).

(4) The attitude also offers some pragmatic advantage, at least in the beginning, in its contribution to union solidarity and hence to the power of the union and its leaders. If the members are morally committed to fighting management, they are less apt to be turned aside from union aims by the prospect of this or that incidental advantage or disadvantage.

The adoption of a morally discriminating attitude has important consequences for any community. For the sake of survival a morally discriminating in-group assumes that it is justified in adopting the tactics that it sees the "evil" adversary using against itself. It does to its adversary what its adversary does to it. The non-discriminating observer may then find it difficult to distinguish the tactical ethic of the in-group from that of its adversary. It seems probable that the in-group is not unambiguously "good" nor the adversary unambiguously "evil." However, the in-group is not interested in this non-discriminating critique. Non-discriminating language is seen as giving aid and comfort to the adversary; it also, therefore, is evil. Morally discriminating thought, speech, and action tend more and more to drive out non-discriminating thought, speech, and action. The cumulative effects are serious. The in-group's mistrust of, and hence its isolation from, all other groups tends to become extreme. In this context of mistrust and non-communication, the in-group's ability to assess the practical significance of situations and their implications for in-group interests tends to be undermined. Moreover, in this context of mistrust and bitter struggle it becomes more and more important for the in-group to maintain a disciplined front against a hostile world. The in-group, therefore, becomes less tolerant of diversity within its own ranks and it tends to take adverse action against "weak" elements within itself.

CUPW's mistrust of postal management and of the government as its employer became a matter of doctrine proclaimed and practised with enthusiastic certainty. The most damning piece of evidence cited against Canada Post was the ill-fated concession on technological changes in 1975. In December 1975, Bryce Mackasey, the postmaster general, settled a long, drawn-out strike with a generous concession on technological changes. Article 29 offered to eliminate all adverse effects on employees, to consult with CUPW on all proposed changes, and to guarantee employment, classification, and pay. In 1976 Canada Post drew back from this commitment and Treasury Board lawyers handed down their opinion that the concession involved matters that were excluded from bargaining under the Public Service Staff Relations Act. The matter was very important. Canada Post no doubt was very much afraid that a highly antipathetic CUPW would spike its massive program of technological innovation, which was at this point in its most dynamic stage. However, if it could not live with the concession, it clearly should not have made it. In any case, Canada Post made the concession and quickly thereafter reneged. CUPW thenceforth cited the reneging as irrefutable evidence that Canada Post and the government were not to be trusted.

The extent to which CUPW carried its mistrust of Canada Post's management reflected the tendency of the morally discriminating approach to run to extremes.

(1) CUPW met with management for formal contract negotiations and for formal grievance hearings only. It refused to meet with management for informal consultation on any matter whatsoever.

(2) John Paré, who was appointed assistant deputy postmaster general in charge of personnel in 1976, offered a radical new approach to labour-management relations with active consultation on all significant problems, with a mutual problem-solving approach to issues affecting unions and management, and with a strong quality of work-life emphasis. CUPW treated Paré's approach as a hypocritical attempt to co-opt the workers into accepting further exploitation.

(3) CUPW strongly objected to management communicating to the workers (except through the union) either its general plans and objectives or its interpretation of matters currently in dispute.

(4) CUPW objected to any fraternizing between union officials and members on the one side and management on the other. The 1977 CUPW constitution provides that the national directors for the four postal regions shall

> ensure that any suspicion of collusion with the employer is avoided by refusing any participation in recreational or sporting events, dances, presentation of trophies, contributions to employer newspapers, etc., in such manner that the integrity and independence of union leaders be safeguarded vis-à-vis the representatives of the employer and that members themselves be guided accordingly (Article 4.65 (a)).

(5) CUPW objected to members accepting promotion to managerial posts. As we have noted, CUPW members appointed to acting supervisory positions were stripped of their seniority. Reflecting this attitude, the *Atlantic Postal Worker* of April/May 1981 reported, under the title "The Judas Principle," that a former president of a CUPW local had accepted promotion to supervisor. "It seems," the report said, that he "has decided to sell his so-called principles for thirty pieces of silver."

(6) CUPW objected to Canada Post setting up the Employee Assistance Program, which was designed to assist employees experiencing various types of trouble such as drug use, alcoholism, marital problems, or financial difficulties.

A bulletin in June 1980 from a regional national director of CUPW concluded with the uncompromising statement: "The Canadian Union of Postal Workers is greatly opposed to the Employee Assistance Program, and we must ensure that our workers do not participate."

(7) If the adversary is not to be trusted to carry out legal commitments (cf. the 1975 technological changes commitment), then the in-group may assume that the legal structure does not adequately protect its interests and that it is justified, therefore, in adopting extra-legal tactics. In both 1977 and 1978 CUPW was on strike at one or more post offices for more than sixty days. In addition, in 1978 when the federal government legislated the union back to work after a legal strike, Jean-Claude Parrot, the president of CUPW, defied court orders and was sentenced for a short time to jail.

CUPW's practice of extreme mistrust severely isolated the union from other groups as well. For unions, the most generous interpretation of the boundaries of the in-group is "all workers." Thereby the union expresses its solidarity with the working class in general. The readiness of CUPW to employ productivity-deflating tactics suggests that the union was not concerned with the impact of its activities on other Canadians. The deflated productivity meant that the unit cost of mail services for Canadians was roughly double what it could have been. In an unguarded moment in 1975 Joe Davidson said that if the Canadian public did not see the justice of CUPW's case, "Then to hell with the public!" This was a major public relations gaffe; but there was little in CUPW's practice that gave the Canadian public any assurance that CUPW had any concern for it.

Being somewhat less generous one might suppose that a postal union could include in the in-group all postal workers. However, by 1975 CUPW was already more or less estranged from other postal unions. Earlier, when sortation of mail on railway cars was closed out and railway mail clerks were transferred to regular sortation duties, CUPW made clear that they would not accept the railway mail clerks into CUPW because it would affect CUPW's seniority lists. In 1968 the Public Service Staff Relations Board placed CUPW and LCUC together in the one bargaining unit, the Council of Postal Unions (CPU). The life of CPU was marked by jealousy, suspicion, and growing tension. In January 1975 the Public Service Staff Relations Board gave in and recognized CUPW and LCUC as independent bargaining units. In the latter 1970s all of the postal unions collaborated at least to some extent with John Paré's mutual problem-solving approach—with the exception of CUPW. The exception of the largest postal union, of course, seriously undercut the effectiveness of Paré's fresh approach.

A morally discriminating in-group, which habitually listens to itself alone, places itself in a very bad position for assessing what is happening around it and for deciding how its interests are affected by what is happening. John Paré offered the union a golden opportunity to grapple with the matter of key interest to the workers, namely, agency-sufficiency—without surrendering its traditional concern for whether or not the work offers good wages. To respond to this offer, however, CUPW would have had to surrender its morally discriminating approach, and this it refused to do. Accordingly, it mobilized its moral forces to oppose the insidious Paré threat. (This opposition was carried to an extreme limit. For example, in 1979–80 Jean-Claude Parrot, president of CUPW, received an invitation to participate in one of a series of seminars in Canadian studies at Carleton University. Parrot referred the matter to his national executive and finally gave a negative decision on the grounds that John Paré was participating in the seminar series some weeks later. John Paré evidently cast a long shadow.)

The "natural" environment for a morally discriminating in-group is one marked by bitter struggle. The more intense the struggle, the more is felt the need for a disciplined front against the adversary. The need for discipline encourages in practice a certain autocracy in leadership style even though the in-group may be very democratic in formal structure. Moreover, the leaders may tend to move against the "weaker" elements in the in-group—that is, the elements that habitually tend to be poor followers. Consequently, mutuality within the in-group now tends to break down.

There is some evidence of this happening in CUPW. The CUPW constitution empowers the National Executive Board to discipline a union local "that does not comply with the Constitution, the policies and decisions of the Union or whose conduct may cause prejudice to the welfare or interests of the Union or its members" (Article 4.08, National Constitution, 1977). Moreover, the local may be disciplined by being merged with another local or by being placed under trusteeship. The National Executive Board has frequently exercised such discipline.

The intent of discipline is illustrated in a letter written by a national official to postal clerks in Thompson, Manitoba, in March 1978. The Thompson local had been merged with another local many miles away after the Thompson clerks had returned to work before the end of a strike. The official pointed out that they had acted as if they were not members of the union, that the union was seeking closed shop, and that when the union achieved closed shop it would know what to do with the Thompson clerks. The implications were clear.

The Thompson clerks might be classed as "weak" members of the union. At the expiry of the contract imposed on CUPW by Parliament in 1978, the union negotiated a restriction for a whole class of "weak" members, namely, the part-time workers. The part-timers are members of CUPW, but for a number of reasons are not regarded by the union as "good" unionists. Some are men with a part-time job elsewhere as well. Some are married women who are quite pleased to have part-time rather than full-time positions. In general, they are "better workers" than their full-time colleagues and are not so interested in the adversarial activities of the union. The union, therefore, negotiated a cutback in the maximum hours for part-timers from thirty to twenty-five hours a week. Disregarding productivity implications again, and showing no more consideration for the rights of a whole class of its workers than the union, Canada Post's management agreed to the cutback.

6.6 The Elixir of Immortality: Monopoly and Government Ownership

In section 6.4 we asked the question, "What are the prospects for survival of an organism with two heads—two heads of somewhat comparable power and related to each other as adversaries and not as partners?" The answer clearly is that the prospects for survival are not good at all. Nonetheless, the post office in its "time of troubles" was made over in the likeness of this two-headed monster, and yet it survived. Why has the post office been able to survive? The answer is not difficult to discover. The elixir of immortality for the post office in its "time of troubles" has been the alchemical compound of monopoly and government ownership.

Any service corporation that drives its unit costs up to roughly double what they could be and at the same time offers a substantially poorer quality of service is in deep trouble. Given a measure of competition, trouble of that sort would be fatal. The competition would quickly gobble up the clientele and the corporation would be out of business. Combatting a typically fatal trouble, Canada Post was saved by its monopoly status. Where Canada Post has a monopoly, namely, in letter-mail, the corporation has survived as a producer of mail service; where Canada Post does not have a monopoly, for example, in parcel-mail, the corporation has been largely driven out of business by the competition. Without the monopoly services, the non-monopoly services of Canada Post would completely collapse.

However, the monopoly status of Canada Post is not the only factor in its survival: the fact that it is a government-owned monopoly and not a private monopoly is also important. A private monopoly would have had to increase the price of its services in line with the rise in its unit costs. In the case of the public monopoly, the impact of rising unit costs can be masked by higher and higher government subsidization. As we have seen, by the mid-1970s the subsidy to Canada Post had risen to a peak of over 45 percent of total costs (Table 3.4E). One can imagine the hue and cry that would have been raised if in the course of a few years a private monopoly let the quality of its services slump badly and at the same time increased its prices far beyond that of general inflation. In the contemporary Canadian political context, it seems improbable that a private monopoly could survive politically in such a situation.

There is another way that the intelligent citizen might look at public monopoly. Given its "time of troubles," public monopoly enabled Canada Post to survive. But the matter might be put another way: Canada Post had its "time of troubles" only because its public monopoly status made it possible for Canada Post to afford it. That is, if Canada Post had had a status that rendered it impossible to survive trouble of that kind, would it not have nipped the trouble in the bud rather than go under?

CHAPTER 7

The Impact of the Marxian Ethic

7.1 A Preview

The beginning of the postal "time of troubles" coincides with the development in the post office of unions with strongly adversarial atittudes. Given the results—a disastrous drop in productivity and in the quality of mail service, coupled with a restless, unhappy postal work force—one is led to question the efficacy of the adversarial approach to labour-management relations. However, one cannot delve very deeply into this question without confronting the major system of thought and practice in contemporary culture that advocates and promotes a militantly adversarial approach, namely, Marxism.

Marxism is important, of course, because in the first half of the twentieth century it became the official doctrine of the "Second World," a world, we may note, with a much greater population than that of the "First World," the industrial West. However, Marxism is important also in the West. In Europe, the United Kingdom, and to a lesser although still significant extent in Canada, the theory behind union practice has frequently been Marxist or partly Marxist in orientation. This has been true even of unions that are explicitly anti-communist, but that retain nonetheless the characteristic Marxist attitude of class struggle. Within the post office itself there is a small but influential minority passionately committed to the class struggle. Since 1974 the leadership of CUPW, the largest postal union, has been consistently Marxist-minded in the sense of advocating a militantly adversarial approach. Outside the labour unions Marxism has an important niche in the universities of the West, including the universities of Canada. Especially within the social sciences there are influential groups that are essentially Marxist in outlook.

An adversarial attitude is a symptom of breakdown in community. Hence, it is as old as human community and is not an invention of Marxism. However, since Marxism is a prominent system of thought and practice in the contemporary world and since it insists that a militantly adversarial approach is imperative to progress in non-communist countries, we cannot grapple with the limitations of the adversarial approach without grappling with the Marxist system of thought and practice.

Because Marxism is a *system* of thought and practice, it is unsatisfactory to wrestle with isolated aspects of it. Hence, if we are to engage intellectually with the proponents of the class struggle both inside and outside the post office, we must attempt an evaluation of Marxism as a total system of thought and practice. This is what we seek to do in this chapter.

By "ethic" in this context we mean a set of imperatives derived from commitment to an ultimate good. The definition is consistent with Max Weber's

91

usage in *The Protestant Ethic and the Spirit of Capitalism*. From devotion to their secular vocation as fulfilling the will of God, early Protestants derived a set of imperatives for behaviour that contributed to the creation of the modern industrial order. Analogously, from their commitment to the pursuit of science as the ultimate good, some modern thinkers have derived an ethic of scientism that treats all other approaches to reality as nonsense. And, similarly, from their commitment to a classless society, or to what we have called a non-discriminating community, the Marxists have derived a set of imperatives for behaviour that foster the class war, the breakdown of capitalism, and the establishment of socialism. Section 7.2 discusses the interplay of ethics in the contemporary world and in particular the interplay of the Protestant ethic, the ethic of scientism, and the Marxian ethic.

Marxism purports to be a science of social development and not simply an ethic derived from an idealistic vision of the ultimate good. Section 7.3 attempts an evaluation of this Marxian science/ethic.

If the Marxist-oriented workers constitute a small minority in the post office, we may ask why we need to concern ourselves with the impact of the Marxist ethic on the postal problem. Two reasons can be suggested for this concern. First, the Marxist ethic, particularly in its central imperative, the class struggle, has an influence on social thinking far beyond the boundaries of groups explicitly committed to Marxism. Second, committed minorities because they are committed can have an impact quite out of proportion to their numbers. Section 7.4 discusses this second reason for concern with the impact of the Marxian ethic.

7.2 The Interplay of Ethics in the Contemporary World

By the term "imperative" we mean a rule of behaviour which for one reason or another we accept as obligatory. A set of imperatives derived from commitment to an ultimate good constitutes what we shall mean by the term "ethic." There are, of course, imperatives other than ethical imperatives. For example, there are imperatives adopted for prudential reasons, that is, imperatives based on expectations of reward or penalty in perceptual or communal experience. Prudential imperatives are closely correlated with the rewards and penalties that are built into the perceptual/communal system. Consequently, if the rewards and penalties that are built into the system change substantially, then the prudential imperatives may be expected to change. Ethical imperatives, on the contrary, since they are based on an ultimate good, may prevail even when the rewards and penalties built into the perceptual/communal system fail to support them.

The close correlation of prudential imperatives with the rewards and penalties built into the perceptual/communal system may be expressed in the language of B. F. Skinner's behaviourism. Certain kinds of human behaviour are conditioned by the presence in the system of relevant positive or negative reinforcers. If the set of positive and negative reinforcers is changed, then other kinds of human behaviour will be conditioned. We might argue, for example, that a relatively high level of industriousness on the part of both managers and workers is essential if modern industry is to operate effectively. The practice by managers of hiring, retaining, and promoting the more industrious workers provides a strong positive reinforcer conditioning industriousness among workers. The practice by managers of not hiring or of firing the less industrious workers provides a strong negative reinforcer of industriousness. At the same time an *absence* of social security measures, such as unemployment insurance providing alternative economic support for those without employment, greatly enhances the impact of the positive and negative reinforcers conditioning industriousness among the workers. However, if the positive and negative reinforcers are in large part removed by collective bargaining and by changes in social policy, as we discussed in the case of the post office in Chapter 6, then industriousness as a conditioned form of worker behaviour will tend to disappear. It might even be suggested that Canada Post is a great "Skinner-box" conditioning postal workers to chronic non-industriousness.

Is it probable in the contemporary setting that the erosion of industriousness as a prudential imperative will be offset by industriousness as an ethical imperative?

The renowned German sociologist Max Weber has advanced the thesis that, from their commitment to the will of God, early Protestants derived a set of imperatives that contributed to the creation of the modern industrial system. For all Christians the ultimate good is the will of God. For Catholic Christianity the *highest* form of commitment to God had traditionally been held to involve a measure of renunciation of the perceptual/communal world. This renunciation was embodied in the monastic imperatives of poverty, chastity, and obedience. Martin Luther broke with the monastic ideal and proclaimed that Christians could fulfil the will of God by devoting themselves to their secular occupation as a calling from God. Hence, one might fulfil the will of God by being a committed scientist. Indeed, the early scientists conceived of what they were doing as thinking God's thoughts after him. They were discovering in nature the designs God had chosen to use in creating the universe. This was an exciting incentive to scientific investigation. However, one might also participate in fulfilling the will of God by being an inventive technologist or a venturesome industrial entrepreneur, or, simply, a responsible, industrious worker. This was precisely what the modern world needed to break the forms of the past: committed scientists, inventive technologists, confident entrepreneurs, and industrious workers. To pursue these vocations, not just for their economic reward but as imperatives derived from one's commitment to the ultimate good, gives to such pursuit a persistence and strength which surmounts all kinds of impediments. Out of such imperatives are new worlds created.

Strangely, Weber related the Protestant ethic to the Calvinist doctrine of predestination. According to this doctrine, it is by the predestination of God and that alone that we are elected for ultimate salvation. However, if we are elected for salvation by God and, moreover, called by God to a certain secular vocation, then we may enjoy success in that vocation as a *sign* of God's election and favour. Therefore, Protestants may *pursue* success in their vocation as a proof of God's election and favour. We may note that this pursuit implies a contradiction: what is a consequence solely of God's predestination does not *logically* call forth active agency on the part of mankind. However, this contradiction in the Calvinist version of the Protestant ethic—on the one hand, complete predetermination, and on the other hand, active human agency—is shared, as we shall note, with other modern ethics. What is logically contradictory operates psychologically, at least for some, to enhance commitment to the appropriate set of imperatives.

If the Protestant ethic helped to create the modern industrial system, can we turn to it again as the prudential imperatives that sustain the system begin to crumble? Two reasons suggest that we cannot expect a rescue operation from the Protestant ethic in the contemporary period. First, a new prophetic ethic has developed within Christianity that is highly critical of the modern industrial system. This new prophetic ethic has some points of correspondence with the Marxian critique of the modern industrial system, which we discuss below. Second, in more recent years the development of science has tended to debunk commitment to God and, indeed, to.cast some shadow on all aspirations to participate in an ultimate good. We may call this view "scientism." With scientism there has developed an influential, new, hidden ethic.

The appropriate setting of modern science is the sphere of perceptual objects. Since conformity to specific limits is the character of all objects, the fundamental faith of all scientists is in perceptual reality as displaying conformity to limits, or as we might also put it, as displaying predetermined order. Thus, scientists are sustained in their pursuit of perceptual objects by their faith in order in the perceptual world. Our commitment to order is appropriately called "faith" because we *presuppose* order. We bring our presupposition of order *to* all of our experience. What experience adds to our presupposition is confirmation that there is order in the perceptual world, and that in this or that case the order has this or that specific character. Hence, as our experience accumulates we are able to embody our "faith" in order in a set of "beliefs" specifying the character of that order. In the scientist's career the set of "beliefs" is open to development and, hence, to that extent is variable while the "faith" itself remains constant.

The appropriate setting of commitment to an ultimate good is a community of selves aspiring to make their existence creative and their lives ultimately meaningful. If there are "goods" correlated with specific perceptual and communal conditions, then human existence can assume conditional meaning. However, only with an ultimate good can human existence assume ultimate meaning. Thus we are sustained in our pursuit of ultimate meaning by our faith that an ultimate good is to be found in the fullness of reality. Again, our commitment is "faith" because we *presuppose* an ultimate good; and we bring our presupposition *to* all of our experience. What experience adds to our presupposition is some confirmation that there is an ultimate good and that it may have this or that specific character. Hence, as our experience is enriched we are able to embody our "faith" in an ultimate good in a set of "beliefs" specifying the character of that ultimate good. In the career of persons seeking ultimate meaning, the "beliefs" are open to development and, hence, to that extent are variable, while "faith" in the ultimate good may remain constant.

One of the reasons for the development of scientism in the contemporary West is that Christian theologians have tended to identify "faith" and "beliefs." When certain traditional beliefs were found to be inconsistent with newly emerging scientific beliefs, theologians clung to their traditional beliefs, claiming that they were indispensable to their faith. Taking them at their word, many scientists responded by discarding theological faith along with the untenable traditional beliefs.

For example, Jews and Christians traditionally "believed" that God, the ultimate good, created the world and that he did so in six days as recorded in Genesis 1. When geologists and biologists postulated the evolutionary development over many millenia of the earth and of life upon the earth and found more and more evidence for their postulate, the traditional Judaeo-Christian "belief" became untenable. If in this context the "belief" is understood to be indispensable to the "faith," then the "faith" itself also becomes untenable. In any case, many orthodox believers contended that the "belief" was indispensable to the "faith," and in response many scientists accepted their contention, but rejected rather then accepted both "belief" and "faith."

The overall consequence of this was that many scientists, because of their commitment to science, came to feel that they *ought* to reject faith in an ultimate good. For example, Sigmund Freud contended that his ancestral faith was wishful thinking that a committed scientists could not accept. Since he did not propose an alternative set of beliefs in an ultimate good, we may assume that he intended to reject "faith" in an ultimate good. Nonetheless, a hidden faith and hidden ethic tended to appear in practice: Freud is committed to the pursuit of science as the ultimate good; and the first ethical imperative is, "You shall have no other ultimate good before it." This, at least, effectively eliminated the traditional faith in God as the ultimate good.

One can see this tendency to dispense with the traditional faith emerging with Pierre-Simon Laplace. Napoleon is said to have chided Laplace with writing a celebrated work on the origin of the heavenly bodies without once mentioning their Creator. "I had no need of that hypothesis," Laplace replied. Less than two centuries later there are few citizens who would even think of asking astronomers Napoleon's question.

In contemporary times scientists such as B. F. Skinner have carried scientism to its logical conclusion and have discarded all subjective being. As we no longer need the hypothesis of God to account for the movement of the heavenly bodies, so we no longer need the hypothesis of the self as the subjective source of human behaviour. The ethic of scientism acquires a second imperative: "You shall recognize objective being only as real and, accordingly, shall deny all subjective being."

The position is contradictory: its commitment with its imperatives makes no sense unless it involves a self with capacity to transcend objective conditions; yet, it denies subjective being, which alone has such capacity. The results are conflicting and confusing. (1) The hidden ethic is a powerful one and provides scientists with a strong working hypothesis as they investigate without fear or favour the objective aspects of all sorts of phenomena including human behaviour. (2) Because this working hypothesis is relevant only to the objective aspect of things, scientists are inclined to develop a distorted view of reality whenever the subjective aspect becomes important. (3) Whenever scientific-minded thinkers accept the position of scientism, they are left without anything to sustain their own subjective being. If human beings are merely complex objects conforming to predetermined limits, then the aspiring self which conceives itself as fulfilling a creative and meaningful role in the order of things is mere illusion. This, surely, is a prime recipe for alienation.

There is no lack of evidence of alienation among our more thoughtful contemporaries. Viktor E. Frankl in his various works on logotherapy, the therapy of meaning, speaks of the "existential vacuum" characteristic of our age. "The mass neurosis of today," he says, is "the feeling of meaninglessness. Patients no longer complain of inferiority feelings or sexual frustrations. . . . Today they come to see us psychiatrists because of feelings of futility. The problem that brings them crowding into our clinics and offices now is existential frustration, their 'existential vacuum.'"[1] Dr. Kenneth Keniston, professor of psychology and psychiatry at Yale, writes of contemporary society when he states: "Alienation, estrangement, disaffection, anomie, withdrawal, disengagement, separation, non-involvement, apathy, indifference, and neutralism—all of these terms point to a sense of loss, a growing gap between men and their social world."[2] And closer to this study, Peter Taylor in his "Working in the Post Office" paints a classic picture of himself and his colleagues as estranged, alienated workers.

The main source of this alienation, we suggest, is meaning-deprivation, to which the ethic of scientism is an important contributor. This meaning-deprivation is least among the scientists, technologists, and industrial managers—the agents of modern society. For them the ethic of scientism offers a strong working hypothesis that guides and justifies their agency-filled work. However, for the many others—the patients of modern society—the ethic of scientism is a life-sentence to non-significance and meaninglessness.

It is in this context, where the tide of the Protestant ethic has clearly ebbed and where the ethic of scientism infects the "patients" of the contemporary world with alienation, that the Marxian ethic exercises a strong attraction.

---

[1] Frankl, *The Unheard Cry for Meaning*, p. 23.
[2] Kenneth Keniston. *The Uncommitted.* New York: Harcourt Brace & World, Inc., 1965, p. 3.

(1) Marxism understands itself to be a *science* of social development. It is not simply an idealistic vision of what ought to be. Its hypotheses are said to be verified by what is happening around us. Hence, the Marxian ethic picks up scientism's attachment to objectivity and the moral values related to objectivity.

(2) Marxism, nonetheless, offers commitment to an ultimate good, a classless society, or as we have called it, a non-discriminating community. From this commitment is derived a set of ethical imperatives. This commitment with its ethical imperatives provides a powerful antidote to the existential vacuum suffered by "patients" of modern society and fills out one's existence with both immediate purpose and ultimate meaning.

There is, we may note, a contradiction here in the Marxian ethic. If the movement of history is determined by the interplay of economic forces and relations that human beings are powerless to prevent, as Marx explicitly contends, what is the logical sense in the Marxian ethical imperatives that promote intense human agency? However, as we have seen, this is a form of contradiction that the Marxian ethic shares with the Calvinist ethic. The Marxists have tended to take their assumption of economic determinism simply as assurance that their ethical imperatives are indubitably sound. This delivers Marxists from the burden of doubt that plagues most thoughtful people in our age.

(3) The Marxian ethic conceives the contemporary age as building up to an apocalyptic event, the revolutionary overthrow of the bourgeois ruling class. The Marxian ethic accordingly assumes three phases: a preliminary phase, an interim phase, and an ultimate phase. In the preliminary phase the Marxian imperatives are directed to awakening workers to an adversarial class-consciousness, to organizing workers to promote their adversarial interests, and to mobilizing the workers, finally, to seize control of the state and to expropriate the bourgeois ruling class. In the interim phase, that of the so-called dictatorship of the proletariat, the Marxist imperatives are directed in theory to consolidating the rule of the workers and to eliminating all residual bourgeois tendencies. In the ultimate phase, that of the classless society, the ethic achieves its ultimate form. It is then that one contributes to the common good as one is able and receives from the common product as one has need.

We are primarily concerned with the Marxian ethic in its preliminary phase. In this phase the Marxian imperatives are directed to intensifying the adversarial attitude of the workers. The problem of good and evil is solved here in a morally discriminating way. The promise is that if you join the forces of good in fighting the forces of evil, then, when the time is ripe, the forces of evil will be overthrown and only the good will remain. This is a solution of the problem of evil that ties in with late Jewish and early Christian apocalypse. The solution has a number of very attractive features. One, to ally oneself with the "good" gives one a sense of meaningfulness, a participating in an ultimate good. Two, it gives one community, mutuality, with those similarly committed. Three, it enables one to objectify one's shadow elements—one's sense of non-mutuality, hate, etc.—and to direct them against an existing target. And, four, it promises, finally, what the self longs for in the depth of its being, a community of pure mutuality.

It is important, therefore, to scrutinize the Marxian imperatives. Can they in fact deliver? Are they based on sound scientific foundations? And, apart from their connection with science, do they tend in practice to promote the classless society to which ultimate commitment is made?

7.3 An Evaluation of the Marxian Science/Ethic

Marx's thought in his mature years was shaped in terms of the model of science. His objective in writing *Capital*, he said, was "to lay bare the economic law of motion of modern society."[3] It is this science of social change that constitutes the ultimate foundation of the programs of all Marxist groups.

The fundamental features of this Marxian science of social change may be briefly summarized as follows:

(1) *The labour theory of value and the appropriation of surplus value by private owners of property.* Economic value is the amount of labour that is incorporated in a commodity. Commodities will tend to exchange, therefore, according to the amount of socially necessary labour required to produce them. Labour, or rather labour-power, is also exchanged like a commodity, and its value is the amount of labour that is incorporated in the commodities that are required to sustain the worker and the worker's family. The family comes into the picture because workers must be allowed not only to sustain themselves, but also to reproduce themselves, thereby maintaining the labour force. Surplus value arises whenever and to the extent that labourers can produce value in excess of the value of their labour-power, that is, in excess of the value required to sustain themselves and their families.

Where private property is a basic institution of the society—as it is in a highly developed form in capitalism— surplus value is not appropriated by the labourers, but by the owners of private property. In a capitalist society the workers typically command no property, but only their own labour-power. Private owners, i.e., capitalists, own the means of production, buy labour-power at its value, and appropriate the whole product including the surplus value incorporated in it.

The appropriation of surplus value is a taking by the property owners of that which they did not produce; that is, it is an exploitation of the labourers who did produce it. It is also the source of the capitalist's ability to accumulate more and more capital—an accumulation which permits mechanization and other approaches to production that enhance productivity and increase the rate of surplus value.

(2) *The class war.* In a competitive, capitalist system there is a kind of Hobbesian war of all against all—capitalists against capitalists, labourers

---

[3]David McLellan, ed. *Karl Marx: Selected Writings.* Oxford: Oxford University Press, p. 417.

against labourers. However, more fundamentally, there is a class war arising out of the antagonism between the interests of the labourers and the interests of the capitalists. This antagonism arises out of the appropriation by the property owner of the surplus value produced by the labourer. As the labourers become more and more conscious of their class interest, they will forget their competitive struggle against each other and unite to overthrow the property owners.

In the meantime, the period of class struggle is marked by a world-wide expansion of industrialization as capitalists seek new markets and new fields for investment, by a growing concentration of ownership as weaker firms are competed out of existence, and by a growing proletarianization of the population as small business people are forced to become labourers. At the same time, the capitalists as a class are being pressed by the impact of the law of the declining rate of profits, and the labourers as a class are being forced into a deeper and deeper misery.

(3) *The revolution and the abolition of private property*. The population as a whole becomes more and more proletarianized, more and more miserable, and more and more conscious of its interests as antagonistic to those of the property owners. The property owners become fewer and fewer, yet they control an ever vaster industrial structure reflecting both the continuous accumulation of capital and the progressive advances in science and technology. The proletariat unites against the property owners, the tension builds to explosive levels, and the revolution occurs. The state is torn from the control of the property owners and private property is abolished. The proletariat is led throughout by the Communist Party, a group distinguished both by its understanding of the science of social change and by its superior resolution. The Communist Party has no interests other than those of the proletariat.

(4) *The dictatorship of the proletariat*. The state is the instrument of the ruling class. In the capitalist society, although the state may assume a democratic form, it serves in fact the interests of the property-owning class. After the revolution it will be necessary to retain the state as the instrument of the proletarian class for a transitional period. Under the leadership of the Communist Party the proletariat in this period will carry out the abolition of private property, purge society of its antagonistic attitudes and practices, and prepare for the classless, co-operative society.

(5) *The communist society*. This is the goal of the science of social change— the classless, co-operative society. Classes, the state as the instrument of the ruling class, and force as a means of exerting the will of the ruling class, all will have withered away.

It is our hypothesis that Marx's science of social change is deficient, and deficient in aspects that are fundamental to the Marxian approach. Some of these deficiencies will be discussed here.

(1) The Marxist theory of value and surplus value is erroneous. This strikes at the foundation of Marx's economic theory, a theory that displayed capitalism as *inherently* and not just accidentally exploitative.

Marx defined value as the amount of socially necessary labour incorporated in an economic product. By definition, therefore, the suppliers of land and capital contribute nothing to the production of value. Hence, surplus value, the value of product in excess of the value paid for labour-power, is created by labour. Landlords and capitalists in appropriating surplus value are, therefore, appropriating what not they but the workers have produced. However, in criticism of this theory we may point out that human contributions to the production of economic value are essentially of two kinds: working and waiting. The Marxist reduction of the human contributions to working only is a fundamental error. The reduction fits well the revolutionary intention to overthrow the capitalist system, but does not accord with the economic realities of either capitalist or communist production.

Let us suppose a farmer together with one hired hand *work* the farmer's land for one month, cultivating and planting, and then for three months leave their inputs invested in the land *waiting* for the harvest. The purpose of both working and waiting is the anticipated return. Does the waiting-for-return add to the working-for-return another kind of input? If the hired hand is offered, say $500 at the end of his month of work, should he be offered something more if he waits until the harvest for payment? In the latter case, should he be offered payment not only for working-for-return, but for waiting-for-return as well? There seems to be little doubt that the waiting-for-return involves a further imposition on the hired hand that warrants an additional payment.

In the case of both working and waiting there is (a) a subjective cost on the supply side and (b) an objective benefit on the demand side—and typically the objective benefit provides the wherewithal to compensate the subjective cost. The subjective cost of working is not necessarily suffering. Workers may or may not enjoy their work; however, they *may* enjoy it, and hence work is not essentially suffering. Work means rather the sacrifice of options one would otherwise have. One might otherwise: (a) expend one's energies playing (and there are a great variety of ways of playing and many play much harder than they work); or, (b) idle away one's time (keeping all options open so to speak); or, (c) choose to work elsewhere (and, of course, the more options are open here the less attractive any particular work may seem to be). The sacrifice of all other options is the essential subjective cost of work. Therefore, it will typically require a positive return of some sort to ensure a particular choice of work. Objectively, on the demand side, working provides this, that, or the other product from which a positive return may be made to the worker.

Similarly, the subjective cost of waiting is the sacrifice of options one would otherwise have. One might otherwise: (a) take the value on which one has a claim and consume it (and here there are typically many options); or, (b) hold the value in the form of money (and hence maintain the nominal value with minimum risk and at the same time keep options open); or, (c) invest the value elsewhere (and here again there are typically various options). The sacrifice of all other options is the subjective cost of waiting. Therefore, it will typically require a positive return of some sort. Objectively, on the demand side, waiting means the producer has more options, including options with higher productivity than the producer would otherwise have. That is, a clear objective benefit is provided the producer through waiting. From this objective benefit the producer may offer the waiter compensation for the subjective cost of waiting.

It would appear, therefore, that there is no scientific ground whatsoever for denying that waiting contributes to output. Working and waiting are the fundamental inputs, the co-creators of output. Surplus value is not "surplus," but rather value paid for the input of waiting. This is not to say that in the vying between waiters and workers for the highest possible share of return there may not be historical circumstances that place the waiters in an exceptionally favourable position so that the social moralist is compelled to say, along with the Marxists, that the waiters are exploiting the workers. However, what we must say is that this exploitation is not *inherent* in the system; and, indeed, historical circumstances may be imagined where the workers rather than the waiters become the exploiters of society.

Marx is wrong, therefore, both theoretically and practically in his doctrine of value. He is wrong theoretically because waiting is a genuine input demanding, as does working, sacrifice of options one would otherwise have. He is wrong practically because products tend to exchange not as he contended according to the input of working per unit of output, but rather according to the input of working *and* waiting per unit of output.

Marx is equally wrong about the value of labour-power. The value of labour-power according to him is the amount of labour which is incorporated in the commodities that are required to sustain workers and their families. Real wages are determined, therefore, in the long run by what is required to sustain the workers and their families. Although he acknowledges here and there that what is recognized as necessary to sustain workers and their families may change, his usual assumption, explicit or implicit, is that improvements in productivity all go to enhance the surplus value appropriated by the capitalist entrepreneurs. In any case, he contends, real wages "never rise proportionately to the productive power of labour."[4] Statistics relating to the Canadian economy over the past thirty-five years (the period for which we have relatively well-developed data) demonstrate that real wages have enjoyed a remarkable increase and that the increase has been almost exactly proportionate to the increase in labour productivity (see Table 3.4A). However appropriate the Marxian model may appear to be in a primitive capitalist economy, it has no relevance in a developed mixed economy. (Further discussion is included in Appendix A.)

(2) The Marxist fixation on private property as the *sine qua non* of exploitative power is tragically misleading. It is power, not property as such, that enables one person or group to lord it over others. Private property is an

---

[4]Quoted in Paul M. Sweezy. *The Theory of Capitalist Development.* New York: Modern Reader Paperbacks, 1968, p. 102.

important medium of power, but it is by no means the only such medium. The abolition of private property may mean little more than that the search and the struggle for power will take other forms; it does not mean that the negative possibilities of the exercise of power are removed. On the contrary, it may mean that the power game will be played out in other media in even less socially creative ways.

Personal power is in part dependent on personal attributes— physical strength, mental capacities, education, and training. However, we do not travel far along the road to power on personal attributes alone. For substantial power we are dependent on social arrangements whereby acknowledgment by others bestows further powers upon us. The institution of private property is one such social arrangement. If our society in general does not acknowledge our right to exclusive possession and use of certain property, then our property with its powers cannot exist. However, given such acknowledgement, private ownership of the means of production bestows on the owners control of the product and of the workers. Private property is thus a social institution whereby the control of one class of persons by another class is acknowledged and made effective. However, the abolition of private property does not mean the end of control of person by person or class by class. No advanced civilization can function without a complex network of controls exercised by persons with varying degrees of acknowledged authority. What the abolition of private property means, therefore, is that a new medium of power must be found for that area where controls were previously exercised by those who owned property.

In the present case we do not have to look far for the alternative medium of power. A position in any organizational hierarchy, particularly when this is combined with superior personal attributes, is a very important source of power. The communist revolution does not take place without substantial organization. Indeed, the hierarchical organization of the Communist Party is typically definite and the discipline rigorous. In the transitional state, moreover, there will be a vast organizational network: the party, the civil administration, and the military. A position in this network will give the holder power. The higher the position, the greater the power; the greater the power, the more possible and more probable it is that the holder of the position will lord it over others.

Officials are appointed to high positions to serve the purposes of the organization. There is typically, however, the other side as well: the organization serves the purposes of the officials. That is, the organization provides its officials with high material rewards and with an opportunity to exercise their creative talents and, indeed, to enjoy the exercise of power itself. Officials can confuse the two sides—indeed, there is a very strong temptation for officials to do precisely that. The needs of the organization are then identified with the needs of the officials and plausibly then with what maximizes the power of the officials. In this context it becomes very annoying to the officials to have "grass roots" opposition from those who do not see things as they do. Official power is then exercised to bring the opposition into line. The power of the officials is thereby consolidated and entrenched.

Fixation on private property as the medium of exploitation of class by class has hidden from Marxists the grim reality of other power bases—power bases that establish the social dominance of a new class of party members and officials who are able to exploit all other classes in the society.[5] Consequently, the Marxist who is hard-headed about capitalist power is peculiarly soft-headed about socialist power, and is theoretically and practically completely unprepared for the naked power struggle and cruel exploitation that tend to take place once the revolution has been "successful." It is no accident, therefore, that Marxists around the world for decades did not believe—they could not believe—what was actually happening in communist Russia, the first Marxist state to be established.

We may illustrate our thesis with reference to this pioneer Marxist state. Did the dictatorship of the proletariat, established in Russia in 1917, turn out to be in fact a dictatorship *by* the proletariat? Were the workers, the proletariat and the peasantry, given greater and greater opportunity to engage in running the country and their own lives? This we may suppose was the promise. In fact, promise and fulfilment stand out in stark contrast.

The fate of the long-suffering Russian peasants, constituting the bulk of the total population, was to suffer even more outrageously. The revolution originally won their support by expropriating the feudal nobility and distributing their land among the peasants. Thus the revolution to abolish private property made millions of peasants new property owners. However, this contradiction was destined in little more than a decade to be corrected by another contradiction—the contradiction of the party of liberation and reform playing the role of the ruthless oppressor. In 1928 Stalin moved to collectivize the farms and, meeting with opposition as could be expected, did not draw back from using naked, bloody, military force. As the despot ruthlessly reshaped the countryside in the image of property-less, classless society, millions of peasants were allowed to starve to death or were killed, shipped to Siberia, or sentenced to slave-labour camps. The slave-labour camps came to include many others than peasants. Solzhenitsyn advises us that

> we can assume that *at any one time* there were not more than twelve million in the camps (as some departed beneath the sod, the Machine kept bringing in replacements). And not more than half of them were politicals.[6]

Marx had deplored the heartless driving of the peasants off the land and into the cities that accompanied the enclosures of land for sheep-raising at the beginning of the industrial revolution. Legal ownership of land gave the landlords power, and they exercised this power without regard for the claims of social morality. Stalin, the great Marxist reformer, likewise had power, the

---

[5]See Milovan Djilas. *The New Class.* New York: Frederick A. Praeger, 1957.

[6]Aleksandr Solzhenitsyn. *The Gulag Archipelago, 1918–1956*, Vols. I and II. New York: Harper & Row, 1974, p. 595.

power that control of a great state gave him, and he too used this power without regard for the claims of social morality. Offence against morality kept pace with power: because Stalin's power was in fact much greater, his acts were in fact that much more monstrous.

The fate of the heralded new masters of the state, the proletariat, was less tragic, but humiliating nonetheless. By 1921 Lenin made clear that a worker's opposition would not be tolerated. The labour movement was to have no independence whatsoever of the Communist Party and the body of state officials. The unions now were effectively "company unions"; that is, they existed to carry out the will of management.

The principle behind the party's exercise of authority over the unions and other organizations came to be called "democratic centralism." In theory the will of the people was filtered upward from the workers, and then further upward from the rank and file membership of the party to the party's central committees, which constituted but a small fraction of the party. The leadership of the central committees made decisions that were then transmitted downward through the various organs of the state and society; and faithful conformity to these decisions was expected and enforced at all levels. Democratic centralism emphasized the unity of the people in action, and hence independent factions were forbidden. The cardinal rule of party ethics was strict conformity to party decisions once made. Thus in principle there could be free discussion of a matter up to the point of decision, but not thereafter. However, since *new* decisions are typically made in the context of a network of *old* decisions, it is not always clear when free discussion of a matter *in anticipation of a new decision* may be interpreted as breaking discipline with respect to one or other *old* decision. In practice, therefore, freedom naturally evaporated—except among the top leadership. Just how many were included in this top leadership depended on many things, but the temptation for ambitious leaders was to make it smaller. The logical limit to this was the establishment of a single undisputed leader—a logical limit which the Russian Revolution attained in little more than a decade. At this point what democratic centralism in practice meant was *decisions* by the despot at the centre and *obedience* by all the people from centre to periphery.

Echoing the doctrine of the classical economists that a harmony of interests obtains between the various participants in a freely competitive economy, the Marxists have assumed that a harmony of interest obtains between the workers and the new ruling class in the Soviet state. The assumption clearly serves the interests of the ruling class—the party and state officials—for it is this class, and not the workers, who define what these mutual interests are. The decision taken in 1921, and adamantly adhered to since that time throughout the Soviet system, against independence in the labour unions means that the workers have no practical way to protest what is decided for them. Solidarity, the Polish workers' movement of the early 1980s, sought to break with this established practice. What its struggle reflects is that the control of the workers by the ruling class throughout the Soviet system is at least as great as that of the ruling class in the heyday of capitalism, and far in excess of any control currently exercised over workers in the mixed economies of the democratic West.

The power-game is played whether the rules allow or disallow private property. Marx saw that the game played with private capital meant competition among the players, with a long-run tendency toward progressive elimination of players. The maturing of capitalism thus tended to bring about a concentration of economic power in the hands of a relatively few corporations. What Marx and his disciples failed to consider carefully enough was that the successful establishment of the "dictatorship of the proletariat" immediately achieved in principle by political means what the capitalist system had not achieved by economic means over many decades, that is, the concentration of economic power in the hands of a single organization. What the Marxists saw as an ominous possibility under capitalism, they themselves produced by their political action. There now existed in principle one corporate body, the state, with control of all economic matters.

However, the establishment of the one corporate body by no means brought to an end the competition between individuals for control of, or for a greater share in, the control of that corporate body. The stakes in the power-game had been vastly increased; they were now far beyond those of the millionaires and billionaires of capitalism. Lenin began to worry about this crucial problem when his own natural powers began to fail owing to illness. It was then that he suffered Stalin's rudeness to his wife. Pathetically he wrote his final testament, advising his colleagues that Stalin was too crude a man to lead the party and the nation. With Lenin's death in 1924 the struggle for power naturally intensified. Stalin, rude or crude as he might be, shortly proved himself the most adept at the power-game. An important source of growing power for him came from his ability as secretary of the party to appoint men favourable to him to key positions. By 1929 Trotsky, Stalin's most powerful rival, had been exiled and Stalin was left dominating the field.

In the history of man's quest for a better society, Stalin is clearly a tragic figure. A genuine tragedy occurs when the happenings are not accidental but are related in a consistent way to flaws in the leading characters. Stalin is such a character, and the flaws are not only in himself but in Lenin and Trotsky and in the nature of the revolution that they with others made. It was Lenin after all who took the lead in crushing the independence of the workers in 1921; it was Lenin who established the principle of democratic centralism; and in all this Lenin had the strong support of both Trotsky and Stalin. It is doubtful that either Lenin or Trotsky would have, or could have, resisted the momentum of the movement toward further centralization and elimination of opposition. Stalin simply carried the movement to its logical limit. Hence the tragedy.

We must conclude, therefore, that what Marxism tragically lacks is a realistic doctrine of power. If it is power that enables an individual or a class to lord it over others and if, given power, we *tend as a matter of fact* to lord it over others, then no individual or class should be granted power unconditionally. "Power tends to corrupt and absolute power corrupts absolutely," as Lord Acton's memorable words tell us. Hence, no person or class of persons should be granted power without definite limiting conditions. This is the essence of the doctrine of power which was emerging from the practice of political democracy in Marx's own day. Providence, of course, observes this rule: we are all mortal and the mightiest among us is not granted indefinite tenure. The democratic doctrine proposes for our collective life that we should imitate and reinforce Providence. Democratic constitutions therefore provide and enshrine mechanisms whereby those holding the top positions of power may be removed every four or five years. By artifice, tenure at the top takes on an insecurity which parallels that at the bottom.

There is an ancient Chinese doctrine which declares that a ruler has the mandate of Heaven so long as he rules well. However, should he become corrupt and unjust, his subjects are then justified in taking action to depose him—an action that heaven approves by transferring the mandate. Western democracy has moved one step beyond the Chinese doctrine by providing for a "peaceful rebellion": every four or five years the old rulers may be thrown out and the mandate transferred as part of a peaceful political process.

The movement toward democratic political practice was particularly remarkable in the Britain that afforded Marx a peaceful haven for the gestation of his revolutionary theories. Marx, however, failed to discern the significance of the doctrine of power implicit in this movement. His mind was set, rather, on the ravages of exploitation effected through private property—a mind-set that he passed on to his disciples. Consequently they were left pathetically defenceless before the forces that tended to place the post-revolutionary society on new pathways to exploitation.

(3) The doctrine that property relations successfully resist evolutionary change and give way only in periodic, revolutionary leaps distorts history. Marx's abstract explanation of revolution is that the forces of production (science-technology, capital, labour, etc.) change in a continuous, evolutionary way; whereas the relations of production (property relations) are transformed only when tension with the evolving forces of production have built up to explosive levels. The Marxian theory of revolution thus requires that property relations successfully resist evolutionary change. However, we note to the contrary that property relations in the democratic, industrialized West have in fact evolved very substantially in the century since Marx.

The requirement of revolutionary theory perhaps explains why Marxists seem to insist on using a stereotype of capitalism and capitalist development that ignores major changes occurring in property relations. They look at Western economies as if nothing had happened in the structure of property relations since Marx. As a matter of fact, they prefer to look at capitalism in newly developing countries; and it is indeed there that their stereotype seems most persuasive.

Property relations in the industrial Western economies have evolved very substantially. Western economies, as Western economists have recognized for some time, are no longer in any strict sense "capitalist;" they are *mixed* economies, capitalist in some respects, socialist in other respects. For example, it is not unusual for the modern state to appropriate 50 percent of the net earnings of a private corporation; to establish natural products marketing boards that fix production quotas and prices; to enact labour laws that give workers the right to organize and to become exclusive bargaining agents with respect to wages and working conditions (and hence to become co-determiners of product prices as well); to set up publicly owned enterprises either as monopolies or in competition with private enterprises; to operate huge social welfare schemes; and in general to enact legislation and establish institutions to control the operations of the economy. The owners of the means of production can no longer simply do what they please with what they own. The state and labour unions are partners in almost everything they do.

Moreover, it is not unusual for a modern corporation, which has distributed half of its earnings to the state, to distribute only half of the remainder to the owners. To a significant degree there has been a divorce of ownership and management. Management emerges as in effect a third party between the owners of capital and labour.

The divorce of ownership and management is abetted by the dispersal of ownership; and in this dispersal workers have become owners to a greater extent than they sometimes realize. It is not unusual in the 1980s for workers to be metamorphosed on retirement into capitalists; they and their dependants now live on the capital and earnings represented by investment in insurance and retirement plans.

The obvious must be said: we have come a long way from the capitalist and worker of the Marxian stereotype. The capitalist is no longer the laissez-faire owner and the worker is no longer the labourer who owns nothing but labour-power. In the century since Marx, productive forces have indeed continued to evolve, but so have property relations. The consequence is that tensions have not necessarily built up to explosive levels; on the contrary, a complementary evolution of productive forces and relations of production has taken place. This is disconcerting for the Marxists. They are tempted, therefore, to fall back on anachronistic stereotypes.

(4) Marx failed to recognize the limitation of any *science* of social change. He failed to recognize, or at least to give sufficient weight to, the fact that human selves not only immanate limits, but also transcend them. Hence, human history is made not only by the immanence of limits of a multiplicity of objects, but also by the transcendence of limits of a plurality of selves. There is a dimension of creative/destructive indeterminacy in all history. Marx's science of social change opposes to this a hard scientism. "It is not the consciousness of man that determines their being," Marx insists, "but on the contrary, their social being that determines their consciousness."[7] However, the outcome of this theoretical

---

[7]McLellan, *Karl Marx: Selected Writings*, p. 389.

underplaying of transcendence and hence of the partially independent role of human agency is not quite what one would expect. Ironically, the independent power of human understanding and resolution is flagrantly displayed in modern communism, although camouflaged as historical necessity. The successful communist revolutions of this century have all been piped in to the tune of historical necessity, but have in fact blatantly exercised the independent power of collective human commitment. According to Marx's theory, revolutions occur only when history is materially ripe for them. However, Russia in 1917 and China in 1948 were "ripe" in Marxian terms only for bourgeois revolutions. The feudal structure was in both cases in decay and capitalist industrialization in its infancy. What happened in fact, however, is that Lenin and Mao and their colleagues, with their fervent commitment to communism, *made* communist revolutions instead. A whole stage of what was historically necessary according to Marxian science was lept over in the name of Marxism.

In jottings in his notebook in 1845 Marx says, "Man must prove the truth, i.e. the reality and power, the this-sidedness of his thinking in practice."[8] What the success of various communist revolutions around the world proves in practice is not that material necessity consistently determines history, including the understanding and practice of man in society, but rather that human understanding combined with resolution—i.e., collective commitment—can sometimes determine material conditions. Communism in the present century has had some startling successes: within a sixty-year period communist parties have gained control of the state in countries embracing over a third of the world's population. This third of the world, however, was not that third where the modern forces of production were most advanced. These communist advances sprang, therefore, not out of the implacable movement of material forces, but out of the commitment of party members. It was this that gave them amazing collective strength in spite of the absence of the material forces that Marx held were indispensable to the communist revolution. A firmly held faith, it appears, may move mountains even when the theory on which it is based is deficient.

(5) The morally discriminating ethic of Marxism is a false guide to reform. It is false because in practice it does not tend to lead toward a classless society.

Marxism, as we have noted, is not only a science, but an ethic—a set of imperatives derived from commitment to an ultimate good. A central imperative is the waging of the class war of the proletariat against the bourgeoisie. In this war there is no doubt which side is good and which is evil. The proletariat is arrayed against the bourgeoisie as good against evil. The Marxian ethic is thus clearly a morally discriminating ethic. The consequence is that faithful adherence to the ethic brings into play the principle of moral-discrimination, that is, that *moral-discrimination tends to drive out non-discrimination.* The classless society is one which practises non-discrimination. The practice of

---

[8]McLellan, *Karl Marx: Selected Writings,* p. 156.

moral-discrimination, on the contrary, tends to drive out non-discrimination even within the in-group.

If the out-group is identified as "evil," then the "good" in-group assumes that it is justified in adopting the practices of its adversary in order to defend itself from its adversary. Hence, the in-group does to its adversary as its adversary does to it. Or, since the morally discriminating group tends to exaggerate the "evil" of its adversary, it may in fact treat its adversary more severely than its adversary treats it. It becomes more and more a mirror-image of its own image of its adversary.

In this context the non-discriminating observer may find that the in-group is not unambiguously "good" and the out-group is not unambiguously "evil." However, the morally discriminating in-group is not interested in the critique of the non-discriminating observer. Any such critique is immediately identified as emanating in one way or another from the adversary. The only language that is now tolerated is morally discriminating language, that is, language that serves the interests of the "good" in-group. "Truth" is now "that which serves the interest" of the "good" in-group.

But what in specific terms is in the day-to-day interest of the "good" in-group? Leaders emerge in the in-group who define what the morally discriminating "truth" is. Since to oppose the "truth" once declared is to ally oneself with the "evil" adversary, the followers quickly learn to accept such declarations uncritically. In such a context the group of leaders who can critically examine issues pro and con tends to become smaller and smaller. For example, if one of the leaders has in the past opposed that which is now declared to be the "truth," he may be regarded with some suspicion, even though he now outwardly toes the line. He is threatened with rejection from the leadership group. It is important, therefore, to be on the winning side in the determining of day-to-day "truths." However, just what that side is, is not settled until one among the group is recognized as the paramount leader. The morally discriminating approach thus naturally gravitates toward autocratic leadership with an uncritical following.

The foundations for mutuality within the in-group are now seriously undermined. The uncritical following are dependent on the leader to declare their interests. But the leader who has survived the struggle for paramount power has done so by overcoming competitors *within* the in-group. His adversaries, therefore, have been chiefly *within* the in-group. He continues to be orientated toward sustaining his power against potential adversaries within the in-group. What sustains the leader's power against others is, therefore, now declared by the leader to be in the in-group interest. In this context the leader is chronically suspicious of any colleague who attains any degree of prominence. Consequently, from the top down suspicion and mistrust, rather than mutuality and trust, permeate the in-group.

With the withering away of mutuality within the in-group, assessments of all the factors of reality that do not respond to the will of the leader tend to become less and less reliable. Because there is no one among his colleagues who is free to correct him when he is in error, the leader is tempted to exaggerate his power and to confuse what he wills to be the case with what is in fact the case. This gives rise to outrageous errors of judgment. The leader is also liable to bouts of anxiety when he sees his own followers as bent as much on asserting their power against him as he is against them. This gives rise to tragically oppressive actions against his own followers.

In this context the defeat of the "evil" out-group does not usher in the ideal community where "from each according to his ability, to each according to his need" prevails, but rather, its opposite. "Evil" is now actively generated from within: pathetically it is attributed to the poisonous remains of the "evil" out-group.

Illustrations of the tragic loss of mutuality within morally discriminating Marxist states are not difficult to find. In 1917 in the name of the Russian workers a small band of Bolsheviks took over the reins of power from a decadent and decrepit Czarist regime. A little more than a decade later Stalin, who had now attained supreme power, initiated his campaign against the non-proletarian workers, i.e., the peasants. At the cost of millions of lives he proletarianized the peasants—that is, he turned them into property-less employees. Shortly thereafter, in anxiety concerning the power aims of his colleagues, he turned against his own party and liquidated everyone who had attained any degree of prominence and power.

The experience of Marxist China was in some respects similar. As a consequence of his outrageous error of judgment in the Great Leap Forward in 1958, Mao, the supreme leader of the People's Republic of China, found that his power was slipping into the hands of other senior party officials. The "good" which he willed was no longer pursued as a matter of course. In the mid-1960s he therefore created a "cultural revolution" which, completely against Chinese tradition, pitted youth against age. Anyone who had become anything either within or outside the party was subjected to cruel harassment by hastily activated bands of naive, volatile youth. Neighbours were encouraged to inform on neighbours; colleagues were encouraged to denounce colleagues. The foundations for mutuality and trust were perilously undercut. Because an old man's dreams were being frustrated, the most populous nation in the world was thrown into tragic turmoil for a decade.

What then can we conclude concerning the application of the Marxian model to labour-management relations in Canada Post? With respect to the workers who apply this model, we can only conclude that they don't understand what they are doing. They seek presumably more freedom and power for the workers. However, if they succeed according to their model in attaining control of the state, then the accumulated evidence of sixty years of experience in a variety of countries around the world, plus the weight of the theoretical considerations we have advanced, suggests that they will very soon thereafter lose whatever worker freedom or power they now have. If, on the other hand, they do not succeed in attaining their model's goal, but nonetheless render effective performance in the economy impossible by their antagonistic stance, then another kind of state, democratic or otherwise, will be forced to cut back on their present powers and privileges. Hence, those who seek to extend labour power in this way will tend to lose for labour the power it has. The price of greater freedom and power for labour is, rather, greater responsibility in wielding the not inconsiderable power that it already has.

7.4 The Disproportionate Impact of a Committed Minority

The direct impact of Marxism on events in Canada Post is, of course, that initiated by committed Marxist postal employees. It is difficult to know just how many postal employees actually fall into that category. Not all committed Marxists are anxious to declare that commitment; and hence, in the nature of the case, there can be no accurate statistical data. The assumption of this chapter is that the number of committed Marxists among postal employees is relatively small. Moreover, this relatively small group is divided among a number of competing, and sometimes fiercely competing, factions. There are almost as many denominations these days among Marxists as among Christians. One is tempted, therefore, to write off Marxist influence in Canada Post's affairs as relatively slight. We recommend, however, that this temptation be resisted. History plays favourites: it is consistently on the side of the committed. By exploiting the possibilities inherent in various circumstances—some of which we note in what follows—a committed minority may greatly enhance their effectiveness and exert an influence quite disproportionate to their numbers.

The Principle of Differential Commitment

In a democratic organization power tends to gravitate away from the uncommitted and toward the committed. If the majority of the members of the organization tend to be uncommitted on most matters, then a committed minority may easily acquire effective control of the organization. We may call this the principle of differential commitment.

In any democratic organization, although there is equal right of all members to participate in the running of the organization, there is by no means an equal interest and commitment of all members to this process. A substantial concentration of power is possible in labour unions, as in most democratic organizations, largely because of this differential commitment of members to participation in running the organization. If a local postal union, for example, has a membership of several hundreds, but only fifteen to twenty turn out to regular meetings, and of these only about a dozen regularly turn out, then it is this dozen, out of the several hundreds, who know what is going on, who decide routine matters, and who decide in significant respects how important issues will be presented to larger meetings of the membership. If at an important meeting a hundred turn up, then it is natural that the twelve, who know what is going on and who because of their superior preparation can more easily rebut contrary views, will carry considerable weight, weight probably sufficient to determine the decision of the meeting. Normally, of course, it will be from the twelve that nominations for executive positions will be chosen. Given a little talent for leadership there is then a sense in which it is true to say that labour leaders choose themselves. They commit themselves to work for the union and their work justifies their election to the executive.

Our hypothetical twelve may use a number of devices to exercise an even greater control over large meetings. If they wish to enhance their already considerable psychological impact, they may by prior agreement seat themselves in different parts of the assembly and then "pop up all over the hall" at tactically appropriate points to promote the "right" decisions. If the "twelve" unexpectedly are having a hard time carrying the day, then they may adopt the tactic of prolonging the meeting. Points of order are particularly effective here— especially when used by one who knows the rules against less rule-trained opponents. Given enough time the opposition may be greatly weakened by deserters in the ranks who find the attractions of going home to dinner or bed rapidly escalating as seen against the claims of a confused and acrimonious meeting. Time is on the side of the committed! If things are going very badly, the meeting can be recessed for resumption at the call of the chair. The chairperson may call for resumption at a time or place that is not convenient for the opposition.

The legitimate and almost legitimate practices of concentrating power may be supplemented by clearly illegitimate ones, e.g., violence, threats of violence, telephone harassment, etc., directed against opponents and their families. However, given that participation in running the union has a very low priority with the bulk of the union membership, substantial concentration of control can easily occur without the use of explicitly illegitimate means. Hence, it is sometimes possible for a small group of committed radicals to appropriate the power of a large local when the bulk of the membership is *not* radically inclined. This has been true from time to time in a number of the postal union locals, e.g., Ottawa, Halifax, and Toronto.

A committed radical minority may exert a great deal of influence even when it is excluded from top executive positions. A workplace populated by alienated workers is, we may suppose, fertile ground for Marxist proselytizing. However, whether or not conversions to Marxism can be effected, alienated workers have a high propensity for trouble and for making a lot of whatever trouble they may find. They are, therefore, a ready source of recruitment for local battles planned by Marxists. These skirmishes add a touch of drama, some echo of life with a serious purpose, to a routine experienced as drab, repetitious, and restrictive. For this reason radicals with a bit of talent for dramatizing their current objective can normally count, in an alienated workplace, on a substantial if perhaps only temporary ad hoc following.

As we note elsewhere, illegal wildcat strikes were an important factor in labour-management relations in Canada Post from 1965 onward. These constituted a very important kind of pressure by labour on management. In this respect in particular, small Marxist groups with their ad hoc following have played a very important role in Canada Post's affairs.

Potts's Principle

In the early 1970s when H. L. Griffin was director of personnel for the Ontario region of Canada Post, he had occasion to negotiate settlement of an illegal, wildcat strike with John Potts, the Toronto local CUPW vice-president. It was agreed that Griffin would arrange a simple concession and Potts would get the workers back on the job. A day later Griffin called Potts and chided him for not keeping his side of the bargain: the strikers had not returned to work. "You see Herb, it is like this," Potts responded, "if you come out of the Post Office and see the mob rushing down the street, then you run like hell around the block to get in front of them!"

The principle graphically enunciated by Potts here is quite significant: a union executive even when it is not radical itself may find it expedient to move toward more radical positions in order to outflank the radicals and thereby maintain a greater semblance of unity in, and control of, the union. In such circumstances the whole union tends to take on the coloration of the radical minority.

Potts's principle has been an important factor in Canada Post's affairs. It was evident in the use that CUPW and LCUC made of wildcat strikes initiated by union radicals. In general, we can say that these unions found the Marxist radicals useful so long as they did not get too far out of hand. The principle was also evident in the response of the national executives to the Québécois radicals. This will be discussed further in the next chapter.

It is clear, of course, to the intelligent citizen that if the Potts's principle is invoked too often by non-Marxist unionists with respect to Marxist initiatives, then the overall posture of the union will take on more and more a Marxist appearance. David Lewis, one-time national leader of the New Democratic Party, is said to have remarked that if something looks like a duck, waddles like a duck, and quacks like a duck, then there are grounds for assuming that it is a duck. However, it is not always easy to tell: man has a great talent for imitation. In any case the postal unions—and particularly CUPW since 1974—have sometimes waddled and quacked like Marxist radicals. However, this is no doubt in part due to the fact that non-Marxist unionists have from time to time been caught up in the exigencies of battle and have adopted Potts's principle.

The Asymmetry of Creation and Destruction

Creation and destruction are not symmetrical: what takes many an arduous effort to build may take only a few a very short time to destroy. It may take the co-operative effort of many to enable a large enterprise to operate smoothly and effectively, but only a few to render its operations rough and ineffective. Since in the present Canadian context the primary aim of Marxist radicals is to destroy the system, the odds are not so heavily stacked against a committed minority achieving their ends as one might at first be inclined to think.

The common characteristic of Marxists whatever their denomination has been an uncompromising adversarial stance with respect to management. Their intersectarian quarrels are frequently couched in terms of the "we" who maintain a consistent adversarial approach and the "they" who don't. The adversarial stance is, of course, a fundamental Marxist position: workers should become conscious of their class and of the unethical interests of management as representing the capitalist class. The eventual outcome of class consciousness is seen to be the seizure of the state by the workers, the abolition of private property, and the inauguration of the classless society. The postal radicals as Marxists, therefore, are not only in principle anti-postal-management, but even more fundamentally, anti-system: their fundamental objective is the overthrow of the existing Canadian economic and political system. With respect to Canada Post's affairs, the Marxists, therefore, always have ulterior motives: their objective is not in any straightforward sense the welfare of Canada Post or the postal workers. That is, the achievement of excellent labour-management relations in Canada Post might not contribute—in fact probably would *not* contribute—to the coming of the revolution against the economic-political system. For this reason Marxist postal workers have to treat any reasonable approach to the resolution of labour-management tensions in Canada Post as a threat. Hence when John Paré, appointed assistant deputy postmaster general, personnel, in 1976, explicitly offered the unions a co-operative, problem-solving approach to outstanding labour-management questions, the Marxist had no option but to oppose it as a most insidious threat.

This paradoxical position of Marxists *against* reasonable approaches to resolution of labour-management problems is illustrated in Robert Andstein's articles on industrial democracy.[9] Robert Andstein, a Marxist radical, was president of the Halifax CUPW local for a number of years in the 1970s. One would think that industrial democracy in the broad sense of the term is what the labour struggle is all about. This turns out, however, not to be the case. Labour is not going to receive anything gratuitously from management, even lollipops of industrial democracy. If management offers anything, then its intention is to seduce the worker. Labour will fight for what it wants and force management to deliver. Co-operation, it is clear, tempts desertion from the class war.

As will be discussed at greater length in the next chapter, in the period 1974 to 1981 CUPW adopted the uncompromising adversarial stance of the Marxist radicals and along with it Andstein's denunciation of industrial democracy. John Paré's proposals for co-operative problem-solving were treated with contempt. Management was damned whatever it did "good" or "bad": the "bad" was forced upon the workers, confirming what the union had been saying about the management all along; the "good" revealed the depth of management's insidious hypocrisy. Given a divided, hence inconsistent management, blunders were naturally made which fed the wrath so cherished by the radicals.

---

[9]See, for example, The Halifax Postal Worker (the newspaper of the CUPW Halifax local), Vol. 2, No. 1, May 1977.

W. J. Turnbull, deputy postmaster general, 1946 to 1957, could year after year in his annual reports acknowledge with sincerity the great devotion to duty and efficiency of the postal employees. In his final report he wrote: "Departmental and field staffs have at all times during the year shown great devotion to duty and efficiency in their work, a fact which is greatly appreciated by myself and the senior officers of the service." Ten years later the deputies could not make such statements sincerely—so the statements ceased. The last such statement, significantly enough, was for the year 1964. Beginning with the national strike of mid-1965 the workers devoted themselves to rights—duty and efficiency became more and more exclusive management concerns. More and more, two sets of public servants warred in the bosom of a single enterprise.

Anyone who has had anything to do with team sports knows how important yet delicate a thing team spirit is. Given that a group, even a relatively small group, is committed to directing whatever team spirit there is into ways that are destructive of the central purposes of the enterprise, it is not at all surprising that a dramatic shift in the effectiveness of the enterprise could occur.

The Curvature of Human Space

In the period since World War II the general climate of opinion in Canada has been favourable to strengthening the hand of labour. During this period labour legislation in Canada was greatly strengthened. The Public Service Staff Relations Act of 1967, granting with a few exceptions full union rights including the right to strike to federal employees, reflects this climate. Incorporated in provincial and federal law, therefore, and in the network of labour-management contracts based on the law, there are now numerous provisions protecting workers against unfair and arbitrary action by management. The "good" worker is protected from "bad" management by rules carrying the force of law and by a powerful institution, the union, which stands ready to see that these rules are observed. This is undoubtedly good. Power tends to corrupt and the power of management needs this kind of limitation and constant surveillance.

However, there is a problem: the problem is that in practice there is a progressive strengthening of defences against the impact of a bad manager, but a progressive weakening of defences against the impact of a bad worker. This is a strange reversal of the "old days" when the manager's whim was the law. This consequence arises it would appear from too much of what was a good thing. A good thing pushed too far becomes a bad thing: human space is sometimes curved. Social critics who have difficulty in reading this curvature are frequently one generation behind in diagnosing what the crucial issues are.

The question, for example, of what to do with the woefully incompetent worker has always been something of a problem in the public service sector. In the private sector the manager knows that if efficiency falls, profits fall, and if efficiency falls seriously relative to competitors, the firm is out of business. Mortality sits heavily upon the shoulders of the private manager; hence, he or she moves quickly to deal with the case of the incompetent worker. In the public sector the situation is quite different. The public service manager who watches the paper-plowman plodding a wasteful way into the sunset knows very well that the enterprise is not going to collapse in consequence. His or her weary worker is mortal; the enterprise is immortal. The manager's human sympathies, therefore, are with the worker. If we add to these natural advantages of the incompetent public servant all of the protections of the new labour system—and the Public Service Staff Relations Act of 1967 did precisely that—then the incompetent public servant is made nigh invincible.

The intelligent citizen may confirm that proposition by asking senior public servants whether, having found all other approaches of no avail, they have ever tried to fire an employee for incompetence. The typical answer will be, "No! Never!" or, perhaps, from the more conscientious, "Yes, once, but never again!" The "once" will have arisen from the completely exasperating case where the contribution of the employee was not merely low, but actually negative. The "never again" will have arisen from the time gobbled up by, and the strain of, the dismissal process—the personal complaints of the employee, the formal grievance through its various stages, the appeal of grievance decisions, possible court action, and throughout it all memoranda and meetings *ad infinitum et ad nauseam*. If, in addition, the besieged employee is ethnically neither English nor French, or is an officer of the union, or is a member of a radical group, then the "union" knows that it has a case of "blatant discrimination" that justifies sustained attention and possibly strike action. Reading the signs of the times, senior executives may decide that the battle is not worth it and simply transfer the worker to another long-suffering division.

Given these conditions, it is relatively easy and safe for a committed radical to harass management and relatively difficult and time consuming for a manager to control a radical. Given also that destruction and creation are asymmetrical, the radicals, who are few in number but are consciously committed to destroying the system, have some surprising advantages.

CHAPTER 8

The Impact of the Québécois Ethic

8.1 The Québécois Ethic: Three Versions

In Chapter 6 the dramatic drop in postal performance is related to the contemporary enhancement of worker alienation. This alienation is accompanied by a withering away of the industrial work mores initially promoted, according to Weber, by the Protestant ethic. In Chapter 7 the postal problem is related further to the presence of what we call, in its various guises and disguises, the Marxian ethic. The postal situation in the 1960s and 1970s is affected by yet a third very important factor—a factor which, by analogy, we may call the Québécois ethic. In this period very significant developments were taking place in Quebec society. An important correlate of these developments was a growing consciousness on the part of Québécois[1] of their minority position as a French-speaking people in a predominantly English-speaking Canada and North America and of the significance for them of the tendency of this English-speaking majority to assert economic, political, and cultural dominance. The commitment of Québécois in the 1960s and 1970s to doing something about this situation is what we are here calling the Québécois ethic. As one studies the history of labour-management relations in the post office in the post-1964 period in some detail, one is more and more impressed with the leading roles played by Québécois—and especially by Montrealers. One is more and more inclined, therefore, to accord the Québécois ethic a prime place among the factors shaping the postal situation in this period.

With respect to its impact on the post office we may speak of the Québécois ethic in terms of three versions, which we shall refer to as A, B, and C. The Québécois ethic-A may be expressed in terms of a resolve of the Québécois, who have become sensitive to the economic, political, and cultural dominance of the English-speaking majority, not to be second-class citizens in any respect any longer. In the postal unions this ethic is reflected in a resolve to have a Québécois presence second to none and, moreover, to have a union that in its effectiveness is second to none. This ethic tended to promote the development of strong Gompers-type unions with strong Québécois presence. By Gompers-type unions we mean unions which are adversarial in character, which aim to wring the maximum possible for labour from the modern industrial system, but which, nonetheless, support the system and do not intend its downfall. Roger Decarie, who as president of the Montreal local of the letter carriers association was responsible more than any other for the 1965 postal strike and who as national

---

[1] In this chapter the term "Québécois" is used to refer to French-speaking residents only.

117

president of the LCUC for the next ten years created a strong Gompers-type letter carriers union, is a prime example of a Québécois motivated by this ethic.

Québécois ethic-B may be expressed in terms of a resolve to make the Québécois "maîtres chez nous" by means of the political separation of Quebec from the rest of Canada. In the postal unions this ethic was reflected in a readiness to carry on a struggle against management because it was the *federal* management of a conspicuous federal institution. It was reflected further in a readiness to push the Québécois position within the national unions to the breaking point. Québécois driven by this ethic did not care all that much whether or not their actions broke up the national postal unions, or for that matter the postal system itself.

Québécois ethic-C may be expressed in terms of a combination of ethic-B with a new radical leftist stance which ethic-B does not necessarily imply. The Québécois who were motivated by this ethic were resolved to become masters in their own house by winning their independence not only of English-speaking Canada, but of exploitative capitalism as well. Within the postal unions, or at least within CUPW, the radical stance was frequently expressed in essentially Marxist language. However, adherents of ethic-C were not necessarily committed to Marxism in all respects. For example, adherence to this ethic was not always found to be incompatible with adherence to the Roman Catholic Church.

Jean-Claude Parrot, for many years a member of the national executive of CUPW and national president since 1977, is a prime example of a Québécois apparently motivated by ethic-C. Even better examples possibly are Marcel Perrault and Clement Morel who have exercised power within CUPW from behind the scenes. Perrault has exercised power, as Willie Houle before him, from his base as president of the Montreal local of CUPW, a post which he has filled from the time Willie Houle vacated it to become national president in 1968. Frequently it would seem the Montreal tail has wagged the national dog.

The history of labour-management relations in the post office in the post-1964 period can be viewed as determined to a remarkable degree by the dynamics of the impact of Québécois ethic-A and ethic-C and of the conflict between them. Roger Decarie, a strong adherent of ethic-A, is *the* father of the modern LCUC. Decarie, with his strong, consistent leadership, built up a solid Gompers-type LCUC and excluded ethic-C radicals from top union positions. Under his skillful leadership the LCUC quietly won a number of remarkable concessions. Robert McGarry, who succeeded Decarie in 1975, only needed to follow in the steps of the founding father. LCUC success was made the easier as it mastered the technique of coasting in on the slip-stream of CUPW radicalism.

On the other hand, Marcel Perrault, Clement Morel, and Jean-Claude Parrot, strong adherents of Québécois ethic-C, are the fathers of the modern CUPW. Willie Houle, who as president of the Montreal postal workers joined Decarie as president of the Montreal letter carriers in making the 1965 strike, had the chance subsequently of doing for CUPW what Decarie was doing for

LCUC. He was elected president of CUPW in 1968. However, Houle was not as long-headed and circumspect as Decarie and the Québécois-C forces pitted against him were perhaps stronger. In any case at the 1971 convention he was edged out by the Québécois-C forces who teamed up with the ambitious Vancouverite, Jim McCall, to vote him out of office. Jim McCall thereafter tried for three years to outflank the Québécois-C radicals and to gain some control as national president over the union. Early in 1974 he was forced to give up in defeat. Joe Davidson from the Toronto local then enjoyed three years of troubled glory as president of CUPW—but only by capitulating to the Québécois-C faction. In 1977 Jean-Claude Parrot was elevated to the position of president and Québécois-C leadership explicitly acknowledged. Outside Quebec the attraction of Québécois-C leadership was not, of course, in its veiled separatism, but in its radically militant stance. As the Québécois-C gained more explicit control of CUPW, the separatist aspect of their ethic was further muted.

In 1968 the Public Service Staff Relations Board made the Council of Postal Unions the sole bargaining agent for both CUPW and LCUC. So long as Decarie was president of LCUC and Houle president of CUPW (1968–1971) joint bargaining seemed feasible. However, in the troubled transition period of McCall's struggle for survival (1971–1974) deep rifts appeared between the unions. Even if other causes of friction had not been present, an LCUC made in Decarie's ethic-A image and a CUPW being remade in Perrault's ethic-C image could not long remain in harness together. In January 1975 the Public Service Staff Relations Board granted LCUC and CUPW separate certification.

In the sections that follow we trace the impact of the Québécois ethic in its various forms on labour-management relations in the post office in four periods: 1965 to 1968, the years of the 1965 strike and its immediate aftermath; 1968 to 1971, the early years of the Council of Postal Unions under "moderate" Québécois leadership; 1971 to 1974, the final years of the Council of Postal Unions and the challenge to moderation by radical Québécois; and 1974 to 1981, the years of steadfast radicalism on the part of CUPW.

8.2 1965–1968: The 1965 Postal Strike and Its Aftermath

This is the period of the 1965 strike and its immediate aftermath including the Montpetit Report on working conditions in the post office and the passage of the Public Service Staff Relations Act. The period witnessed the transformation of the typically "civil" postal service associations into full-fledged unions with an adversarial posture. Symbolizing this transformation, the largest postal association, the Canadian Postal Employees Association (CPEA), changed its name to the Canadian Union of Postal Workers (CUPW), and the second largest association, the Federated Association of Letter Carriers (FALC), changed its name to the Letter Carriers Union of Canada (LCUC). Significantly the name-changing took place within a few months of the successful conclusion of the 1965 strike.

It is interesting to note that the 1965 strike was initiated by local CPEA and FALC units against the advice of the national executives of CPEA, FALC, and the Postal Workers Brotherhood which embraced the two associations together with the remnants of the declining Canadian Railway Mail Clerks Federation (CRMCF). At the same time the strike was not so much against postal management—postal management by and large sympathized with the demands of the postal workers—as against the government as employer. The Treasury Board, the legal employer, had not raised postal salaries for two to three years, seemed to be taking a penny-pinching approach to possible raises, and moreover seemed to be moving at glacial speed. In the meanwhile, industrial wages generally were rising steadily and rising prices were steadily eroding the real value of money wages established many months earlier.

The strike was led off by Montreal. Here the key man was Roger Decarie, president of the FALC local. Decarie had been irked by the jibes of colleagues in other unions that FALC was not a genuine union since it could not go out on strike or, at least, had never done so. He chided members of his Montreal local into making a motion to consider a strike and thereafter proceeded methodically, with the support of Louis Laberge of the Quebec Federation of Labour, to prepare for a strike. The effervescent Willie Houle, president of the Montreal local of the CPEA and a member of the CPEA national executive, quickly joined forces with Decarie. Hence, much to the dismay of the national offices of FALC, CPEA, and the Postal Workers Brotherhood, within a few days of the official announcement of salary raises of $300 to $360 per year the Montreal postal workers and letter carriers were out on strike. Vancouver and Hamilton went out with Montreal immediately, Toronto joined in the strike a day later, and shortly most urban post offices across the country, with the exception of the Atlantic provinces, were out on strike.

Decarie tended to be quiet, long-headed, and resolute; Houle tended to be more outgoing and volatile. The latter created some confusion among his colleagues by alternating between accepting moderate proposals in Ottawa and more radical actions in Montreal. In the course of the strike government officials and Judge J. C. Anderson, who was appointed as a commissioner to negotiate a settlement, tended to overrate Houle's command of the Montreal situation and to underrate Decarie's role. In consequence the Anderson proposal, which the striking locals across the country in general found acceptable, and which Houle initially accepted, was rejected by Decarie, and Montreal remained out more than a week after other locals had returned to work. Decarie's chief objection to the proposed settlement, other than not being consulted in advance, was that it granted the postal clerks a larger absolute increase than the letter carriers. Decarie did not intend to be treated as second-class to anyone—postal clerks included.

Anderson's final salary recommendation granted increases of $510 to $550. In retrospect it seems clear that if something approaching these reasonable salary levels had been offered a month or so earlier no strike would have taken place.

During negotiations Rene Tremblay, postmaster general, offered to have an outside expert look into working conditions. Judge Montpetit, heading a three-man commission looking into working conditions in the post office, found much to concern him. He made two hundred and eighty-two recommendations. High on his list of priorities was the need for more active consultation between management and workers to discover together mutually satisfactory solutions to their diverse problems. He was something less than complimentary about the apparent aptitude of some traditional postal managers for such consultation and was a little apprehensive about the new militant mood of some of the postal workers. It is interesting to note that when Judge Montpetit was asked to review working conditions in the post office a couple of years later he reported great progress—over 80 percent of his recommendations had been implemented.

When the postal strike was launched in 1965 the exact legal status of public service strikes was somewhat unclear. The postal workers had received the opinion of Professor F. R. Scott of McGill University Law School that since strikes in the public service were not specifically forbidden they were not illegal. Given the postal strike, the time had clearly come to establish the ground rules for union activities in the public service. The Pearson government had earlier appointed Arnold Heeney to chair a commission to recommend on such matters. The commission reported in July 1965, just before the postal strike. It recommended that the public service be granted the right to unionize, but that if bargaining and then conciliation procedures failed, points of disagreement should be submitted for compulsory arbitration. However, given the postal strike as a fait accompli, strong objections from the unions, and arguments from parliamentarians such as David Lewis, the government was persuaded to accept a two-options proposal: *either* compulsory arbitration *or* strike action. The Public Service Staff Relations Act was passed in March 1967. The Public Service Staff Relations Board determined such matters as union jurisdiction and set up tribunals to hear and decide unresolved grievance cases. Certain matters, however, remained the exclusive preserve of the government, e.g., job classification and appointment, appraisal, promotion, demotion, transfer, lay off, or release of employees. These were not opened up for union-management negotiations.

The postal workers accepted the outcome of the 1965 strike as a resounding victory. They were also inclined to deduce that something less than civility can sometimes pay in the civil service. Pragmatic-minded workers were moved, therefore, in the direction of supporting strong Gompers-type unions. The national presidents of the postal workers and the letter carriers at the time of the strike were quickly replaced by less cautious types. Roger Decarie was elected national president of LCUC, a post which he then held from 1965 to 1975. Willie Houle, who had raised mixed feelings by his more militant Montreal behaviour and his more conciliatory Ottawa stance, was retained on the national executive of CUPW but not elevated to the presidency until 1968. In the meanwhile Bill Kay, a Vancouver activist was elected CUPW president.

Early in 1968 the Public Service Staff Relations Board finally certified the Council of Postal Unions as the sole bargaining agent for CUPW and LCUC.

The Railway Mail Clerks, now numbering about four hundred, were rejected by CUPW lest their seniority lessen the chances of CUPW members getting preferred shifts or assignments.

8.3 1968–1971: "Moderate" Québécois Leadership

This is the first half of the period in which the Council of Postal Unions acted as the sole bargaining agent for the postal workers, letter carriers, and railway mail clerks. We may note in particular three developments in these years: the first involving a significant shift in the approach of management and a shake-up in senior management itself; the second involving the apparent establishment of strong Gompers-type postal unions under Québécois-A leadership; and the third involving a definite threat to this leadership from Québécois-C groups.

Eric Kierans was appointed postmaster general in 1968 and immediately set about to transform the post office. He authorized a set of studies whose main thrusts were summarized in *A Blueprint for Change*, tabled in the House of Commons in December 1969. The *Blueprint* recommended that the post office be transformed into a Crown corporation, that certain headquarters functions be decentralized by the creation of four regions (Ontario, Quebec, Western, and Atlantic), and that a massive program of modernization and mechanization be initiated. Patronage–loving parliamentarians were not yet prepared to see the post office slip out from under their direct surveillance by becoming a Crown corporation. Kierans, however, proceeded with the other two recommendations and, in addition, shook up the existing senior management by bringing in some dozens of new executives, who had proved themselves successful outside the post office, to occupy most of old and new senior posts. Kierans evidently felt that new times required new faces. The weakness of this clean sweep at the top, however, was that it naturally provoked some resentment in the upper and middle ranks of management and that it catapulted a whole set of executives inexperienced in postal matters into top management at the very time that the pressures on the post office from strongly adversarial-minded unions and anxious politicians were becoming particularly acute. In the circumstances the new top management was called upon to learn how the postal system operated from veteran postal executives who had some reason to resent their intrusion, to plan a massive modernization program, to cope with a strongly adversarial and peculiarly turbulent labour situation, and to submit to the uncertain directives of politically sensitive Cabinet ministers as they vacillated between labour peace at any price and law and order whatever the cost. The new top management could not have been expected to have had previous experience with all elements of this peculiar mix. As it happened, Kierans's Cabinet colleagues found him too strong a proponent of his views of what the situation demanded, and he was eased out of the post office in September 1970. However, the "technological transformation" of the post office proceeded and became the central focus of CUPW as it adopted a more radical stance in the next period.

In this period (1968–1971) LCUC and CUPW were led by the Montrealers who had figured so prominently in the 1965 strike: Roger Decarie and Willie Houle. In Decarie and Houle, and other leaders of their unions, the desire to create first-class unions and to be pioneers in the public service sector was very strong. In consequence they may have felt it necessary, after their recognition by the Public Service Staff Relations Board in January 1978, to establish a strong identity by another strike. In any case by a narrow vote they decided to strike in 1968, again over a matter of pay scales. After being out three weeks, they settled for a further small increment. Again in 1970, attempting to break the federal government's 6 percent wage guidelines, they engaged in rotating strikes for several months. The settlement finally accepted was just slightly above the guidelines. The cost in lost revenue was estimated by the post office to be in the vicinity of $35 million.

The Council of Postal Unions' leadership in this period was characteristically Québécois-A. However, the presence of Québécois-C sentiment and its inherent antagonism to the Québécois-A ethic began to emerge in a peculiarly complex way in what came to be called the Lapalme Affair. The trucking of mail within Montreal was contracted out by the post office as in other cities. As early as 1952 Rod Services had obtained this trucking contract. In October 1965 the Rod Services drivers were organized by the CNTU, a Quebec-based union outside the Canadian Labour Congress and the Quebec Federation of Labour. In July 1968, two hundred and fifty Rod Services employees were laid off during the three-week Council of Postal Unions strike. At the end of the strike the Rod Services drivers refused to return to work because of a dispute with Rod Services concerning their pay during the postal strike. It may be noted that the Rod Services strike was not a strike against the post office, but merely against one of the companies doing contract work for the post office. However, the mail in Montreal was not moving so Kierans announced a plan for contracting out the trucking in four separate sectors of the city, and the Rod Services drivers accepted a week's pay in lieu of notice of layoff and returned to work.

The CNTU strike shattered Rod Services' interest in the mail contract. G. Lapalme Company was organized to take over the Rod Services mail contract and the CNTU agreement for the fiscal year 1969–70. Sweetening the contract was a healthy 20 percent hike in the contract price. However, even with the sweetener G. Lapalme Company with its turbulent CNTU drivers exhibited no interest in continuing the contract. Early in 1970, therefore, Kierans signed five-year contracts with five different Montreal trucking firms for a period beginning April 1, 1970, at an overall savings of well over one-third.

The Lapalme Affair presumably should have ended there, but in fact it was just beginning to heat up. On February 2, the CNTU began a political lobby backed by a slowdown in mail transportation within the city of Montreal. The issue was in part one of job security for the Lapalme drivers; but it became more and more one of retention of the CNTU affiliation of the drivers whether they worked for private contractors or directly for the post office. The problem for the government was, first, if it opted to stand by Kierans's contracts with five different Montreal companies, then the union affiliation of their drivers would depend on their respective labour contracts; and, second, if on the other hand it opted to cancel Kierans' contracts and have the post office take over urban mail transportation in Montreal, it was tied to the Council of Postal Unions contract, which included mail service couriers. The federal government was accused by the CNTU of union-busting. It would have been accused of union busting by the Council of Postal Unions if it had given in to the demands of the CNTU.

The CNTU had some reason to expect a favourable hearing in Ottawa. Prime Minister Trudeau at one time had been a legal advisor to the CNTU, and Jean Marchand, an influential Cabinet minister, was a former president of the CNTU. However, as it might be expressed in our terms, Trudeau, Marchand, and others in Ottawa were moving in an ethics-A direction, while the CNTU in Montreal was moving in an ethics-C direction. It is interesting to note that while Decarie and Houle in the national offices of LCUC and CUPW strongly opposed the aims of the CNTU in this affair, Marcel Perrault, president of the Montreal CUPW local, strongly supported them.

The peaceful lobbying of the CNTU in Ottawa was supplemented by mounting violence in Montreal. By March 16–17, tension in the federal Cabinet had built up to crisis proportions. Kierans stood by his resolution of the issue as reasonable and efficient. In this he was strongly backed by management of the post office and by a number of Cabinet colleagues. Bryce Mackasey and Marchand, on the other hand, proposed that it be stipulated that the striking drivers should all be rehired by the new contractors. Lacking adequate support, Kierans presented his resignation to Trudeau. However, he reluctantly accepted instead the compromise of the appointment of a Montreal labour mediator, H. Carl Goldenberg, to investigate and make recommendations concerning the situation in Montreal. On March 25, Goldenberg recommended that Kierans's five contracts be cancelled and that the post office assume operation of the mail transport service in Montreal with the drivers now working on the routes to be integrated into the post office.

This decision solved the issue of job security for the Lapalme drivers, but did not resolve the deeper issue for CNTU of continued CNTU affiliation of the drivers; or, rather, it decided the latter issue in the negative. Violence mounted during the spring and summer and came to an end only with the October crisis and the imposition of the War Measures Act.

H. L. Griffin has described the consequences of the final months of the Lapalme affair as follows:

> Between February 2, 1970, when the Lapalme drivers began their fight, and mid-August 75 persons had been injured and 824 incidents recorded. There had been seven dynamite bombings, 28 fire bombings, 646 postal trucks damaged, 104 postal installations hit, 41 employees injured, 18 postal employees assaulted, 16 private truck escorts injured and five attacks on the homes of postal employees. The injuries to 75 persons included broken bones, cuts, burns and bruises.
>
> Damage to the trucks was inflicted mainly with rocks, tire irons, and ball bearings fired from catapults. Two hundred and ninety-six

windshields were smashed, 680 tires slashed, 125 side windows broken, a number of radiators punctured, door handles torn off and ignition keys broken in the starter switches. In addition to the property damage a large amount of mail was burned in the fire bombings. In two cases fire bombs were deliberately thrown into the backs of loaded trucks to destroy the mail. Twenty-six of the fire bombings were at postal stations. Four hundred and ninety-two relay boxes and 754 letter boxes were damaged. Quick-drying cement was used in many cases to fill the locks.

Of the 102 men arrested, 99 were freed on bail and three were acquitted for lack of evidence. Later five men were fined and placed on probation and one man was sentenced to 30 minutes in jail and fined $15.00.

The Lapalme violence finally ended in the state of "apprehended insurrection" we remember as the October crisis. In that month the kidnapping of the British Commissioner James Cross and the murder of Pierre Laporte, Quebec's Minister of Labour, by cells of the FLQ, led to the imposition of the War Measures Act. Laporte in his Labour Day message had expressed hope for sane and harmonious relations between workers, employers, union leaders and legislators. Instead he was killed. The War Measures Act put an end to the violence. The Lapalme affair was allowed to fade away. Charges were dropped and those drivers courageous enough to seek employment were quietly hired by the Post Office.

The drivers had been callously exploited by the CNTU in its effort to gain a foothold in the Federal Public Service at the expense of the postal unions and their affiliation with the QFL and the CLC. They were used by the FLQ in its effort to foment a revolution and by a few politicians to further the cause of a separate Québec. The CNTU's attempted coup in Montreal was halted, but the idea of a separate Québec postal workers union remained a threat to the national unity of the CUPW and a source of unusual power to the leaders of its Montreal local.[2]

As the Lapalme Affair concluded it appeared that Québécois-A forces had finally been successful in stemming the attack from Québécois-C forces centred in Montreal. Nonetheless, a price was paid. Kierans, representing too much the voice of reason in an unreasonable time, was eased out of the post office at the end of September. As the post office hired former Lapalme and other drivers, the radicals of the Montreal CUPW local accused the Council of Postal Unions of signing on scab labour. Willie Houle, the CUPW national president, was in their view compromised and they waited impatiently for the 1971 convention to take their revenge.

---

[2]Unpublished manuscript, Institute of Canadian Studies, Carleton University, Ottawa.

8.4 1971–1974: The Challenge to Moderation by Radical Québécois

This, a key period of transition in labour-management relations in the post office, is explicable in large part in terms of the power-plays of Québécois-C groups and especially of Marcel Perrault and his Montreal CUPW local. The pressure of Québécois-C activities tended to maximize tensions in a diversity of contexts: (1) within CUPW itself between the national office and the Montreal local—and especially between the national president, Jim McCall, and the Montreal local president, Marcel Perrault; (2) within the Council of Postal Unions between CUPW and LCUC; and (3) within the post office between unions and management as the former effectively spiked the manning policy that alone made the massive modernization program a sensible undertaking.

Jim McCall became president of CUPW in 1971 by means of the support of Marcel Perrault and the Québécois-C group, the intent of the latter being to get rid of Willie Houle. McCall, an ambitious unionist from Vancouver, had no intention of being a yes-man for Montreal. However, he found it increasingly difficult as national president to assert any kind of authority over a turbulent Montreal. In the 1972 negotiations of the Council of Postal Unions with the post office, McCall appointed himself and the regional representatives on the CUPW wage and contract committee to the Council of Postal Unions negotiating team; but not Marcel Perrault who was chairman of the CUPW committee. Perrault retaliated by having his local picket the national office for failure to keep the local informed of developments in negotiations. Later in the summer the Montreal local refused even to distribute copies of the CUPW constitution to its workers and dumped them back in bulk at the national office door. In September the Montreal local picketed a labour relations seminar at McGill University at which Eric Kierans was speaking and prevented embarrassed and humiliated national CUPW officers from entering the campus. The intra-union struggle came to a climax in April 1974 when Jim McCall and Jean-Claude Parrot proceeded to negotiate a settlement of the suspensions and strike in Montreal. Montreal refused to negotiate except through Parrot; and McCall, lacking adequate support in his national executive, tendered his resignation.

Joe Davidson, acting-president of CUPW, quickly sought the support of his own local, Toronto, and then in effect committed the national union to the radical Montreal position by calling a national, illegal strike in support of their position. Davidson, confirmed as national president at the 1974 CUPW convention, thereafter followed the radical Québécois lead. In the 1971 convention and throughout the 1971 to 1974 period the Québécois-C group had not wholly hidden their separatist predilections. Ironically, unity was restored to CUPW by a more general acceptance of the radically militant aspect of the Québécois-C stance. After 1974 the Québécois spirit, with its separatist theme somewhat muted, reigned victorious in CUPW.

In the period 1971 to 1974 relations between CUPW and LCUC were so strained that it became difficult for them to work together in the Council of Postal Unions to negotiate a common contract with the post office. There was much talk in principle of the desirability of a single union; but in practice the two unions distrusted each other. In fact there were strong underlying reasons for a difference in attitude between the two. Most of the problems with which we have wrestled in this study apply to the internal workers, but not so certainly to the external workers, the letter carriers. One might even argue that, unlike the policeman in the "Pirates of Penzance," the lot of the letter carriers is indeed a happy one—or, at least, had become so by the time Roger Decarie retired from the LCUC. Unlike the postal clerk, the letter carrier is out most of the day, without close supervision and working at his or her own speed. Unlike the postal clerk, the letter carrier may work faster and reap the benefit of a self-imposed speed-up by going home early. Moreover, by negotiating a very favourable definition of the standard walk in 1970, the average letter carrier can complete a daily walk without too much hurry in six hours. Letter carriers' effective work week is thus thirty hours. To frost this cake, the letter carriers negotiated that when they assumed responsibility for an additional half-walk in the afternoon their extra pay would be at overtime rates. Thus in an actual eight-hour working day an active letter carrier covering one and a half walks can earn fourteen hours' pay. We may note also that the letter carrier, unlike the postal clerk, is not concerned with evening, night, and weekend shifts or, at this point in time, with the impact of modernization and mechanization. In addition, letter carriers can feel assured that without much struggle on their part their PO3 salary and benefits are going to follow very closely the PO4 salary and benefits of the postal clerks. In general, therefore, one would expect the letter carriers to whistle while they work!

Hence there are underlying reasons why one might expect LCUC to develop a more moderate approach to management. Indeed, one may ask why the LCUC did not become more moderate. The plausible answer is that they could not do so given the invitation of Québécois-C groups to more radical stances. It is to be noted that Decarie went along with the illegal national strike in 1974.

One source of annoyance to CUPW was that in the Council of Postal Unions the LCUC was given equal say with CUPW although the former had a considerably smaller membership. On the other hand, what Decarie feared respecting any merger was that the letter carriers would be swallowed up by the postal clerks. In any case by 1974 both unions were anxious for a divorce. LCUC applied for separate certification and CUPW for jurisdiction over the whole Council of Postal Unions field. In January 1975 the two unions were issued separate certification by the Public Service Staff Relations Board.

The period 1971 to 1974 was of crucial importance to postal management as it began to transform the postal system according to its billion-dollar modernization plan. A prerequisite of the new system was public acceptance of the postal coding scheme. CUPW initiated a campaign to boycott the postal code. As a matter of fact, this campaign was an important aspect of the problem in Montreal in April 1974. A number of postal clerks there began to wear boycott-the-postal-code T-shirts and were suspended by management. CUPW closed the Peel Street post office. When McCall and Parrot proceeded to negotiate with the postmaster general and his deputy, Montreal refused to negotiate through McCall. McCall resigned and Davidson broadened the illegal Montreal strike into an illegal national strike.

A prerequisite of reasonable relations between workers and management as the new postal system was being introduced was consultation between them with respect to the impact on the workers. J. C. Corkery, general manager of the new Ontario region, and H. L. Griffin, director of personnel for the region, therefore set up worker-management committees with the co-operation of local CUPW offices to plan MAPP-Toronto (Major Processing Plant, Toronto). Since Ontario was considered at this time to be a pilot region, the precedent was important. However, Jim McCall, invited to a planning session in Toronto in the hope of developing a communication link with national union headquarters, walked out of the meeting and ordered the local officers thenceforth to refuse co-operation. McCall had decided that these matters should all be *negotiated* at the national level. In view of the Montreal situation he was possibly oversensitive on the point of maintaining centralized national control. In any case we see here the beginning of what later became a hardened CUPW policy: no consultation and co-operation with management at the local level; everything decided by official negotiations at the national level.

At the national level everybody—union and management— seemed to agree in principle on union-management consultation on modernization and mechanization. However, in practice the *content* of consultation fell by the wayside as union and management, in a highly adversarial atmosphere, battled over the *form*. The form, of course, was important because it determined who would *control* the matter. In general CUPW and management never did get beyond the battle over form. Postal management was loath to bend very far on the form lest a contentious union effectively block the whole modernization program. The union, on the other hand, was unwilling to move until it was clear what its rights were to be. In the 1972 contract negotiations the main issue for CUPW was automation. Owen Shime, appointed to chair the Conciliation Board, recommended a Manpower Committee, with an equal number of management and union members and a third party chairperson, to consult on automation. However, through 1973 and into 1974 the committee involved itself mainly with form, that is, its own terms of reference, and thus made itself ineffective.

Another prerequisite of the success of the new postal system was an appropriate manning policy. As we have noted, the new system *could not* improve productivity unless the number of workers was reduced relative to output. Output could be expected to increase, but with various work-stoppages and a serious decline in the quality of service, output was not increasing as much as anticipated. To allay the fears of the postal workers, Postmaster General Kierans promised them that no *person* would lose his or her job because of the modernization program. This promise was renewed by succeeding postmaster generals. Given this promise as a precondition, what was required was a steady reduction by attrition of permanent employees beginning in the early 1970s. However, in the period in which the new system was being introduced a certain amount of double-staffing was required. The obvious answer to this requirement was the appointment of explicitly temporary employees, that is, casuals. In the past the post office had frequently abused the category of casuals by appointing workers as casuals for year after year. But now it was essential to hire most new employees explicitly as casuals if the modernization program was to succeed. During the 1970 negotiations in Ottawa CUPW accepted the assurance of personal job security and agreed to co-operate in the matter of the appointment of casuals in return for a pay increase for casuals raising them to the starting rate of the regular position they covered. However, they quickly reneged and thereafter supported widespread agitation on the casuals question. They persistently distorted the promise that no *person* would lose his or her job on account of technological change into a promise that no *position* would be lost. Abolition of a permanent position became a cause for agitation. In the years 1971 to 1974 over one hundred unlawful local strikes took place—in many, if not most of which the issue of casuals was uppermost. The trouble in Montreal in April 1974 was connected with an aggressive campaign of that local against part-timers and casuals.

There seems little reason to doubt that the unions knew here what they were doing: blocking the modernization program in a way that at the same time built up union membership and financial strength. For the sake of some peace in their time and, on occasion, at the urging of Cabinet ministers, the postal managers gave way somewhat, now here, now there. The overall percentage of casuals to permanent employees did not increase, and hence the absolute number of permanent employees increased alarmingly. CUPW was winning the battle to spike the benefits of the modernization program.

8.5 1974–1981: Steadfast CUPW Radicalism

In April 1974 Jim McCall resigned as president of CUPW, completely frustrated by the behaviour of Marcel Perrault and his Montreal local, and Joe Davidson took over as acting-president. In October 1981 Canada Post became a Crown corporation. The one completely stable factor in the postal situation in the intervening years was an undeviating adherence of CUPW to a militantly adversarial stance vis-à-vis management. The LCUC in this period was also adversarial in its general stance: it did not hesitate to confront management when that suited its tactical purposes. Although LCUC engaged in no official nation-wide strike in this period, there were numerous unlawful LCUC local strikes. However, it also involved itself extensively in consultation with management as requested by management. This process of consultation it also turned to its own advantage. Hence, LCUC's adversarial stance was a pragmatic one: it was adversarial or co-operative as best suited its interests as it currently conceived them. CUPW's adversarial stance in this period was fundamentally different: it was a steadfast stance of deep conviction. It permitted no fraternizing with the enemy in the form of consultation, even if this seemed currently advantageous. If LCUC's motivation may be said to have been basically commercial, CUPW's motivation was highly moralistic. CUPW was empowered by a paradigm, a model, a vision of how things are and ought to be, which transcended immediate, pragmatic, commercial interests. The paradigm was in essential features that which we described in Chapter 7 in relation to the Marxian ethic. The Marxist element among the postal workers across Canada joined with the radical left element among the Québécois to overwhelm the basically alienated, perhaps largely commercially minded, majority of postal workers.

To classify the CUPW thrust in this period as essentially Marxist in character will no doubt be flattering to some and offensive to other members of this union. To yet others it will seem a capitulation to the wolf-crying of the radical right. And it must be admitted that in a context where the far-right and the far-left distort terms to serve their own ends, it is difficult for the centre to use certain terms with assured rectitude. Nonetheless, the attempt must be made, and the reasonable test would seem to be, with respect to any group, what they actually *say* and actually *do* rather than what they say they *are*. The hypothesis then is that CUPW in this period was essentially Marxist in that what they *said* corresponded in very important respects with Marxist theory and what they *did* corresponded in very important respects with Marxist practice. We do not contend that CUPW leaders in this period necessarily understood themselves to be Marxists; however, what we do contend is that the thrust of CUPW during this period was essentially Marxist whether or not they would have chosen to apply this term to themselves.

The speech by CUPW President Jean-Claude Parrot to the Labour Day rally in Hamilton, Ontario, in September 1979, illustrates this orientation of CUPW. The speech is published in the September issue of the CUPW paper. Three quotations separated from the main body of the text faithfully represent the tenor of the argument.

> We are confronted with a situation where virtually all of our rights are being openly threatened.

> The trade union is the only force which can mobilize the power of workers against the employers.

> We have a choice. We can place our faith in the good will of the employer or we can organize the entire labour movement into an effective fighting force.

With respect to the first point Parrot speaks of

> . . . three elements of the attack on workers which has been jointly waged by corporations and governments.
> *Cutbacks* in our social rights;

Rollbacks in acquired rights; and
Reduction in our real wages.

In the immediately preceding paragraph he exclaims,

> Yet, while a generation of workers is witnessing a reduction in their standard of living, THE AVERAGE INCREASE IN PROFITS IN THE SECOND QUARTER OF 1979 WAS 37%. Is there anyone here whose wages are 37% ahead of last year, or 30% or 25%?

The Marxist theory of the state is that it is simply the handmaid of the ruling class. Parrot says here that the attack on workers is "jointly waged by corporations and governments." He fails to note that governments in the mixed economies have moved a long way in the past hundred years and that corporations are frequently as unenthusiastic about government actions as he is. The increasing misery of the working class is a standard claim of Marxists. Parrot says here that "a generation of workers is witnessing a reduction in their standard of living." He fails to note that in the thirty years ending in the time that he is speaking real labour compensation per person *more than doubled*. Moreover, the decline in real labour compensation per person after 1977 is related to the failure of productivity to increase and to the fact that for some years prior to 1977 improvements in real compensation per person had been outrunning productivity (see Table 3.4A). Since there may be sharp fluctuations in profits in the short run, *both up and down*, a comparison of profit changes and wage changes in the short run are meaningless. Parrot, moreover, fails to note that over the past thirty years the percentage distribution of income between labour and non-labour recipients has remained remarkably stable (see Table 3.4B).

With respect to his third and concluding point, the workers choice, Parrot leaves no doubt as to where he stands. It is standard Marxian doctrine, as we have noted, that property relations successfully resist evolutionary change and give way only in periodic, revolutionary leaps.[3] The captains of modern industry are leopards who do not change their spots. If they seem to do so, it is simply camouflage hiding the law which determines their persistent, exploitative behaviour. The contemporary employer, he says (and he is thinking of persons such as John Paré, assistant deputy postmaster general, personnel),

> would like to see our leaders unite with them and substitute industrial democracy programs and quality of worklife programs for the collective bargaining system.
>
> They say they want to end confrontation. They say they want a more rational system. But what they really want is to see consultation replace negotiation. They would like to replace the democratic character of collective bargaining—where the membership makes the final

---

[3] See Chapter 7 (section 7.3).

decision—with a system in which the members are often not informed of the deals that are made and certainly not able to vote on them.

And now, they say they want to give us power. They say they want us to be on the Board of Directors. Isn't that great. After 100 years of struggle, now the employers are going to let us help them to maximize their profits.

If we think the corporations' greed for greater and greater profits will disappear as soon as we put a trade union leader on the Board of Directors, then the answer is easy. If we think that changing the attitude of management will eliminate the fundamental law that governs a "free enterprise" system—a law which states that the success of management is measured by their ability to extract the maximum amount of surplus from *our* labour—then our answer is easy. So we have a choice. We can place our faith in the good will and intelligence of the employers or we can turn to ourselves and begin the long and difficult task of organizing the entire labour movement into an effective fighting force.

As Jean-Claude Parrot completed his speech we can almost hear the closing words of the *Communist Manifesto* echoing in our ears: "The proletarians have nothing to lose but their chains. They have a world to win. WORKING MEN OF ALL COUNTRIES UNITE!" The inherently exploitative nature of capitalism as taught by Marx is affirmed. The labour theory of value and surplus value as developed by Marx is referred to as a fundamental law. The courageous alternative to being taken in by the blandishments of the employer is for the workers to gird themselves up for the class war. The very title of Parrot's speech lamely echoes the Marxist Manifesto: "Attack on workers—Worker unity needed now."

If the most remarkable feature of the postal situation in the period 1974 to 1981 was the undeviating adherence of CUPW to a militantly adversarial stance, a further remarkable feature was that, with the appointment of John Paré as assistant deputy postmaster general, personnel, in 1976, the post office offered the workers a genuine, new choice—the alternative that Parrot was so anxious to disparage in his 1979 speech. A post office that was traditionally authoritarian and that lived according to the directives of the postal manual offered the postal unions a joint problem-solving approach. In place of, or at least supplementing, the adversarial mechanisms, procedures were established enabling management and the unions to identify, define, and work out the resolution of issues together.

John Paré had considerable success with Intergroup, his joint problem-solving approach with the various postal unions, CUPW excepted. However, from the beginning he had a number of serious difficulties.

(1) The exception of CUPW was a major one. It was in this jurisdiction that the key problems lay. CUPW adamantly refused to engage in joint consultation procedures from the very beginning. Indeed, it is clear that if the co-operative approach can be made to work, the class war has come to an end and something is happening which is not foreseen by the Marxist model. However, Parrot and

his colleagues were too committed to the model and its battles to risk letting any other model succeed. CUPW "religiously" kept itself aloof from anything that even hinted at a co-operative approach. As late as 1981 Parrot refused to participate in a seminar on postal problems at Carleton University because John Paré was participating some weeks later.

(2) A traditional, authoritarian organization is not converted to joint problem-solving ways overnight. There were difficulties in communicating proposals from headquarters through regional offices and district directors to the local workplace and equally great difficulties in translating consultative theory into consultative practice.

(3) The initiation of the joint problem-solving approach by management followed hard upon some backtracking on what the 1976 annual report cryptically called "new language on technological change with access to a third-party tribunal." This "new language" was offered as part of the settlement of the crippling six-week CUPW strike at the end of 1975. John Mackay, deputy postmaster general, and his staff were very unhappy with the "new language," but Bryce Mackasey proceeded with the settlement nonetheless. The "new language" was incorporated in Article 29, Technological Changes. Paragraph 29.02 provided that "in carrying out technological changes, the Employer agrees to eliminate all injustices to or adverse effects on employees." Stated in this very general and inclusive way the stipulation invited trouble. Paragraph 29.05 provided that the employer and union were "to hold constructive and meaningful consultations in an effort to reach agreement on solutions to the problems arising from [technological change] in the presence of and with the assistance of an independent and qualified third person." And paragraph 29.07 provided, in the case of disagreement, that "the parties shall refer such matters to a special adjudication committee." After some months of wrangling Treasury Board lawyers expressed the opinion that the article encroached on matters that were excluded from bargaining under the Public Service Staff Relations Act and hence was not legally binding. CUPW lawyers evidently accepted the legal point, but the union naturally felt they had been "taken in" by the government on this matter. CUPW is inclined on principle to distrust employers whether private or public; this particular issue happily confirmed for CUPW its general distrust.

Given CUPW's doctrinnaire distrust of management and management's capacity occasionally to come up to expectations, it is not surprising that CUPW–Canada Post relations in this period did not excel in peace and good will. Living up to its reputation, in April 1975 the Montreal local again initiated a vigorous campaign against casuals. The post office responded by issuing three hundred suspensions. This time, however, the Toronto local dragged its feet and national action in support of Montreal evaporated. Six months later, however, within a week of the passage of the Anti-Inflation Act, CUPW was legally out on a national strike. The strike lasted for six crippling weeks and was finally settled for a wage offering extending to mid-1977, which matched the LCUC agreement reached without strike many months earlier. In addition, the union won the "new language" on technological innovation, and improved shift premiums, weekend premiums, etc.

The long strike drained CUPW and discouraged nationwide action for a few years. However, as CUPW and LCUC wound up for negotiations in 1977 as the current contract ran out, local illegal strikes multiplied. In the two years 1977 and 1978 there were well over a hundred of these. In addition, CUPW in particular used a flood of formal grievances as a method of harassing management. At the time of the strike in October 1978, there were approximately 56,000 outstanding grievances. The Liberal Cabinet lost patience, and when CUPW went out on strike they legislated them back to work after nine days, provided for compulsory arbitration of unsettled issues (which included virtually everything), and declared a ban on strikes until the end of 1979. Jean-Claude Parrot, refusing to perform what was demanded of him by the Act, finally spent a few months in jail, thereby becoming one of the select company of modern martyrs of labour. The arbitration among other settlements restored to the post office the right of individual work measurement.

Again in July 1981 CUPW went on strike and remained so for six weeks. A curious feature of the settlement was a limitation placed on part-timers negotiated by CUPW. Part-timers were cut back from a maximum of thirty hours a week to twenty-five hours a week. Part-timers are members of the union, but by reputation are good workers and indifferent unionists. Given that part-timers are typically those who have *chosen* to be part-timers, the settlement was highly discriminatory.

8.6 Political Expediency versus Legal Rectitude

The Public Service Staff Relations Act (PSSRA) passed in 1967, set forth the rules of the game for workers and management in the public service. As we have reviewed the history of labour management relations in the post office it has become all too apparent that unions and management have frequently been prepared to operate completely outside these rules. In the 1970s there were between two and three hundred illegal, local strikes in the post office. In the typical case the workers involved lost pay for the time they were off—but nothing else. In 1974 the whole Council of Postal Unions went on strike illegally. Assisted by the chairman of the Public Service Staff Relations Board, the post office negotiated a settlement, the first point of which was "no reprisals."

So long as the law was broken "collectively" it seems that the postal management and the federal government were prepared to find it politically expedient *not* to invoke the penalties provided in the law. No doubt an important part of the reason for this was the political sensitivity of the situation in Quebec where so much of the postal trouble originated. However, it does not take an acute observer to see that the postal unions were being conditioned to invoke the rules of the PSSRA system when it suited their purposes, and to ignore these rules when it suited their purposes. The consequence, of course, was that the PSSRA rules applied in practice in a discriminatory way to the two sides of the labour-management relation. In practice the PSSRA protected the unions; but because the government typically found it politically expedient *not* to enforce the law against the unions, it failed to protect management.

In comparing Canada Post and the U.S. Postal Service in the post-1964 period, one is struck by the dissimilarity in productivity performance in spite of the similiarity in most general conditions. However, there were two general conditions that were explicitly different: the postal unions in the United States were not given the right to strike; and the U.S. government adopted a quite different approach to illegal strikes. On one occasion when the New York City post office struck illegally the President of the United States sent in the army to process the mail. It may be politically expedient in the short run to sell the unions indulgences for illegal strikes; in the long run, however, the social costs may be very high.

PART 4

CONCLUSIONS

CHAPTER 9

A Proposal

9.1 Counts Against the System

Since working for wages is a *quid pro quo* activity, we may assess working in any enterprise in terms of both *quid* factors and *pro quo* factors. Workers are hired to produce something: a key *quid* factor, therefore, is the effectiveness of working in producing what is intended, i.e., productivity. However, workers are not simply instruments of production, that is, objects that may be manipulated to produce other objects. They are also creative beings: each is also a self transcending as well as immanating the world of objects. If the creative nature of the worker is not to be seriously repressed, then working must provide the worker with opportunity for expressing what we have called agency. Another important *quid* factor, therefore, is the opportunity that the system of working affords for expressing creative agency. Moreover, workers are not simply creative beings isolated from each other by their power of transcendence. They are also communal beings: the one self actualizes itself only in complementary relation with other selves. If the communal nature of the worker is not to be seriously repressed, then working must provide the worker with opportunity for expressing community with other workers. The key *quid* factors in working, therefore, are productivity, agency, and community. The key *pro quo* factor is, of course, the money wage; but since inflation may erode the purchasing power of the money wage, inflation may also be added as a *pro quo* factor.

Assessing working in the post office in terms of these five factors—productivity, agency, community, money wages, and inflation—how well does it fare? Apparently, very badly indeed! Productivity fell disastrously for more than a decade, then failed to make significant recovery. The quality of agency, which was low enough by the early 1960s, was further degraded by gradually dispensing with memory-skill sortation and by the introduction of machinery that left workers with work as mechanical as that of coding desk operators. The quality of community fell to abysmal levels reflecting the contemporary enhancement of worker alienation and the development of militantly adversarial labour-management relations. One might say that the opportunity for expressing agency and community passed from the organized working context itself to union activities; or, if Peter Taylor is correct, to the anarchic struggle of workers against work.

We are left with something positive to say about the *pro quo* factors only. Even Peter Taylor, writing in the early 1970s, says the money was not too bad. And in the later 1970s, as we have noted, money wages were substantially increased. With respect to the erosion of money wages by inflation, CUPW and LCUC won cost of living adjustment clauses as part of contractual wage settlements as early as 1976. In terms of *pro quo* factors, therefore, working in the post office was quite good by the later 1970s. Even here, however, caveats must be added: given the abysmal productivity performance, the improved *pro quo* benefits of postal workers were acquired at the expense of reduced real *pro quo* benefits for other Canadian workers.

If Maslow is right, and there is surely something in what he says, once basic physiological and safety needs are met there is not much motivational power to be got by means of increased *pro quo* benefits. Modern enterprise must turn, therefore, to *quid* factors. It is here that Canada Post, management and unions together, failed miserably. Management attempted to solve the productivity problem by technological assault. It failed to see that what was imaginative and bold for engineers and managers was potentially destructive of agency and community for the general run of postal workers. Moreover, it failed to see that the technological revolution itself might be neutralized by the concurrent revolution in union-management relations. This neutralization was explicitly stated by CUPW in 1977, as we have noted.

The unions, in turn, attempted to resolve their problems by organizing for counter-assault. In public, they approved in principle any intimations of productivity improvements; but in practice, they opposed such improvements as a threat to union numbers and hence a veiled kind of union busting, or as a kind of speed-up threatening the health and welfare of the workers. They failed to see that efficiency is an important positive factor in both self-esteem and the esteem of others. In public, they damned the new technology for robbing the workers of agency, but in practice, they did little to resolve the deepening agency and community crisis. On the contrary, union leaders seemed to be more concerned with maximizing the power correlated with a more militant, adversarial stance over against management. A variety of union demands tended to exacerbate the productivity-agency-community problems. To cite some examples: (1) Provision that a group of workers less than ten could not be assessed for productivity meant that no workers could display their proficiency either to themselves or to others. The natural tendency was a decline in both productivity and mutual esteem. (2) CUPW won for the coding desk operators high PO4 salaries, but nonetheless, left them sitting high and agency-less at their coding desks day after dreary day. (3) Provision that a worker who temporarily accepted a supervisory position would lose his or her seniority on return to normal duties symbolized rather blatantly that workers should not allow ambition to lure them into fraternizing with the managerial adversary. The natural tendency was a lowering of incentive among the most competent workers, a deepening of the division between postal workers and supervisors, and a dampening of esprit de corps.

The adversarial management–union system failed, and failed dismally, in coping with the crucial deficiencies in *quid* factors: productivity fell dramatically and remained low in spite of the technological transformation; agency, which was already low at the postal workers' level, was lowered even further;

community among the postal workers and between the workers and the post office as a corporate entity was replaced by the disunity of alienation, class struggle, and a general factionalism. In this forbidding context Roger Bouvier's story in Chapter 4 shows us both how easy it is to find a solution and how difficult it is to hang on to that solution once found. Bouvier as supervisor introduced some humanity into his relationship with the postal workers and gave the workers individually and collectively some incentive for working efficiently and harmoniously together. His work group multiplied their productivity, participated in managing the process (even to the extent of manhandling slackers out of the washroom), built up an impressive esprit de corps—and frequently went home two to two and a half hours early as a reward for increased efficiency.

The solution on the face of it was ideal. The workers worked much more efficiently and were happy doing it. The post office got much more for its money and the workers, instead of being the source of a steady flow of formal grievances, took some interest and found some satisfaction in their work. Nonetheless, the solution, temporarily fruitful as it was, failed to survive. There was apparently somewhere a fatal flaw.

The Achilles heel of the Bouvier solution of the postal problem was that it involved bending the rules of the system. The intelligent citizen should note that in the modern labour-management system rules play a role analogous to the law of gravitation in the Newtonian system. What nature failed to impose, two groups of persons meeting in an adversarial spirit contract to impose on each other. Like gravitation, the rules are intended to have a uniform and universal application. Immersed in a network of rules established by the contractual agreement, everybody is safe, life is orderly, and novelty is subject to formal grievance. The fatal flaw in the Bouvier solution was that the rules said that the worker worked eight hours a shift: the Bouvier worker sometimes worked only five and a half to six hours. The intelligent postal user might say, "Very well, let us wink at the discrepancy!" And this indeed is what the union steward and lower-rung management did for a time. However, as we might have learned from the Buddhist practice of the Four Unlimiteds where Sympathetic Joy is a hard-won discipline, not everyone is enthusiastic about the happiness of others. The shift that succeeded the Bouvier workers frequently found little left over for them to do, and this raised the spectre of redundancy. Besides, if some workers were getting off two or more hours early, why should other workers labour the full eight hours? The principle of uniformity was raising its awesome head. Idiosyncrasy, even very successful idiosyncrasy, hints at loss of control—and that cannot be tolerated for long by either a control-conscious management or a control-conscious union. Senior union and local management officials therefore reverted to type, and Bouvier was ordered to cease and desist. Bouvier, through the creative use of agency and community in his role as first-line supervisor, had solved the postal problem. "The System," like a dragon spouting uniformity through two fiery nostrils, reared back and gobbled up the Bouvier experiment.

9.2 A Proposal

Where a system by its very structure prevents creative resolution of its own basic problems it is clearly destined for destruction. If the post office had been a private, competitive enterprise then *either* its performance would have been radically different *or* it would have gone bankrupt within a few years of its 1965 change in direction. Its survival has been dependent on a combination of very substantial increases in constant-dollar postal rates and enormous subsidies. Given an efficiency that is roughly half of what it apparently could be, and a community of workers that is among the highest paid and most discontented in Canada, the postal system has very little to commend it. Since the postal users in their capacity as citizens are in principle the masters of the system, who or what should stand in the way of an abolition of the system and its replacement with an alternative system both more efficient from the point of view of the users and more satisfactory from the point of view of the workers?

Two important questions require answering: What should the alternative system be, e.g., a mild modification of the old system or a radical change? Who, whether or not they *should*, will *actually* oppose the transformation? The two questions are interrelated in that the design of the alternative system will have to take into account the possibility that the effective operation of the alternative may be neutralized by the opposition to it. As we have noted, the technological revolution of the 1970s failed largely because its planners failed to assess realistically the power of the opposition to neutralize it.

A possible choice is the surrender of the government-owned postal monopoly to competitive private enterprise. Entrance of private firms into the postal trade could be controlled by licensing. Competition could be assured for all the main corridors of postal transmission by setting up Crown corporations to compete with private enterprise. If it is felt socially desirable to keep inter-urban and rural postal rates in line with each other, then inter-urban mail could bear a small tax and rural mail receive an appropriate subsidy.

A major objection to this alternative is the waste involved in duplicating collection, processing, and delivery services. However, the cost of duplicating some of these services could be minimized. For example, the government could construct sets of delivery boxes for postal users in each locality and grant access to these boxes to various licensed postal enterprises at an appropriate rental fee. Under this system unit costs would no doubt be higher than what they *could* be under an efficiently operating government monopoly. However, in view of the fact that actual monopoly unit costs are roughly double what they *could* be, it seems probable that competition would bring *actual* unit costs down significantly. Even more important, competition would bring a significant improvement in the quality of mail service—mail again would be transmitted reliably and quickly.

Opposed to this alternative system would be those who wield power within the present system: senior management and union officials. It takes only a little experience to confirm that it is a rare official who willingly presides over the dissolution of his or her own power. Both sets of officials would argue cogently that national disaster would follow choice of such an option. Of the two sets, senior management officials are closer to the postmaster general and hence the Cabinet; but union officials are better organized to exert a more broadly based political influence. Twice in the contemporary period the federal government has seen fit to submit senior postal management to a radical shake-up: first, under Eric Kierans, in anticipation of the technological revolution of the 1970s, and, second, under Michael Warren, to effect the reorganization of Canada Post as a Crown corporation. In both cases a completely new set of senior managers displaced the old, in some cases exceptionally competent, senior management. It would seem that the power of top management is not inviolable. It is yet to be demonstrated, however, that the power of top union officials is equally subject to radical shake-up. It is true that Parliament has from time to time ordered the postal workers on strike back to work; but, in general, both the Public Service Staff Relations Board and the Cabinet have been exceedingly reluctant to invoke sanctions against the postal workers, even when their actions are clearly illegal. Legal rules have applied to postal management; political expediency has applied to postal unions.

Turning over the postal monopoly to competitive enterprise would mean that the present postal unions would be dissolved and new unions formed in the new enterprises. However, if the purpose of introducing competitive enterprise into the postal system is to be realized, then it is essential that not only management be demonopolized, but labour as well. Legislation effecting postal reorganization would provide, therefore, that no postal union could extend its jurisdiction beyond the workers of a single enterprise. If the unions condemned this as union-busting, the charge could be admitted in the sense of monopoly-union-busting. Both unions and management would be denied the right of becoming a monopoly. To protect postal users, the right of workers in one postal enterprise to strike while the workers of another postal enterprise are already on strike would be severely curtailed.

It is our hypothesis, therefore, that a competitive postal system would be superior to the present postal monopoly in almost all respects. Efficiency would increase significantly: real unit costs would fall, and even more important, the quality of service would greatly improve. The opportunity for postal workers to express agency and community would improve and the real wages of Canadians generally would be raised. However, this is not the option that we would recommend as a first choice. Our proposal is simpler, if not less radical in some respects: namely, that the Crown corporate structure of Canada Post be retained, but that appropriate segments of mail collection, processing, and delivery in each locality be contracted out to small, independent, co-operative enterprises organized for this purpose. That is, the bulk of the work of Canada Post's sixty thousand employees would now be done by small, independent, co-operative enterprises, while Canada Post as a Crown corporation would be retained as the overall co-ordinator and planner of the postal system. The rationale of this proposal is (1) that the co-operative enterprises would be small enough and independent enough to stimulate worker initiative and esprit de corps; (2) that contracting-out would provide *pro quo* benefits in a form that would encourage rather than stifle efficiency, agency, and community; and (3) that maintenance of the Crown corporation, Canada Post, as the overall co-ordinator and planner, would make possible, and now probable, economies of scale that are presently possible but improbable. The proposal weds "small is beautiful" with "big is efficient." It is a move to the right in that it establishes private enterprises; it is a move to the left in that it sets private enterprises in the context of a co-ordinating, planning, public body. We might discover to our surprise that in social-political affairs also "right ... left" is the way to march *ahead*.

It may be noted that Canada Post is no stranger to "contracting out." The bulk of transportation of mail by rail, truck, air, and water is contracted out. This includes rural mail delivery. Before the unfortunate Lapalme Affair urban mail collection was contracted out. In addition, the services of the small post offices, which we have referred to as revenue offices, are in effect contracted out. In terms of total expenditures of the post office the contracted-out total is substantial: in 1964–65 transportation constituted 25 percent and revenue offices over 10 percent of total expenditures.

The success of contracting out is underlined by the data presented in Table 9.2A. Here "productivity" in revenue offices and transportation, the contracting-out divisions, is contrasted with that of other divisions. What is presented is productivity in a qualified sense: the indexes of expenditures at constant input prices for each division are divided by the indexes of the volume of output of the total system. What is measured in this way is productivity for the division to the extent that the quantity of mail passing through the division varies with output of the total system. This is more apt to have been the case with transportation than with revenue offices. In any case the data demonstrates that productivity in this qualified sense has flourished in the contracting-out divisions of Canada Post as contrasted with the other divisions. In the fifteen-year period ending in 1964–65 "productivity" in the non-contracting-out divisions barely changed, while "productivity" in transportation rose 45 percent. In the fifteen-year period beginning in 1964–65 "productivity" in the non-contracting-out divisions *fell* over 45 percent, while "productivity" in transportation *rose* another 20 percent or more.

Improvements in productivity in the Canadian transportation sector were taking place during this thirty-year period, and Canada Post by contracting out transportation functions was able to take advantage of these improvements. There is little doubt that the potential for improvement in productivity in other aspects of postal output was also present during this thirty-year period, including the post-1964 period. The technological transformation of Canada Post in the 1970s obviously contributed to this potential. What we are here proposing is a radical extension of contracting out, enabling Canada Post to take advantage of this potential as well.

Table 9.2A "Productivity" in Contracting Out and Other Divisions of the Post Office, 1949–50 to 1979–80.

	Revenue Offices	Transportation[1]	Other	Total
1949–50 = 100				
1945–50	100	100	100	100
1945–55	116	109	97	103
1959–60	140	125	101	113
1964–65	147	145	103	120
1964–65 = 100				
1964–65	100	100	100	100
1969–70	94	105	79	87
1974–75	88	127	58	72
1979–80	94	122	54	68

[1]Including the services in the transportation division of employees paid directly by the post office in 1964–65 and after.

Source: Based on data provided by Canada Post.

The proposed co-operative enterprises would consist of groups organized on a co-operative basis to perform certain specified collection, processing, or delivery functions. Roger Bouvier's group could in some respects serve as a prototype of such co-operatives. Each group would elect or hire its own management, contract with Canada Post to perform specified functions at a specified price for a period of one to five years, and thereafter would be left free (within the limits of broadly defined guidelines) to perform these functions as it saw fit. The group would then have every incentive to work together as efficiently and harmoniously as possible. Within the given context, productivity, agency, and community would be maximized. The management of Canada Post could concentrate on improving the given context—by introducing the kind of productive process and the kind of plant and machinery that would facilitate improvements in productivity, agency, and community. The machinery could be provided to the co-operatives and kept in good working condition by Canada Post, or alternatively, the machinery could be rented to the co-operatives who would be responsible for its maintenance. The latter option would have the advantage of giving the users of the machinery some interest in keeping it in good running order.

Here again we may expect that those who wield power within the present system, i.e., senior management and union officials, will be opposed to the proposal. And, again, although the objections of senior management can be overridden by parliamentary enactment and by directives of even more senior government officials, the objections of union officials may not be so simply dealt with. Many of our parliamentarians may find it politically inexpedient to "be an aggravation" to the unions. And, indeed, this proposal does involve a radical reshaping of worker organization and hence could constitute a major aggravation.

However, since the unions exist for the sake of the workers and not the workers for the unions, it is possible in principle that an alternative worker organization might serve their interests better. In such a case it is clearly the unions, and not the workers' interests which must give way. This, it must be admitted, is not a point that immediately commends itself to union officials. The power of union officials is closely correlated with the power of the unions which they serve; hence, union officials are tempted to identify the power of the unions with the welfare of the workers.

It is our hypothesis that the combination of a Crown corporation and many co-operatives offers the postal workers an alternative form of worker organization that much better serves their interests. Instead of organizing themselves adversarially against a management that is presumed to be hostile, they organize themselves to become, within their own sphere of production, their own management. It is true that the workers so organized are no longer thousands-strong; they are, perhaps, only a hundred-strong or even twenty-strong. But instead of fighting the boss they are now, within their own sphere of work, their own boss. Under this new organization we might expect, therefore, substantial improvements in productivity, agency, and community.

We can imagine how Roger Bouvier's group might have fared as a co-operative. Probably a couple of workers who were refusing to pull their weight would have "either shaped up or shipped out." But there is every reason to suppose that the group would have sustained a high level of efficiency, agency, and community. Indeed, our proposal is one that is devised to allow Bouvier-like groups to "be fruitful and multiply."

It might be objected that the proposal encourages improvements in productivity that would cut down the staff of the system, that is, the Crown corporation and the co-operatives together, by about one half, and that the workers, therefore, would have very good reason for opposing it. The objection is correct in its arithmetic: an improvement in productivity means that less labour is required for a given output. Employment in postal services therefore must fall. We question, however, that this offers the workers a good reason for opposition. Overstaffing does *not* make workers happy. Workers do *not* enjoy slack times more than busy times, but typically the reverse; and they do *not* enjoy the reputation of being careless and inefficient. Moreover, postal workers cannot look their fellow Canadian workers in the eyes and say, in effect, that they expect to be supported half the year by other workers' production. Self-respect and the respect of others are aspects of satisfaction with one's work.

The problem of the transition from overstaffing to optimum staffing remains. It is clear that special provisions to ease the human cost of this transition need to be made for that part of the postal staff whose functions are taken over by the co-operatives, but who themselves do not become members of one of the co-operatives. However, we will not attempt to set forth here precisely what those provisions should be.

One advantage of the contracting-out arrangement is that it should enable allowances to be made for local variations in average wage rates. For example, in the larger, industrial, urban areas where wages tend to be higher, the contractual settlements with the co-operatives could allow for this. The contractual settlements should also allow the co-operative to enjoy some benefit from greater than average proficiency, not only in relation to other co-operatives, but in relation to industrial workers generally. Calculations of appropriate contractual settlement levels could be based, therefore, on estimates of average productivity for postal co-operatives across the nation, some adjustment area by area for local variations in wage rates, and a general proficiency bonus (e.g., 15 to 25 percent), assuming that the proficiency of workers *under these conditions* would exceed that of industrial workers generally. The co-operatives could take their proficiency bonus either in the form of higher pay or, as did the Bouvier workers, in the form of shorter hours. If the co-operatives wanted shorter hours they could adjust the membership of the co-operatives accordingly. A national consultative council to advise on contractual settlement levels could be set up, with one-half the members representing the co-operatives, one-fourth representing Canada Post, and one-fourth representing the federal government.

Under these arrangements, per unit real costs should fall 40 to 50 percent within two or three years.

CHAPTER 10

A Concluding Word to the Intelligent Citizen

It is a strange, strange world into which the study of the post office has taken us. It is indeed strange that by 1980, after the billion-dollar technological transformation of the 1970s, Canada Post was producing at a level of efficiency far below that of fifteen years earlier and scarcely half that which could reasonably have been expected. It is clear that the deficiency was not of resources and know-how, but rather of will: there was a failure of will to produce efficiently; there was a crisis in motivation. But why this crisis? Our answer is that in an age of extraordinary development in human dominion over perceptual objects we have tended to lose touch with human beings as subjects. At the root, therefore, of the postal problems and the correlated problems of modern industrial society, there is a debasement and abuse of human beings as subjects.

A perceptual object immanates limits not set by the subject; hence, it conforms to pre-established form, pattern, or order. A subject, in contrast, transcends as well as immanates limits. That is, like an object the subject remains within limits, but unlike an object it goes beyond limits as well. It is this inherent capacity to go beyond pre-established limits that distinguishes the human subject radically from an object. It is this which constitutes human beings as in some degree creative, free, self-determining.

The perceptual object remains within its pre-established limits. The challenge for the scientist is to discover what these limits are and for the technologist and industrialist to discover how, given these limits, the object may be manipulated to serve our interests. Modern scientists, technologists, and industrialists are experts in dealing with perceptual objects. They excel in this, and in human history there is none to compare with them. However, when they come to deal with human beings who conform to limits insofar as they are objects, but who also create for themselves new limits insofar as they are subjects, the modern scientists, technologists, and industrialists are beyond their field of expertise and are beyond their depths. They are beyond their depths not because they are not themselves creative—since they are creative in a striking way—but because they do not reflect on their own creativity. Their reflections focus on the conformities of perceptual objects; it is in dealing with these conformities that they are experts. However, since they have been extraordinarily successful in dealing with perceptual objects, they are inclined in dealing with human beings to try the same approach: to treat them as conforming to established limits and to take up the challenge of discovering just how complex these limits are. The models of human nature that emerge are a debasement of, and an offence to, human beings as subjects.

We may discuss the debasement of human beings as subjects in terms of three models of humanity: (1) the economist's model, the model of humanity engaged in want-satisfying work; (2) the radical reformer's model, the model of humanity locked in class struggle; and (3) the scientistic culture's model, the model of humanity indifferent to the quest of an ultimate good. A deficiency of the economist's model is that the ultimate objective of this model is a condition that if attained would leave human beings completely apathetic and bored. A deficiency of the radical reformer's model is that the class struggle creates within the reforming class itself the kind of domination from which it seeks to liberate itself. A deficiency of the scientistic culture's model is that indifference to the quest of an ultimate good engenders such a deep subjective insecurity that the human subject is incapacitated for anything but the destruction of the civilization which modern science, technology, and industry have created.

(1) *The economist's model: humanity engaged in want-satisfying work.* In this model human beings seek to maximize the satisfaction of wants with the minimum of work. The difficulty with this model is that the more successful we are in attaining its objectives, the more nearly are we reduced to complete apathy and boredom. As we have shown, complete satisfaction of wants produces a state of absence of wants with a correlated absence of satisfaction, that is, a state of apathy. Likewise, minimal work is correlated with minimal challenge and boredom. Unless, therefore, there is more to the human story than this, mankind is in very deep trouble whenever productivity and affluence approach high levels. Our conclusion is that the industrial West is indeed in deep trouble with the attainment of high productivity and affluence in the post–World War II period, but that the way out is through the "more" which ought to be and can be added to the human story.

As we have noted, various developments in the post–World War II period enabled workers to satisfy their physiological wants and to achieve economic security: (a) a rapid improvement in output per person in the economy made a much higher real income per person possible; (b) a much higher participation of women in the work force created many two-income families; (c) a high sustained level of employment in the earlier decades provided a high degree of economic security; and (d) the introduction of social security measures (workmen's compensation, unemployment insurance, medical and hospital insurance, superannuation, etc.) contributed further to economic security. Although postal workers contributed negatively to the higher productivity that made affluence possible, they participated fully with other Canadian workers in the affluence achieved by the economy as a whole. However, although high motivation on the part of workers contributes to the high productivity that makes affluence possible, affluence with its tendency to apathy reacts negatively on motivation. In the case of the postal workers, growing affluence was accompanied by a widespread apathy and a low morale. As Peter Taylor tells us in "Working in the Post Office" more-for-less was the maxim of the postal workers; but, it is clear, the achievement of more-for-less did not produce a happy workplace.

How is motivation to be sustained in a context of continuing affluence? It would appear that if what the workers get out of work in terms of real income becomes less motivating, then we can only hope that what the workers put into work will become more motivating. Contrary to what is so frequently implied, work can be experienced as typically enjoyable. An important factor in making work enjoyable is the opportunity for creativity in the job, that is, the provision of high agency-content. If workers are to work not so much for the real income obtained as for the responsible involvement and creative challenge of the work itself, then we must look at forms of work not simply in terms of their direct productivity implications, but in terms of their implications for motivation. Agency-content becomes a prime consideration.

We note that Canada Post in its time of troubles moved in the contrary direction. Many routine operations were already minimal in their agency-content. Striving for efficiency, management intensified the agency-deficiency of many jobs. Sortation, for example, was reduced to the simplified ABC method and then converted later to the electronic sortation system. Creative agency was required of the inventors of the new process, but not of those who operated the new process.

Agency-deficiency, we conclude, is a serious abuse of human beings as subjects. Let the inventors in Canada Post and in the industrial system generally turn their minds, therefore, to overcoming agency-deficiency rather than creating it.

(2) *The radical reformer's model: humanity locked in class struggle.* Echoing Lord Durham, we have characterized the postal situation as two classes of employees warring in the bosom of a single public corporation. This is another of the strange aspects of the postal world. The Canadian government appointed certain citizens to produce an efficient Canadian mail service. Instead of devoting themselves single-mindedly to their appointed task, these citizens divided into adversarial groups and spent half their energies fighting each other.

The warfare was curious, moreover, because the concept of class struggle was originally developed in the context of large private corporations where the management was accused of exploiting the workers, keeping their wages down to subsistence levels, and working them to near exhaustion in inhuman working conditions. A much sought-after outcome of the class struggle was expropriation of the private owners and public acquisition of the means of production. In the case of the post office the sought-after public ownership was already in place, the level of real incomes was far above subsistence and rising, the hours of work were relatively short, pressure to work hard was relatively low key, and while certain conditions of employment were certainly improvable the prospects were that with patience they would be improved. In terms of broad historical perspectives Canadian postal workers never had it so good. Why then were the postal workers persuaded to wage a sustained, internal war against management?

What the postal workers got out of the war was, perhaps, something of the order of a 10 percent higher level of real wages and a 100 percent larger work force. The costs of the warfare were an atmosphere of chronic hostility in the workplace, an abysmal quality of Canadian mail service, and a unit cost of service roughly twice what might reasonably have been expected.

An important part of the reason why postal workers were persuaded to wage war was that adversarial labour-management relations were very much in the wind. The postal workers could claim after their doubtfully legal strike of 1965 that they had won for the federal public service the right to unionize and the right to press their claims by strike action. However, they "won" in 1965 only what the government and the people of Canada were at that point willing to "concede." The Pearson government had already been exploring the feasibility of introducing unionization into the federal public service. In 1967 the Public Service Staff Relations Act granted legal status to federal public service unions. With scant regard for the significant differences between the private sector and the public sector, a labour-management structure generally accepted in the private sector was transferred almost holus-bolus into the public sector. A significant difference between the sectors is that the private sector is characterized by a measure of competition, whereas the public sector is characterized by public monopoly. In the case of the post office the consequence of combining a public monopoly with a private monopoly of labour input was disastrous. However, this was a consequence that was not foreseen in 1965 or 1967.

A competitive-enterprise critique of postal performance would point out that efficiency was put in double jeopardy after 1967: (a) given the monopolistic structure of Canada Post there was no competitive incentive to push efficiency in order to stay in business; and (b) when to this was added an effective union monopoly of labour input, there was now covert incentive to promote inefficiency.

Within the competitive, private-enterprise system there is a high incentive to improve efficiency. In the course of time less efficient firms are competed out of business by more efficient firms. This is a theoretical characteristic of the competitive enterprise structure that has proved itself in practice by a phenomenal improvement in productivity over the past two hundred years. However, there is another general factor that contributes to efficiency, namely, the factor of large size. Certain kinds of goods and services can only be produced by very large enterprises, and with respect to most goods and services there are economies of scale to be enjoyed by large-scale producers. To cope with largeness the corporate form of business organization has been invented. Through this form of organization owners of capital can combine their resources; owners of capital otherwise competitive join in a common undertaking. Given the corporate structure and given economies of scale, what happens in the course of time is that not only are less efficient firms competed out of business by more efficient firms, but the latter tend to be larger and larger corporations. Hence, there is a historical tendency in the competitive, free-enterprise system leading toward concentration of economic power in larger and larger corporations and toward oligopoly or monopoly.

Large corporations with a typically hierarchical structure of control place great economic power in the hands of a few directors and managers. If we apply the power principle to the wielders of corporate power we may predict that they will tend to use this power to serve their own interests whether or not the interests of others are also thereby served. Indeed, the authorized wielders of corporate control may exercise this power in partial independence not only of the workers, but of the owners as well. That is, there may be partial divorce of ownership and control. How much more, therefore, may we expect division of interests to appear between management and workers.

To offset this concentration of economic power in the hands of corporate management, with its potentially adverse implications for the welfare of workers, it seems appropriate that the workers also should forego competition among themselves and combine to promote their common interests. The development of labour unions is thus a natural reaction to the development of large corporations. Over the years, therefore, unions have provided a much needed countervailing power offsetting the domination of the economy by a small class of corporate managers. It is in this context that public support for labour unions grew and governments introduced legislation to protect workers as they sought to establish unions.

In the context also the model of human beings locked in class struggle emerged. The workers, organized in unions, were seen to be engaged in a historic struggle against exploitation by the owners of capital. In the Marxian version the workers were destined to be victorious and in their victory to liberate all mankind from the oppression flowing from private ownership of the means of production. Emancipated from Judaism, Marx and Engels anointed the proletariat to be a secular Israel, a chosen people called to emancipate all peoples. In this version labour unions were to be viewed as morally discriminating communities, that is, as bearers of the "good" arrayed against the perpetrators of "evil."

The tendency to view unions as morally discriminating communities has had very important consequences. It has tended to hide from the eyes of labour sympathizers that unions also are centres of economic power and that in this context also the power principle operates. Here also the authorized wielders of power tend to exercise their power to serve their own interest, whether or not the interests of others are served. Union policies tend to serve the interests of the leadership, whether or not the interest of the members, the interests of other workers, or the interests of the citizenry as a whole are also thereby served. In the case of CUPW, for example, we argue that union policy has served the interests of CUPW leadership, but in general, not the interests of the members, other workers, and other citizens. Moreover, the morally discriminating outlook leads to facile rationalization excusing the not-so-admirable behaviour of unions. What is clearly "evil" when done by the adversary is seen as necessary to protect the union or to achieve its ultimately good ends. To the non-discriminating observer of empirical events it does not seem evident that the moral sensibilities of union leaders are of a higher order than those of corporate leaders. Both sets of leaders appear to pursue their own interests within the context of the organizations they lead. Indeed, the more unions emerge as centres of power in the economy, the more do they seem to assume the image of their adversary.

The proponents of moral discrimination continue to insist that we choose sides. The truth, nonetheless, resides in non-discrimination.

With the appearance of big corporations and big countervailing unions, governments have eventually surrendered their laissez-faire stance with respect to the economy and have entered economic life in a big way. Today we are surrounded on all sides by government organizations of one kind or another. Government also is big business and we pay for its services by turning over to it in direct and indirect taxes a substantial slice of the national product.

The public servants who direct large government organizations also wield great power. Here also the wielders of power are tempted to use their power to serve their own ends, whether or not public ends are also thereby served. For example, the status of a public servant may be seen to be correlated with the size of the staff. Public officials, like union bosses, may be more interested in the size of the ship they command than in its paying load.

Since public service staff are appointed by and are subject to discipline by public authority, we might expect them to be more "civil" in providing citizens with services than their private sector counterparts. Unhappily, civil servants frequently appear less civil than their private sector counterparts. If we should be tempted to suppose that this is merely the product of the alienation suffered by public servants in a capitalist state, then we need only to experience the studied indifference of service in a socialist state (such as the Soviet Union) to be disillusioned. The indifferent service of civil servants seems to be correlated with the monopoly context. In the private, competitive sector the situation is: If you do not like my kind of service then you can go to my competitor, but in that case I am competed out of a job. The civil servant's public monopoly context is more arrogance-inducing: If you do not like my kind of service then you can do without.

If one should insist in viewing citizens as locked in class struggle with a dominating class, we might excuse the non-discriminating citizen for some hesitation. From which class of dominators do we most wish to be liberated? The more orthodox reformers would at once answer: from those who wield the massive power of private corporations. However, less orthodox reformers who have assessed carefully both the positive and negative sides of corporate power, union power, and government power, and have noted the discernible shift to union power and, in particular, government power in recent decades, may be uneasy with this answer. The problem is that we may use union power and government power to mitigate the negative aspects of private corporate power, but thereby reap the negative harvest of union and government power. The responsible reformer weighs very carefully the pros and cons of the distribution of power among these three centres of power. In the contemporary setting overweaning union power or overweaning government power may be as great a threat to personal welfare as overweaning private corporate power.

The proponents of class struggle discern the power principle as operating in and through the private corporate structure. In this they are correct. What they do not discern is that the power principle operates in and through any organization where some persons are authorized to exercise some control over others. And what they do not discern is that in the morally discriminating choice of the workers as the bearers of the "good," setting them up in battle array against private corporate power as the bearer of "evil," they are promoting a kind of organization in which the power principle flourishes. Hence, the class struggle engenders within the exploited class itself the kind of domination from which it seeks to liberate itself.

Proponents of a mixed economy (such as this author) contend that we must keep an ever-updated account of the positive and negative consequences of more or less private corporate power, more or less union power, and more or less government power. A positive side of private, competitive corporate power is its proven efficiency and its greater flexibility and creativity. A negative side is its indifference to losers in the competitive game and its tendency over time to augment size and enhance concentration of economic power. Citizens are wise to be concerned about concentration of economic power even when this results in improved efficiency and higher real incomes. A positive side of union power is that it gives workers some say in their conditions of work in the context of large corporations. A negative side is the thrust toward monopoly of the input of labour. The consequence of this monopoly is reduced efficiency of operations and the attainment of a privileged status for unionized workers at the expense, not of corporate incomes, but of the real incomes of non-unionized and self-employed workers. A positive side of government power is that it can be explicitly designed to serve the interests of all. A negative side is its monopoly character with a susceptibility to low efficiency and a potential for very high concentration of power in the hands of relatively few officials.

A fateful weakness of Marxist theory is its naivete concerning the socialist state. Since the Communist Party is implicitly constituted as a morally discriminating group, no attention is paid to the operation of the power principle within it. Consequently, the Stalinist and Maoist dictatorships of the proletariat became the mirror-images of what the Marxists intended most to avoid: the concentration of economic and political power in the hands of a few self-serving individuals.

Owing to its monopoly position, government power does not have built into it the very high incentive to improve efficiency that we find in the competitive enterprise context. There is a great deal of empirical evidence from both mixed and socialist economies indicating that public monopolies have great difficulty in reaching levels of efficiency that are standard for competitive enterprise. In the case of Canada Post the combination of government monopoly with union monopoly of labour input in the 1960s proved disastrous. The quality of service fell to disgraceful levels, while in quantity terms productivity dropped to half what could have been expected.

It seems clear, therefore, in the case of the post office that the union monopoly of labour input, and possibly also the government monopoly of output, needs to be taken away. Both monopolies have been created by government legislation; both can be taken away by modifying that legislation. That, of course, is easier said than done. Given the aura of moral-discrimination that tends to emanate from labour unions, Canadian governments are loath to subject themselves to the flood of moral invective that would sweep the country were a radical curtailment of the power of the postal unions to be proposed. If a private corporation had produced a disaster of like magnitude in the postal system, there is little doubt that something could and would have been done about it. However, can any Canadian political party explicitly curtail a prominent union's power, however just the cause, and not pay a high political price? In the meanwhile, we the people of Canada by a legislative act of our own Parliament protect the right of a few thousand citizens to act in such a way as to cripple the effectiveness of our postal system. It may be argued that there are occasions when it is permissible for "the union of all citizens" to assert its prior rights over component self-serving groups.

One way of relieving the postal unions of their monopoly of labour input is that proposed in the previous chapter. Operations of collecting, processing, and delivering mail could be contracted out to many relatively small, private, and preferably co-operative, groups. Another way might be to break up the union monopoly in conjunction with the break-up of Canada Post as a monopoly. We have normally assumed that a surrender of government monopoly means the opening of mail service to private competition. As far as I am aware we have not experimented with public corporations competing with each other. However, if private corporations can compete with each other and thereby serve the public interest, why cannot public corporations compete with each other thereby serving the public interest?

Our second proposal, therefore, might take the following general form. Canada Post would be broken into two public corporations, let us say, Canada Post Alpha and Canada Post Beta. Plant and equipment in the urban areas would be divided equally between Alpha and Beta and they would be invited to compete openly for customers in all urban areas. However, Alpha would be given a monopoly of the service in about half the rural areas and Beta in the other half. Postal unions would be authorized in both Alpha and Beta, but the boundaries of any union would not be permitted to extend beyond that of one of the corporations. Any collusion between the unions of Alpha and the unions of Beta and any collusion between the managements of Alpha and Beta in restraint of trade would be declared illicit. If in the course of time reflecting the competitive situation either Alpha or Beta became financially non-viable, then the corporation would be declared defunct. The government would forthwith establish another public corporation, Canada Post Gamma, to compete in the urban market and to assume the rural monopoly. The management and unions of the defunct corporation would carry over no right to employment or any other rights with respect to the new corporation.

The merit of this structure is that both management and unions would have a high incentive to push toward the highest possible efficiency and that the unions would see that in this important respect they have an interest that coincides with that of management, other workers, and Canadian citizens generally. However adversarial management and unions might be in certain respects, the two groups would have a high incentive to work together as a team in the important area of productivity.

It might be argued that the duplication of services in the urban areas would enhance unit costs and push up postal prices. However, let us assume, on the high side, that duplication would tend to push up unit costs by 50 percent. Let us assume further that productivity improvements under the new incentive conditions would tend to reduce unit costs to one-half present levels (a reasonable assumption according to our findings). Unit costs, in this case, would fall by 25 percent ($1.50 \times .50 = .75$). It is clear that now is the time the experiment can be made with very reasonable prospects of cost reduction.

It is very important that we not perpetuate a structure where the interests of management, workers, and citizens on a matter as fundamental as productivity are not in accord. We should experiment, therefore, with the structure of Canada Post, and with the structure of all government organizations in similar plight, until we discover a viable structure where the interests of management, workers, and citizens are in reasonable accord and where there are strong incentives for all to pursue this mutual interest. A negative side of the competing-public-corporation structure is that from time to time there will be losers in the competitive game: both workers and management may lose their jobs. There is a serious loss here only if there is a high level of unemployment with consequent reduced opportunity of finding alternative employment. The possibility of losing one's job is not in itself a structural weakness. On the contrary, if the structure does not in some substantial way reward efficiency and creativity and penalize inefficiency and sluggishness, the structure is deficient. It is not too much to ask of either the workers or managers who individually or in company with others have demonstrated their inefficiency that they look for other jobs. On the other hand, it is not too much to ask of society that it always have available a goodly complement of job opportunities by maintaining a high level of employment. Having two persons doing one person's job, as in the case of Canada Post, is not a substitute for full employment. Contrary to what one might naively expect, there is no evidence that reductions in efficiency reduce overall unemployment.

We have a continuing problem: we must care for the losers, but not in such a way that we make everybody want to be a loser.

(3) *The scientistic culture's model: humanity indifferent to the quest of an ultimate good.* A perceptual object immanates limits not set by the subject and,

hence, conforms to a pre-established form, pattern, or order. If we take away this pre-established order the whole of perceptual objectivity collapses into illusion. We can see, therefore, how important the presupposition of order is in our dealings with the objective perceptual world.

A subject, in contrast, transcends as well as immanates limits and, hence, it may choose between ends to be pursued, between purposes to be realized, between goods to be attained. If, therefore, we take away the presumption that there is good worthy of pursuit, the raison d'être of the subject collapses, the being of the subject is rendered void of meaning. Moreover, given the cycle of birth, growth, decay, and death, the raison d'être of the subject finally collapses unless there is an ultimate good that transcends the apparent perceptual/communal evil of the conclusion of the cycle. We can see, therefore, how important the presupposition of ultimate good is in sustaining the subject in its being in the world.

In contemporary culture there is a curious tendency to promote the first of these presuppositions, the presupposition of order, but to disparage the second, the presupposition of ultimate good. It is as if the modern age wished to make the world secure for objects, but utterly meaningless and insecure for human subjects.

One reason for this state of affairs is that while modern scientists have managed to sustain a constant faith in underlying order as they varied their beliefs concerning the specific form of that order, modern theologians have not been as successful in sustaining a constant faith as they varied their beliefs concerning the ultimate good. Consequently, the advances of science have rendered many traditional religious beliefs untenable and this has been interpreted as showing that faith in an ultimate good is illusory. See, for example, Freud's *The Future of an Illusion.*

Science is concerned with a human subject's knowledge of perceptual objects. However, in their fixation on objects modern scientists somewhat uneasily have tended to ignore the subject. The behaviourist psychologist B. F. Skinner has gone further and proposed that we deny subjective agency in human beings altogether (in analogy, he suggests, to what intelligent moderns have already done in denying subjective agency in the heavens). In this cultural context the human subject is made exceedingly insecure. Are we as human beings merely complex objects of no ultimate value in the scheme of things? Perceptive psychologists have pointed to the widespread sense of meaninglessness, of existential vacuum, in the modern age. Contemporary existential philosophy has focused on the anguish of the human situation, and Edvard Munch has painted it for us in "The Scream." In an age in which science, technology, and industry have made life objectively more secure than ever before, we have been made subjectively exceedingly insecure.

This subjective insecurity is reflected in Peter Taylor's "Working in the Post Office." Taylor has good reasons for criticizing working in the post office, for example, its gross agency-deficiency. However, he goes so far in his objections to curtailment of his liberty that one gets the clear impression there is no practically viable modern system that could possibly meet his demands. Taylor resigns his postal job without confidence that he will find things any better outside the post office. "Working in the Post Office" is thus a cry of anguish, a scream, reflecting the extreme subjective insecurity of our age.

Max Weber has pointed out how, in the early years of the modern industrial system, industriousness in the workplace was associated with Protestant aspirations for eternal salvation. It is to be noted that workers imbued with the Protestant ethic were able to bear the much more severe disciplines and the much more restrictive conditions of employment of these early times. Peter Taylor and his colleagues are as far removed as can be imagined from workers imbued with the Protestant ethic: not devoted industriousness, but a struggle against work marks their quest for ultimate liberation. Deeply insecure in their subjectivity, they are sensitive to and unable to bear the slightest restriction on their freedom. Consequently Taylor and his colleagues are effectively incapacitated for anything but the destruction of the world which modern science, technology, and industry have created.

There is, of course, another peril in the existential vacuum of derogated subjectivity. Nature abhors a vacuum: into the vacuum many kinds of things will flow. An important filler of the vacuum in the modern industrial world is Marxism. In the post office the impact of Marxism was represented (a) by a variety of small, sometimes mutually antagonistic but ever turbulent, groups of radical employees chiefly in the large urban centres; (b) by the Marxist leanings of the union leadership, especially in CUPW after 1974; and (c) by the highly adversarial stance of the two main postal unions. Through the class struggle and the victorious expropriation of private ownership of the means of production, Marxism promises an ultimate good: a classless society in which each contributes according to ability and each receives according to need. Marxism is atheistic only in the sense that all previous visions of the ultimate good are rejected so that the Marxist ultimate good has no other ultimate good before it. Marxism thus does offer human subjects an ultimate good, restores the subject's sense of ultimate worth, and provides the creative challenge of pursuing its good.

The peril associated with Marxism as a filler of the vacuum is that its promises also turn out to be empty. There is scarcely a single tenet of Marxism that can withstand non-discriminating criticism: the doctrine of value and surplus value, the doctrine that real wages remain at subsistence levels, the doctrine that the social relationships reflecting the private ownership of the means of production do not yield to evolutionary modification, the doctrine that the interests of the Communist Party are identical with those of workers, and the doctrine that the dictatorship of the proletariat leads to the withering away of the state and the advent of the classless society. Moreover, Marxism as such has nothing to offer on the fundamental question of the apparent evil of the end of the natural cycle of birth, growth, decay, and death.

$$* \quad * \quad * \quad * \quad * \quad *$$

We end our postal study leaving behind vivid impressions of vast unresolved problems. The problems reach far beyond the boundaries of Canada Post. We offered the opinion that one of the reasons postal workers were persuaded to wage war against management in the 1960s and 1970s was that adversarial labour-management relations were very much in the wind. The post office in many respects is a sensitive weather-vane reflecting the strong currents sweeping the wide expanse of the democratic-industrial world. Such vast problems call for profound solutions. At the same time, the postal problem is a local problem, one not so large that it cannot be grasped. Perhaps if we have the social vision and social courage to resolve the postal problem, we can go forth with confidence to meet the challenge of problems in the vaster setting.

Along the way we may hope that we will not be distracted by tinkering with peripheral matters. Since 1980 the Canadian government has transformed the postal department into a public corporation, an organizational change that was long overdue. Also since 1980 Canada Post's management has introduced a number of modifications intended to enhance the corporation's financial viability. However, in terms of what is needed these modifications are merely cosmetic: the basic structural disorder of the post office remains intact.

APPENDIX A

The Concept and Measurement of Productivity

The concept of productivity is relatively simple. However, the measurement of productivity can involve a set of factors, each of which is simple enough in itself, but which in combination may appear complex and confusing. Consequently we set forth our definition of productivity and its measurement in five steps. As we take these steps it is well to keep in mind that the relationship between the factors displayed, however surprising they may sometimes seem, are simply implications of a consistent definition of productivity. That is, the relationships follow *by definition*. After these five steps in definition we present two *assumptions* respecting general *tendencies* in the national economy. These assumptions suggest what is normal with respect to certain key relationships, hence what we can expect to see usually, although not always. Whenever these normal relationships are not approximated, the deviations call for explanation. Hence, the relationships of the five steps are such by definition, whereas the relationships of the two assumptions are proposed as normal but not invariable. Attention to these definitional and normal relationships is important not only to understand what is meant by our measures of productivity in Canada Post, but also to understand the significance of variations in the economic performance of Canada Post for the Canadian economy in general.

Definition Step 1

$$D = \frac{O}{I},$$

where D is the productivity, O is the quantity of output, and I is the quantity of input involved in an economic activity. However, since we shall be concerned with relative productivity, that is, performance in period t_n compared to performance in the base period t_o, we may move directly to the equation

$$D' = \frac{O'}{I'}$$

where D' is the productivity ratio, O' is the quantity of output ratio, and I' the quantity of input ratio.

That is, $$O' = \frac{\text{quantity of output in } t_n}{\text{quantity of output in } t_o}$$

and $$I' = \frac{\text{quantity of input in } t_n}{\text{quantity of input in } t_o}.$$

In all cases the ratios may be expressed alternatively as index numbers, it being kept constantly in mind, of course, that their arithmetic value is always equal to the index number divided by 100. Hence, if output triples, $O' = 3.00$ (index 300), and input increases by 50 percent, $I' = 1.50$ (index 150), then productivity doubles, $D' = 2.00$, (index 200).

Definition Step 2

O' and I' are assessed by measuring outputs and inputs in constant output prices and constant input prices respectively.

That is,
$$O' = \frac{\text{output in } t_n \text{ in } t_o \text{ output prices}}{\text{output in } t_o \text{ in } t_o \text{ output prices}}$$

and
$$I' = \frac{\text{input in } t_n \text{ in } t_o \text{ input prices}}{\text{input in } t_o \text{ in } t_o \text{ input prices.}}$$

It may be noted that this method of assessing O' and I' provides an answer to the question of how to aggregate diverse kinds of outputs or how to aggregate diverse kinds of inputs whose quantity ratios diverge significantly from each other. If performance in a succession of periods is assessed with calculations using the prices of a single period as the base, as we have done in the case of Canada Post, then the comparison of any two other periods is affected by the particular pattern of relative prices obtaining in that base period, a pattern that would most likely be different if another period had been chosen as base. This, however, is an assessment problem that cannot be avoided. The problem we may note is much less serious in the case of inputs than that of outputs because of the tendency for the relative prices of diverse inputs to remain stable (see below).

Definition Step 3

$$D' = \frac{O'}{I'} \; ; \text{ but also}$$

$$D' = \frac{\text{output in } t_n \text{ in } t_o \text{ output prices}}{\text{input in } t_n \text{ in } t_o \text{ input prices}}$$

or, as we might state it,

$$D' = \frac{\text{constant price output measure of product}}{\text{constant price input measure of product.}}$$

Price in the case of inputs is deemed to include all income accruing to the owners of the inputs; that is, salaries and wages and supplementary labour income with respects to input of work, and interest, dividends, and undistributed profits with respect to non-work input. Hence, output and output prices, input and input prices are so defined that the current value of output and the current value of input are equal. That is, output in t_n in t_n output prices equals input in t_n in t_n input prices. Accordingly, the product of any economic activity may be assessed either in terms of its *output measure* or its *input measure* and in *current prices* these two are *by definition* equal. The basis of the equation is simple enough: value currently created by the production of output accrues as current income to the owners of the inputs.

It follows from this equation that the value of output and the value of input in the base period in that period's prices are equal. Hence,

$$D' = \frac{O'}{I'}$$

$$= \frac{\text{output in } t_n \text{ in } t_o \text{ output prices}}{\text{output in } t_o \text{ in } t_o \text{ output prices}}$$

$$\div \frac{\text{input in } t_n \text{ in } t_o \text{ input prices}}{\text{input in } t_o \text{ in } t_o \text{ input prices}} \qquad \text{(see Step 2)}$$

$$= \frac{\text{output in } t_n \text{ in } t_o \text{ output prices}}{\text{input in } t_n \text{ in } t_o \text{ input prices}}$$

$$\div \frac{\text{output in } t_o \text{ in } t_o \text{ output prices}}{\text{input in } t_o \text{ in } t_o \text{ input prices}}$$

and, since the numerator and denominator of this last expression are equal,

$$D' = \frac{\text{output in } t_n \text{ in } t_o \text{ output prices}}{\text{input in } t_n \text{ in } t_o \text{ input prices}}.$$

Or, in other words,

$$D' = \frac{\text{constant-price output measure of product}}{\text{constant-price input measure of product}}.$$

Consequently,

$$\frac{\text{current-price output measure of product}}{\text{current-price input measure of product}} = 1,$$

whereas,

$$\frac{\text{constant-price output measure of product}}{\text{constant-price input measure of product}} = D'.$$

Hence, the productivity ratio is a measure of the divergence of the constant-price output measure from the constant-price input measure of product.

Definition Step 4

$$D' = \frac{O'}{I'} \; ; \quad \text{but also}$$

$$D' = \frac{IP'}{OP'},$$

where OP' is the implicit output price ratio and IP' is the implicit input price ratio. That is,

$$OP' = \frac{\text{output in } t_n \text{ in } t_n \text{ output prices}}{\text{output in } t_n \text{ in } t_o \text{ output prices}}$$

$$\text{and } IP' = \frac{\text{input in } t_n \text{ in } t_n \text{ input prices}}{\text{input in } t_n \text{ in } t_o \text{ input prices}}.$$

Proof

$$\frac{IP'}{OP'} = \frac{\text{input in } t_n \text{ in } t_n \text{ input prices}}{\text{input in } t_n \text{ in } t_o \text{ input prices}}$$

$$\div \frac{\text{output in } t_n \text{ in } t_n \text{ output prices}}{\text{output in } t_n \text{ in } t_o \text{ output prices}}$$

$$= \frac{\text{output in } t_n \text{ in } t_o \text{ output prices}}{\text{input in } t_n \text{ in } t_o \text{ input prices}}$$

$$\div \frac{\text{output in } t_n \text{ in } t_n \text{ output prices}}{\text{input in } t_n \text{ in } t_n \text{ input prices}}$$

and since the last expression equals one (see Step 3),

$$\frac{IP'}{OP'} = \frac{\text{output in } t_n \text{ in } t_o \text{ output prices}}{\text{input in } t_n \text{ in } t_o \text{ input prices}}$$

$$= \frac{O'}{I'} \qquad \text{(see Step 3).}$$

It may be noted that when the performance of the economy as a whole is being assessed, D' represents the productivity ratio of the national product, OP' is the overall output price ratio, and IP' the overall rate-of-income ratio. Thus, IP'/OP' yields our assessment of relative change in rate-of-*real*-income in the economy as a whole (that is, rate-of-income after adjustment for inflation). Consequently, the rate-of-real-income index equals the productivity index. Hence, a 10 percent improvement in productivity overall means a 10 percent improvement in rate-of-real-income overall. This equation we may emphasize again obtains *by definition*.[1]

However, the equation holds for the economy as a whole, but *not* necessarily for any particular enterprise or industry within the economy. Indeed it is possible, as we shall illustrate in the case of Canada Post, for an enterprise to enjoy a substantial improvement in rates of real income while productivity actually falls significantly. This involves a big increase in the relative output prices of the products of this enterprise.

---

[1] Assuming there is no change in terms of trade.

Definition Step 5

Inputs are classified in a twofold way as follows:

Inputs (I)	Working	Waiting	Total
Primary	I_1	I_3	$I_1 + I_3$
Secondary	I_2	I_4	$I_2 + I_4$
Total	$I_1 + I_2$	$I_3 + I_4$	$I = I_1 + I_2 + I_3 + I_4$

The distinction of working and waiting may be illustrated in the case of a wheat farmer who in the course of a year puts in 10,000 hours of *working* and on the average one-half year of waiting for return on investment of work. We may assess the *working* in terms of number of persons and time worked, in this case four persons for 2,500 hours each, and the *waiting* in terms of inputs invested and time waited for return on these inputs, in this case 10,000 working hours for one-half year. If in the base period wages paid for working were $5.00 per hour and income for waiting for return on investment 20 percent per year, then the inputs in this period in constant-price input measure would be:

Input of working, $10,000 \times 5.00$	$50,000
Input of waiting, $(10,000 \times 5.00) \times (.20 \times \frac{1}{2})$	5,000
Total input at constant-price input measure	$55,000

The distinction of primary and secondary inputs may also be illustrated in the case of our farmer who, we may imagine, buys irrigation water from another producer. Let us suppose that the water company records with respect to the water sold to the farmer the following inputs in base period input prices:

Input of working	$41,000
Input of waiting	4,000
Total input at constant-price input measure	$45,000

For the water company the $45,000 is an assessment of its primary input at constant-price input measure; for the farmer the $45,000 represents an assessment of secondary inputs at constant-price input measure. Secondary inputs, therefore, are inputs that have their first or primary accounting in another productive entity (or in an earlier accounting period of the same productive entity). The intention of our accounting of secondary inputs is that their sum correspond with that in the primary phase. Thus our twofold way of accounting for our farmer now yields in constant-price input measure terms:

Inputs	Working	Waiting	Total
Primary	$50,000	$5,000	$55,000
Secondary	41,000	4,000	45,000
Total	91,000	9,000	$100,000

Two questions arise with respect to this way of classifying and assessing inputs: (1) Is waiting a genuine input? The Marxists claim it is not. (2) Granted waiting as an input, should the stock of invested products correlated with waiting and the flow of products representing secondary input be assessed in terms of constant-price input measure, as we propose, or in terms of constant-price output measure? Many contemporary economists opt for the latter.

(1) According to Karl Marx, what we have called waiting is a fictional input and hence any income received with respect to it reflects exploitation of the workers. We might imagine our farmer testing this hypothesis of the "inputlessness" of waiting by offering his employed workers the going rate of wages, but now with the variant of a six-month wait for their pay. The explanation to the workers would be that the farmer must wait six months for the growth, harvesting, and marketing of the crop, and the justification for no increment in income for waiting would be that since no extra input is involved no extra pay should be expected. We might imagine that the employer is the government rather than a private entrepreneur and that the workers are in the Soviet Union or China rather than Canada. However, what is difficult to imagine is the workers, whatever their institutional context, being impressed with the justification.

When economic resources are invested in a particular economic activity for a period, all the alternative uses of these resources for that period are surrendered. It is essentially for this surrender of the alternative uses of economic resources that we claim payment. When we are employed for a time, what is surrendered is all alternative activity for ourselves for that time. It is for this surrender of alternatives that we expect to be paid as we go. We may expend less physical and mental energy at work than at play, and we may even enjoy ourselves more at work than at play; nonetheless, we are paid for working precisely because, forsaking all other, we expend our energies in this specific contracted activity. Similarly, if workers are asked in addition to surrender alternative uses of their pay for six months by investing it in the productive process, they will expect an increment in income to compensate for this further surrender of alternative uses of economic resources.

Marx is wrong conceptually and practically. He is wrong conceptually because waiting is a genuine input demanding, as does working, surrender by persons of alternative uses of economic resources. He is wrong practically because products *tend* to exchange *not* as he contends according to the investment per unit of output of inputs of working $(I_1 + I_2)$, but according to the investment per unit of output of inputs of working and waiting $(I_1 + I_2 + I_3 + I_4)$. (See below what we have called the pricing principle).

(2) The question whether the stock of products with which the input of waiting is correlated and the flow of products which represent secondary input should be assessed according to constant-price input measure or constant-price output measure is a fundamental one. The arguments for accepting the traditional constant-price output measure appear persuasive. (a) In *current-*

price terms the input measure and output measure yield identical results. Hence, when we are considering the comparative productivity of alternative combinations of labour and capital in the current period we can safely ignore the input measure. (b) When we are concerned with comparing performance in t_n with t_o there is something "intuitively obvious" in saying the input correlated with a machine in t_n is equal to the input correlated with the same kind of machine in t_o. Hence, if the output price of the machine were \$100,000 in t_o, the machine in t_n should be assessed at \$100,000. That is, investments of capital should be assessed according to their constant-price output measure. (c) If productivity in the machine-producing industry, Dm', has changed between t_o and t_n, let us say $Dm' = 2.00$, then the constant-price *input measure* of the machine in t_n is \$100,000/2.00 equals \$50,000. It appears, therefore, that if we use the constant-price input measure in assessing the inputs in t_n for the purpose of calculating productivity changes t_o to t_n we have used a factor ($Dm' = 2.00$) that already involves productivity changes t_o to t_n. To use elements that are dependent on productivity in the very process of calculating productivity would seem to be a serious methodological error.

However, we may point out that scientific advances sometimes take place through the discovery that the "intuitively obvious" is misleading. Nothing is more intuitively obvious, for example, than that at sunrise the sun rises. Nonetheless, our culture accepts the counter-intuitive explanation that the earth rotates. In our present case the use of the productivity factor $Dm' = 2.00$ in translating the constant-price output measure to the constant-price input measure does not *introduce* a productivity-dependent element into the calculations, but rather *takes out* a productivity-dependent element that would otherwise be in the calculations. That is, the \$100,000 in the above illustration equals the constant-price input measure of the investment *multiplied* by Dm'. The only way to *remove* Dm' from the picture is to *divide* the \$100,000 by Dm'.

This way of understanding the matter is illustrated in Table A.1 in an account of a three-phase productive process: first phase, production of irrigation water; second phase, production of wheat; and third phase, production of flour. We assume that the irrigation water is all used up in the production of the wheat and the wheat all used up in the production of flour. That is, water and wheat are interim products and flour alone is a final product.

Columns 4 and 5 record respectively the accumulated flow of inputs and outputs from which the productivity ratio at the end of each phase is accounted (column 6). To shift some element in column 4 to an output measure would in effect be to mix outputs with inputs, which cannot of course yield an unambiguous aggregate of inputs. The alternative of assessing the productivity of each phase alone (rather than the accumulated results of the process up to the end of a phase) by taking the value-added to output in constant-price output measure terms (column 2) and the value-added to inputs in constant-price input terms (column 1) and dividing the former by the latter (column 3) has some significant weaknesses. First, there is a conceptual difficulty in that there is no

Table A.1 Inputs and Outputs in a Three-Phase Production Process (inputs in constant-price input measure, outputs in constant-price output measure)

	Increment Input	Increment Output	(2) +(1)	Accumul. Input	Accumul. Output	D' (5) ÷(4)
	(1)	(2)	(3)	(4)	(5)	(6)
Period t_o						
Phase 1	45,000	45,000	1.00	45,000	45,000	1.00
Phase 2	55,000	(55,000)	(1.00)	100,000	100,000	1.00
Phase 3	10,000	(10,000)	(1.00)	110,000	110,000	1.00
Period t_n Option 1						
Phase 1	35,000	70,000	2.00	35,000	70,000	2.00
Phase 2	35,000	(30,000)	(0.86)	70,000	100,000	1.43
Phase 3	10,000	(10,000)	(1.00)	80,000	110,000	1.38
Period t_n Option 2						
Phase 1	22,500	45,000	2.00	22,500	45,000	2.00
Phase 2	55,000	(55,000)	(1.00)	77,500	100,000	1.29
Phase 3	10,000	(10,000)	(1.00)	87,500	110,000	1.26

physical counterpart to output value-added. There is a physical counterpart to the constant-price output measure of irrigation water and to the constant-price output measure of wheat; but there is no physical counterpart to the constant-price output measure of wheat *net* of the irrigation water. For this reason the figures in column 2 and column 3 are bracketed in Phases 2 and 3. Second, the value-added productivity results can be misleading for the planners of a production phase as can be seen from a comparison of Period t_n Option 1 and Option 2. Value-added productivity in Phase 2 is substantially *higher* in Option 2 than Option 1 (see column 3), whereas the overall productivity in Phase 2 of Option 2 is significantly *lower* (see column 6). The planners should be guided, of course, by the overall productivity results (see column 6).

We proceed now to consider two assumptions respecting general tendencies in the national economy. These assumptions, and the important relationships they imply, suggest what may be *normally* expected but *not* what will *invariably* be the case. In this respect the relationships we are about to discuss are quite different from the relationships considered in the five steps that are invariable by definition.

Assumption 1: The Pricing Principle
There is a significant tendency for the implicit input price ratio, IP', to be the same throughout the economy. This is not, of course, to suggest that input prices do not change—they are changing all the time—but that diverse input prices *tend* to change proportionately the same. Or to put the matter otherwise, there is

a tendency for the *relative* prices of diverse inputs to remain constant. We shall call this tendency the pricing principle.

Given the operation of the pricing principle certain implications follow:

(1) The ratio of return per unit of waiting equals IP′ only when the profit rate remains constant.

Proof

If the ratio of return per unit of waiting is to equal IP′ (as the pricing principle supposes), then the ratio (t_n **over** t_o) of aggregate profits, F′, over the ratio (t_n over t_o) of inputs of waiting must equal IP′. The ratio of inputs of waiting equals K′cpim, that is, the ratio of stock of capital invested at constant price input measure.

Hence, $\dfrac{F'}{K'\text{cpim}} = IP'$

But, $K'\text{cpim} = \dfrac{K' \text{ at current prices}}{IP'}$

therefore, F′ = K′ at current prices.

This equation will hold only so long as the profit rate (whatever its level) remains constant.

(2) The wage rate ratio, W′, will equal IP′, the general input price ratio, and will everywhere be the same. For this reason W′ may sometimes be used in calculations as a first approximation of IP′.

(3) The real income rate ratio and the real wage rate ratio equals IP′/OP′ and hence correspond to D′, the overall productivity ratio. Hence, the *real* wage rate ratio within a particular enterprise will equal *not* the productivity ratio of that enterprise, but the overall productivity ratio of the economy.

(4) The relative output price ratios of products will vary inversely with their productivity ratios. That is, for any two products X and Y,

$$\frac{OP'_x}{OP'_y} = \frac{D'_y}{D'_x.}$$

Proof

Since $D'_x = \dfrac{IP'_x}{OP'_x}$ and $D'_y = \dfrac{IP'_y}{OP'_y}$

therefore, $\dfrac{D'_y}{D'_x} = \dfrac{IP'_y}{OP'_y} \times \dfrac{OP'_x}{IP'_x}$

and since $IP'_x = IP'_y$ (see pricing principle)

$$\frac{D'_y}{D'_x} = \frac{OP'_x}{OP'_y.}$$

(5) If by *comparative* output price ratio for any product X we mean OP'_x / OP', where OP' is the overall output price ratio for the economy, and if by *comparative* productivity ratio we mean D'_x / D', where D' is the overall productivity ratio for the economy, then the comparative output price of X will equal the reciprocal of its comparative productivity. That is,

$$\frac{OP'_x}{OP'} = \frac{D'}{D'_x}$$

Hence, OP'_x

$$= \frac{D'}{D'_x} \times OP'$$

$$= \frac{OP'}{D'_x / D'}$$

$$= \frac{\text{general inflation ratio}}{\text{comparative productivity ratio of X.}}$$

The pricing principle will tend to be effective throughout the economy to the extent that supply and demand are allowed to operate under competitive conditions. Let us imagine an ideal base period when diverse input prices are so in balance that there is no incentive for resources to shift from one line of production to another. If changes in real wage rates are roughly the same proportionately throughout the economy and profit rates remain constant, there will be no price incentive for labour or investment to shift to other lines of production. However, if some change in demand or supply makes it more profitable to shift resources to a particular line of production, then higher profits will lure investments and higher real wages will lure labour to make the shift. Nonetheless, the more the shift of resources is accomplished, the nearer will profit rates in the expanding line be pushed back to the standard rate and the nearer will wage rates be pushed back to prevailing rates. That is, changes in supply and demand that bring forth some diversity in IP ratios also evoke responses under competitive conditions which tend to push the wayward ratios back toward conformity.

However, if competitive conditions do not prevail, deviations from the pricing principle may be more than temporary. If the enterprise enjoys some degree of monopoly of the product market or if labour-management contracts modify competitive conditions in the labour market, deviations from the pricing principle may occur and the usual counteractive responses be prevented from appearing. Since Canada Post both enjoyed some degree of monopoly of postal services and after 1965 was increasingly affected by adversarial labour-management relations, deviations from the pricing principle in its case could perhaps be expected.

Assumption 2: Neutral Technological Development
For the economy as a whole there is neutral technological development if the relation of stock of capital invested, K, at current prices, to national product, N,

at current prices, remains substantially unchanged. Expressed in terms of ratios, neutral technological development prevails so long as K' at current prices equals N' at current prices.

Given the combination of neutral technological development and the operation of the pricing principle, certain important implications follow.

(1) The relative aggregate income shares of workers and waiters in the national product tend to remain constant.

Proof

If R is the rate of profits, then aggregate profits equal KR. If R is constant (following the pricing principle) then $R' = 1$, and
hence $(KR)' = K' = N'$.

That is, aggregate profits vary with the national product. However, if aggregate profits vary with national product, then the remainder of national product, aggregate labour income, must also vary with national product. Hence, the relative aggregate income shares of workers and waiters remain constant.

Table 3.4B displays to what extent these relative aggregate income shares approached constancy in the post-war years in Canada. It is interesting to note that whereas aggregate labour income increased in the period 1949 to 1979 over fifteen times, the share in total product remained throughout roughly the same. The maximum deviation from the average share of 67.7 percent was minus 2.7 points in 1952 and plus 2.7 points in 1971, that is, plus and minus 4 percent of the average. In this period the *real* wage rates of Canadian workers increased well over 100 percent. Deviations from average share affected real wage rates at a maximum by only 4 percent, and that only temporarily. In this context the income-share distribution appears remarkably steady.

(2) The labour productivity ratio for the economy, LD', will tend to correspond to the overall productivity ratio, D'. For this reason we may sometimes take the overall labour productivity ratio as a first approximation of the overall productivity ratio. (This does not apply, of course, to particular enterprises or industries.)

Proof

If L' is the labour input ratio and W' is the wage rate ratio, then $L'W'$ (the aggregate labour income ratio) equals N' (see (1) above). But I' times IP' equal N' (where I' and IP' represent the overall input and input price ratios respectively).

Therefore, $L'W' = I' IP'$.

But, $\qquad\qquad W' = \qquad IP'$ (see pricing principle)

therefore, $\qquad L' = I'$.

Hence, $\qquad\qquad \dfrac{O'}{L'} = \dfrac{O'}{I'}$

that is, $\qquad LD' = D'$.

It may be noted also that this approach is analogous in some respects to that of Karl Marx. (1) Marx was interested in the input-content of commodities—in his case the amount of labour embodied in commodities. (2) He was interested in making his assessment of input-content essentially in terms of replacement requirements—he called it the socially necessary labour embodied in commodities. And (3) he postulated an economic pricing principle—that the comparative prices of commodities tended to correspond to their comparative input-content, input-content being, in his case, labour-content.

However, this approach also radically differs from Marx. (1) The weakness of the Marxian approach stems from the systematic denial of the primary input of waiting. Our approach, on the other hand, recognizes this primary input and indicates how it may be assessed commensurately with labour input. (2) Marx categorically denied that real wage rates rise proportionately with general productivity. He assumes that real wages are determined in the long run by what is required to sustain workers and their families. Although he acknowledges here and there that what is recognized as being necessary to sustain workers and their families may change, his usual assumption, explicit or implicit, is that improvements in productivity all go to enhance the surplus value appropriated by the capitalist entrepreneurs. Our approach on the contrary assumes a tendency to long-run stability in comparative returns to labour and non-labour inputs and hence an equal sharing in the benefits of improvements in total-input productivity. What Marx categorically denied is accepted as the standard case. Statistics relating to the Canadian economy over the past thirty-five years (the period for which we have relatively well-developed data) demonstrate that, however appropriate the Marxian model may appear to be in a primitive capitalist economy, it has no relevance in a developed mixed economy such as we now have in Canada.

An index of what is called "total-input productivity" is presented for Canada Post (see Table 3.2 E and Figure 3.2 F) although the coverage falls short of being "total." Omitted are (a) an estimate of the primary input of waiting and (b) an estimate of the secondary input of "accommodation." Accommodation consists mainly of the service of post office buildings provided for the most part by the Department of Public Works. This is an important item of real input; but changes in the way accommodation expenses have been accounted make it inadvisable to use the figures in assessing inputs. The percentage of total expenditure attributed to accommodation was 9.0 in 1964–65, 7.4 in 1969–70, 6.3 in 1974–75, and 6.1 in 1979–80. However, provisional input assessments were made respecting (c) transportation services contracted out to other enterprises, and (d) all other goods and services purchased from other enterprises. Expenditures on these goods and services were deflated by the overall index of labour compensation per person for the total Canadian economy. Expenditures on (d) were adjusted where necessary to replace any "capital" expenditures by appropriate estimates of "current" expenditures. These deflated figures were aggregated year by year and combined with the deflated labour expenditure figures to obtain a deflated total expenditure series upon which the index of total input was based.

The use of general compensation per person indexes to assess non-labour inputs may be regarded as make-shift, to be abandoned whenever more reliable data become available—perhaps when a concerted attempt to assess non-labour inputs by industrial sectors is made. In the meanwhile, there are a number of considerations that seem to support adoption for the post office of the total-input productivity index as outlined despite its omissions and provisional nature. (1) The direct expenditure on labour inputs is relatively large and on non-labour inputs relatively small. Hence, a good estimate of labour inputs and any reasonable estimate of non-labour inputs should yield satisfactory total-input assessments. (2) The direct expenditure on labour inputs has become relatively larger and larger and on non-labour inputs relatively smaller and smaller, the former rising from 62 to 77 percent and the latter falling from 38 to 23 percent in the fifteen-year period from 1964–65 to 1979–80. In the context it would seem inadvisable to rest content with the labour productivity measure alone. (3) Even with respect to goods and services purchased by the post office from other firms, the labour-input content (paid for, of course, by the other firms) is substantial and the application of a wage-rate deflator to that part of the price seems not inappropriate. The residual expenditure providing a return to "waiting" in the case of secondary inputs is thus clearly small as a part of total postal expenditure—say, 10 to 15 percent in recent years. The application of a wage-rate deflator to this residual is of less certain accuracy, but nonetheless not without basis as we have indicated. (4) It may also be noted, taking 1979-80 as an example, that an error of 10 percent in this make-shift deflator of the non-labour expenditures of the post office would have changed the total-input productivity index by only $\pm$ 1.4 points, that is, the index would have been 67.1 $\pm$ 1.4 (1964–65 = 100). Given the 6.3 point spread between this index and the labour productivity index in that year, it seems reasonable to assume that the total-input productivity estimate, despite its provisional nature, is still the more accurate indicator of overall productive performance.

From another point of view, the use of a general wage rate index in the assessment of non-labour inputs may be regarded as something more than make-shift. In somewhat the same way that we become accustomed to assessing *real* incomes by deflating current incomes by a *general* index of prices of consumer goods and services, so we might find it useful for some purposes to assess "real" input by deflating entrepreneurs' current expenditures on inputs by a *general* index of input prices. Given the tendency for the prices of diverse inputs to converge, the overall index of labour compensation per person provides a reasonable approximation to such an index. It is true, of course, that the general Consumer Price Index may not be precisely applicable to the basket of products that this or that particular consumer buys with his or her income. A price index specially tailored for a particular consumer would be more accurate in the case of that consumer. However, current income deflated by the

Consumer Price Index represents in a *general* way the power of current income to buy units of output as compared with output-purchasing power in the base period. Similarly, a general input price index may not be precisely applicable to the basket of inputs that a particular enterprise purchases with its current expenditures. An input price index specially tailored for a particular enterprise would be more accurate for that enterprise. Nonetheless, current expenditures on inputs deflated by the overall index of labour compensation per person represents in a *general* way the power of current expenditure to buy units of input as compared with input-purchasing power in the base period. It also might be noted that, given the tendency for diverse input prices to converge, of the two general price indexes the index of compensation per person will normally be more representative of the diversity of input prices than the Consumer Price Index will be of the diversity of output prices.

What we offer here for Canada Post is therefore a hybrid index of inputs. (1) Expenditures on labour inputs are deflated by indexes specially tailored for the post office. (2) Expenditures on secondary inputs are deflated by a general compensation per person index. Deflation of secondary inputs by indexes specially tailored for the post office is possible in principle, but was not felt to be feasible for this study. For the reasons already indicated the productivity assessment based on this hybrid index of inputs is considered superior to the labour productivity calculation, which totally ignores secondary inputs.

APPENDIX B

Human Beings: Creative Agents or Conforming Objects?

B.1 Creative Agents or Conforming Objects?

A rock is a perceptual object; a human being is also a perceptual object, although a much more complex one. The rock and the human being are alike in being perceptual objects. But the human being is also radically different from the rock: it is also a conscious, thinking-acting subject, that is, it is also an agent. Hence, if to postulate agency in the rock is to indulge primitive fantasy, then to postulate no agency in the human being is to indulge modern scientific fantasy.

The renowned behaviourist B. F. Skinner argues in *Science and Human Behavior* that psychology will take a great leap forward when it casts aside the presupposition that human beings are creative agents who behave this way or that as they choose. Meteorology advanced not at all so long as it presupposed agency in the clouds. Analogously, psychology will not advance until the concept of the self as an originating agent is cast aside. "A concept of self is not essential in an analysis of behavior," he says. "The self is most commonly used as a hypothetical cause of action. So long as external variables go unnoticed or are ignored, their function is assigned to an originating agent within the organism. If we cannot show what is responsible for a man's behavior, we say that he himself is responsible for it. The precursors of physical science once followed the same practice, but the wind is no longer blown by Aeolus, nor is the rain cast down by Jupiter Pluvius."[1]

In this study we shall use the term *object* to mean "that which conforms to specific limits." Science is concerned with objects and its aim is to discover the limits to which objects conform. In these terms B. F. Skinner is saying that *if* we are to have an *exact science* of human behaviour—and Skinner commits himself to the task of developing such a science—then the human being *must* be an object, a complex object to be sure, but nonetheless an object, conforming to specifiable limits. "We cannot apply the methods of science to a subject matter which is assumed to move about capriciously."[2] Hence, the self as originating agent is out—it must be out *if* we are to have an exact science of human behaviour. If we use the term *patient* to refer to the opposite of *agent* (that is, a patient passively suffers conformity to limits), then Skinner presupposes that human beings are patients completely devoid of creative agency. The presupposition is arbitrary in one sense, but not in another: it is only on this foundation that Skinner can begin to build an exact science of human behaviour, and to that enterprise Skinner is wholeheartedly committed.

---

[1]B. F. Skinner. *Science and Human Behavior*. New York: The Free Press 1965, pp. 283–85.
[2]Skinner, *Science and Human Behavior*, p. 6.

What Skinner has cast aside, our hypothesis picks up as constituting the heart of the matter. Briefly stated our hypothesis is: (1) that human beings are inherently creative; (2) that they express their creativity in the context of reality experienced as multidimensional; and (3) that the basic problem in Canada Post has been developments that have tended to suppress human creativity, or put otherwise, that have tended to suppress human creativity except in forms that militate against the formal objectives of the organization, namely, low-cost, quick, and reliable mail service.

We experience reality as multidimensional. Within this multidimensionality we discover that we can experience reality in terms of certain dimensions only, ignoring the presence of the others. We experience reality at different levels, the levels being distinguished by their greater or lesser dimensional comprehensiveness. Arraying these levels of experienced reality from the dimensionally less comprehensive to the dimensionally more comprehensive, we shall name them: (1) the imaginal world; (2) the perceptual world; (3) the communal world; and (4) the spiritual world.

These levels of experienced reality are familiar and distinctive. We all know what it is to be lost in imagination. We all know what it is to be immersed in a world of perceptual objects mediated to us by our senses. In imagination and perception we are alone: my imagining and my perceiving are mine alone. However, we all know what it is to have this isolation broken by communication with others like ourselves. We all know, moreover, what it is to strive to reach beyond the relative "goods" of the imaginal, perceptual, and communal worlds towards the ultimate good. This striving typically takes an explicitly religious form; but it may assume a secular form as well. For example, in our own day the quest to ally ourselves with history as it moves toward an ultimately good destiny (e.g., as in committed Marxism) is a very important form of this striving.

Each succeeding level in the array is experienced as including the lower level, but as being itself dimensionally more comprehensive. Imagination is still at work in perception, although perception is dimensionally more comprehensive. Imagination and perception are still at work in communication with others, although communication is dimensionally more comprehensive. Imagination, perception, and communication are still at work in our experiencing of the ultimate good; but the latter is experienced as also dimensionally more comprehensive.

The operational significance of dimensionality may be illustrated from our experience with the sub-dimensions of space-time at the perceptual level. We may experience space-time reality in its full space-time multidimensionality, or we may experience space-time in terms of one or more of its sub-dimensions in abstraction from the others. For example, Case 1, we can experience length, setting aside all other dimensions of space time. Case 2, we can experience a plane surface, having the dimensions of length and width, setting aside all other dimensions of space-time. Case 3, we can experience a solid, having the dimensions of length, width, and depth, setting aside the remaining dimension of space-time. Case 4, we can experience a solid in motion, having the dimensions of length, width, depth, and time. Case 2 includes Case 1 in that it has a dimension of length as well as a further dimension. In a similar way Case 3 includes Case 2 and Case 4 includes Case 3. The more comprehensive *include* the less comprehensive. However, because the more comprehensive are *dimensionally* more comprehensive, the more comprehensive are *not* to be discovered by the mere extension of or extrapolation from the less comprehensive. We can extend length to infinity and we will not discover a plane surface anywhere therein. In each Case 2, 3, and 4, a new dimension is added. From the standpoint of the dimensionally less-comprehensive reality the transition to the dimensionally more-comprehensive reality is a leap. There is *something more* in the dimensionally more-comprehensive reality—but a something more that is not to be found by the most exhaustive analysis or extension of the dimensionally less-comprehensive reality. A basic characteristic of multidimensionality, therefore, is: *we cannot find evidence for the dimensionally more-comprehensive reality in the dimensionally less-comprehensive reality.*

Similarly, as we move from imaginal reality to perceptual reality, we may note that although imagination is at work in perceptual reality, there is *something more* in perceptual reality that the most exhaustive analysis or extension of imagination itself does not and cannot disclose. The transitions from the imaginal sphere to the perceptual sphere, from the perceptual sphere to the communal sphere, and from the communal sphere to the spiritual sphere are leaps. The dimensionally more-comprehensive sphere contains the dimensionally less-comprehensive sphere, but has something more as well, a something more not to be found by the most exhaustive analysis or extension of the dimensionally less-comprehensive sphere.

Our hypothesis, therefore, is that in accord with their inherent nature the primary motivation of human beings is creativity, a creativity expressed in distinctive ways at the imaginal, perceptual, communal, and spiritual levels.

B.2 Creativity at the Imaginal Level

In contrast to B. F. Skinner, another renowned psychologist, Rollo May, acknowledges the seminal importance of creativity and offers an instructive theory concerning its nature. In *The Courage to Create* he writes:

> I wish to propose a theory and to make some remarks about it, arising largely out of my contacts and discussions with artists and poets. The theory is: *Creativity is an act of encounter and is to be understood with this encounter as its center* . . . . The very fact that the creative act is . . . an encounter between two poles is what makes it hard to study. . . . In his book *Poetry and Experience* Archibald MacLeish uses the most universal terms possible for the two poles of the encounter: "Being and Non-being." He quotes a Chinese poet: "We poets struggle with Non-being to force it to yield Being. We knock upon silence for an answering music."[3]

---

[3]Rollo May. *The Courage to Create.* Toronto: Bantam Books, 1975, pp. 87, 89.

Our own hypothesis accepts this characterization of creativity as constituted in the encounter between opposing but complementary poles. For the terms "being" and "non-being," however, we substitute the terms "being-within-limits" and "being-beyond-limits." Hence we say, *creativity originates in the encounter or interplay of being-within-limits and being-beyond-limits.*

Of the two poles being-within-limits seems the easier to grasp. We have defined an object as "that which conforms to specific limits." An object, therefore, is to be characterized as being-within-limits. Human beings encounter objects as objects of consciousness; for example, as objects of imaginal consciousness or objects of perceptual consciousness. We are concerned at this point, therefore, with being-within-limits in the form of objects of imaginal consciousness, that is, the images of imagination.

The second pole, being-beyond-limits, seems more elusive. Our postulate, however, is that being-beyond-limits is as basic as being-within-limits because it is an essential dimension of all consciousness. Consciousness originates in the interplay of being-within-limits and being-beyond-limits. For example, the grasp of the image in imaginal consciousness is possible because consciousness not only enters into the limits of the image, but goes beyond the limits of the image as well. We are conscious of the image because we are conscious of its limits and we are conscious of its limits only if we are conscious of what lies on both sides of the limits, that is, only if we are conscious of both what is *within* and what is *beyond* the limits. Consciousness, consequently, arises only in the interplay of being-within-limits and being-beyond-limits.

Wittgenstein, in the preface to his *Tractatus*, makes the same point with respect to thought, "thought" meaning much the same here as what we intend by "consciousness." We cannot, he says, draw a limit to thought "for in order to be able to draw a limit to thought, we should have to find both sides of the limit thinkable (i.e. we should have to be able to think what cannot be thought)."[4] It follows that however "conformable to limits" objects of thought may be, thought itself has, and, indeed, must have, a dimension which is "beyond limits."

In consciousness of its image, we might say, imaginal consciousness both *immanates* (from Latin, "immanere" meaning "to remain within") and *transcends* (from Latin "transcendere" meaning "to climb beyond") the limits of its image. The movements of immanating and transcending in consciousness are opposed but complementary. As tongs grasp an object by the opposing but complementary movements of its arms, so consciousness grasps its object through the opposing but complementary movements of immanating and transcending the limits of its object. Being-beyond-limits is thus an essential dimension or pole of the consciousness which grasps being-within-limits.

It appears, therefore, that consciousness in its very structure is creative: it emerges in and only in the encounter of being-within-limits and being-beyond-

---

[4]Ludwig Wittgenstein. *Tractatus Logico-Philosophicus.* London: Routledge & Kegan Paul, 1961, p. 3.

limits. Consciousness itself, therefore, is the model and primary evidence for human creativity. This conclusion, that every event of consciousness is a creative event, may seem to assert too much: that which was considered rare and hence highly prized is now made common and of little account. On the contrary, we contend that the discovery of creativity in every event of consciousness serves to elevate human nature, however modest its appearance, above anything and everything merely objective.

Modern science is concerned with objects. Given the remarkable success of modern science in dealing with objects, we are tempted to conceive human nature in the image of objects. Such a conception, however, is a disastrous reduction: that which has its being in and only in the *interplay* of being-within-limits and being-beyond-limits is reduced to being-within-limits alone. This is a misconception. Science is concerned with objects, with being-within-limits; nonetheless science itself is not merely a set of objects but, rather, *consciousness* of objects and of the limits to which objects conform. As consciousness, science both immanates and transcends the limits of its objects. A science that does not acknowledge this dimension of transcendence in scientific consciousness may understand objects, but utterly fails to understand itself. Modern science becomes irrational and goes astray if, in its fascination with deciphering the limits of being-within-limits, it denies being-beyond-limits.

A consciousness that is not only conscious of its objects but conscious of its consciousness we may call a subject. The denial by B. F. Skinner of the self, which we noted, is a radical scientific reduction effectively denying the reality of consciousness and the subject. The logic of this reduction is seductive. The premise is that if anything is real, then it is an object conforming to specific limits. It follows from this premise that anything postulated for which limits cannot be specified is not real. Hence, a subject, for which constant limits cannot be specified, is thrust aside as illusory. The error here is in the premise that the only reality there is, is objective being, i.e., being-within-limits. Our hypothesis is that the being of the subject, a being constituted by the interplay of being-within-limits and being-beyond-limits, is a dimensionally richer kind of being than objective being, which is confined to being-within-limits alone. Whereas objective being passively conforms to specific limits, subjective being, in immanating and transcending the limits of objective being, is actively creative.

Consciousness is in its most unambiguously creative form at the imaginal level. At this level it is our experience that we can imagine what we will whether it be "ships and sails and sealing wax" or "cabbages and kings." In this sphere we propose what we will and it is so. It is true that our imagining is usually mixed up with what we have perceived in the perceptual world and with what we have encountered in the communal world, that is, with the history of our experience at higher levels. However, it is our experience that we can at times so detach ourselves from our higher experience that we can imagine what we have perceived or encountered, or the opposite of what we have perceived or encountered, or something that differs from both. It is to this power of the imaginal consciousness to re-create what we have perceived or encountered, or to create the opposite of what we have perceived or encountered, or to create something that differs from both that we here call attention. Indeed, the fundamental characteristic of the human being at the imaginal level is its omnipotent creativity. The human being is master of the world of objects, the images, which it alone creates and it alone enjoys. We may speak of the imaginal subject and its world as the *Brihadaranyaka Upanishad* speaks of the dreamer and his world:

> There there are no chariots, no spans, no paths; but he brings forth (from himself) chariots, spans and paths. There are no joys, no pleasures, no delights; but he brings forth (from himself) joys, pleasures and delights. There there are no tanks, no lotus-pools, no rivers; but he brings forth (from himself) tanks, lotus-pools and rivers: for he is a creator.[5]

Over the imaginal world hovers the human subject as its omnipotent creator.

B.3 Creativity at the Perceptual Level

In perceptual experience imagination is still at work; but there is something more as well, and it is this something more that distinguishes the perceptual sphere. In imaginal experience the objects, the images, are experienced as created by the subject. Whatever the subject proposes, *is*. The perceptual self, however, experiences a new kind of object—an object *not* under its direct control, an object *not* created by itself. The perceptual self, moreover, experiences *itself* as not simply a subject, but also as a complex perceptual object conforming to limits not created by itself. Perceptual objectivity imposes limitations on the coming into being of what the self proposes. As subject, the self experiences itself as having some control over itself as perceptual object. As complex perceptual object, in interplay with an environment of other perceptual objects, the self experiences itself as having some control over some other perceptual objects. However, the power of the self, as subject, to control itself as perceptual object and the power of the self, as perceptual object, to control other perceptual objects is limited. The subject in its participation in perceptual experience is a finite self; it has fallen into finitude. Hence, in perceptual experience the subject still may, and does, *propose* this and that, but the world of perceptual objects *contraposes* with limitations not created by the self. Creativity is given a new context: in the interplay of subjective proposing and objective contraposing, the self is challenged to creative encounter.

The self may respond in two ways to the limitations imposed on it by the contraposing of the perceptual sphere. First, it may treat perceptual limitations as a deficiency, as a lacking. Consequently, one seeks to overcome the deficiency, to make up the lacking, as far as one's limited powers allow. The goal

---

[5] *Hindu Scriptures*, translated and edited by R. C. Zachner. London: J. M. Dent & Sons Ltd., 1966, p. 66.

here, one might say, is to recover as nearly as possible the condition of imaginal experience where there are no limitations on the realization of whatever the subject proposes. Second, the self may treat perceptual limitations as an opportunity, as a challenge to creative encounter. Consequently, one takes up the challenge of perceptual limitations and enjoys the creative encounter. Here one is enriched by a kind of creative encounter completely denied to pure imaginal experience.

The first response implies a negative evaluation of the system of perceptual limitations: the self would be much better off without this system of limitations. The second response implies an affirmative evaluation of the system of perceptual limitations: the self is given an enriched environment where precisely because systematic contraposing is presented creativity takes place in a context of challenge.

The distinction between the two responses is important. At the level of perceptual experience are we motivated merely to overcome the deficiencies, to make up the lackings, imposed by perceptual limitations? Or are we also motivated to take up the challenge presented by the systematic contraposing of the perceptual sphere and to engage with zest in creative encounter with it? Contemporary opinion, if it recognizes creativity at all, is inclined to acknowledge its appearance in a very select few only. At the same time human beings in general are viewed as anxiously trying to satisfy wants, i.e., to make up perceptual deficiencies, and with no interest in challenges for their own sake. Our hypothesis on the contrary is that creativity is the fundamental characteristic of human beings in general and, consequently, that responding to challenge for the sake of the creative encounter itself reflects a more fundamental human motivation than does the pursuit of satisfaction of wants— "wants" being understood in this context as representing specific deficiencies or lacks.

On the face of it the affirmation of a contraposing system, the preferring of the presence of such a system to its absence, appears to be merely perverse. However, note the implications of such a system. First, it implies, as we have seen, limitation of the self. The omnipotence of the subject of imaginal experience is lost. The self has fallen into finitude. But, second, it implies a realm of purposive activity and all that goes with it: continual selection among options, choice of values, development of character, involvement rather than non-involvement, in short, a dramatic, challenging existence.

Purposive activity implies that it is necessary to do *this* and *this* in order to effect *that*. The *this* and *this* are the means, the *that* is the end. That means are necessary to effect the proposed end implies that something contraposes itself between the proposal and its direct realization. In imaginal experience to propose an end and to realize that end are one and the same thing; nothing contraposes itself between the proposing and its realization. Purposive activity implies contraposing limitations: this and this are required to overcome the obstacles to the direct realization of the end. Now both means and ends must be proposed and promoted and purposive activity is born.

Given a finitude of means, not all ends can be pursued, hence the self must continually select what ends it will pursue and what ends it will reject. Values are chosen and fostered, establishing the kinds of ends to be pursued. Character is developed, strengthening the kinds of perceptual powers which facilitate the attainment of the chosen ends. Within these boundaries one becomes interested, involved, committed. Existence assumes a dramatic, challenging form.

Hence, purposive activity and the qualities of human existence that go with it presuppose that over against our subjective proposing is a contraposing system such as that which we encounter in perceptual experience. In pure imaginal experience there is no purposive activity because no means are necessary to effect proposed ends. Because all things are possible no selection among proposed ends, no choice of values, no development of character, no persistent and consistent involvement of the self is necessary. Because all things are possible nothing has dramatic interest and existence is devoid of challenge.

Given the qualities of existence that are made possible for creative being only by the presence of a contraposing system, we might speculate that were there an infinite creative being it would invent a contraposing system and choose voluntarily to conform to its limits. However, we do not have to resort to infinite being to find such invention: finite human beings are very much given to such invention. They propose arbitrary limitations and engage passionately in purposive activity voluntarily conforming to these limitations. A prime example is games. Games have rules that arbitrarily specify the ends to be sought and arbitrarily add limitations to natural limitations with respect to the means to be used. As arbitrary as the prescription of means and ends may be, human beings everywhere are challenged by games and commit themselves to play with remarkable passion. In the interplay of proposing and contraposing that constitutes play, human beings enjoy the challenge of creative encounter. Without the contraposing provided by the game—by the arbitrary limitations imposed by the rules of the game and by the contraproposing of opponents playing according to the same arbitrary limitations—there would be no challenge. Enjoying the challenge, the committed player confirms that the system of contraposing that the game provides is *good*.

Our hypothesis, again, is that creativity is the fundamental characteristic of human beings in general and that responding to challenge for the sake of the creative encounter itself reflects a more fundamental human motivation than does the pursuit of satisfaction of wants—"wants" being understood in this context as representing specific deficiencies or lacks. The importance of challenge in motivation is partly obscured by the logical form that challenge takes. One is challenged to a purposive activity that has a means/end form. We may call these the formal means and the formal end. If we are asked what we are challenged to do, we can cite the formal end. However, if we take up the challenge for the sake of the creative encounter itself, then the end of the activity *for us* is not the formal end as such, but rather creative involvement in the activity constituting the formal means. Our end is beyond or ulterior to the formal end. It is more closely related in fact to the formal means than to the formal end. For this reason, in the case of purposive activity motivated at least in part by the challenge itself, we shall distinguish carefully the formal end or purpose from the ulterior end or purpose. What may be confusing is that in the transition from the formal purpose to the ulterior purpose there is a kind of inversion of means/ends involved: the ulterior end seeks creative encounter in the activity constituting the formal means, while in the same context, the formal end merely serves as a means to give structure to the challenging activity.

For example, in a game the rules establish the formal means and the formal end (defining what constitutes "winning"). However, the person who wants to enjoy the creative encounter of play is not so much concerned with winning as with the challenge of the activity of playing. The player plays to win, because a good play is one that contributes to winning; but the player is not as concerned to win as to play well, to have a good game, to enjoy the challenging encounter. The player is fundamentally concerned not with the formal end of the game—winning—but with the ulterior end of the game—challenging encounter.

It might be argued that the motive of enjoying creative encounter is not so much characteristic of human beings in general as a vision of what ought to be the case in the minds of idealists far removed from the humdrum reality of everyday human nature. We contend, on the contrary, that the humdrum model of human nature as driven only to make up perceptual deficiencies is an abstract, theoretical paradigm which assures investigators that they are dealing with an object which, as complex as it is, conforms to specific limits and from which, once they know these limits, they can expect no surprises. Let us suppose a seasoned senior hockey team is highly motivated to win every game and in fact wins 80 percent of the games it plays in the senior league. Suppose the team is now invited to give up the senior league and to play against school teams only. They now easily win 100 percent of their games. What effect will this have on the motivation of the team? There is surely little doubt that the motivation of the team will fall disastrously.

The illustration, of course, is absurd: apart altogether from the question of what will be good for the schools, no one in their right mind would make such a proposal to a seasoned senior team. However, proposals equally absurd have not only been made but implemented within Canada Post. Citizens with semi-professional rates of pay have been assigned absurdly simple operations and asked to repeat these operations over and over again, minute after minute, hour after hour, day after day. For example, let us describe with great care precisely what a half-minute of a postal coder's work involves. We challenge the intelligent reader to stick with the description if he or she can. Remember it is only a half-minute!

A Detailed Description of a Half Minute of a Postal Coder's Work
The coder sits at a desk, one of a suite of desks. Before the coder is an electrically powered mechanism that displays an envelope with its address code showing,

and that has a set of keys on which the coder may type the address code, i.e., a letter, a number, a letter, a number, a letter, a number. With the typing, the mechanism imprints the colour code, which is used later to activate the sorting machines. With the typing of the last number the mechanism whisks away the envelope and replaces it with another. Certain frequently used combinations of letters and numbers, e.g., the first three of certain codes, may be typed with a single key. If an envelope is to be rejected for colour coding, e.g., an envelope without address code, a reject key is pressed. Apart from the typing of code combinations and rejects, the postal coder's work consists of the following.

The coder types the envelope's address code—letter, number, letter, number, letter, number—and the envelope is replaced. The coder types the next envelope's address code—letter, number, letter, number, letter, number—and the envelope is replaced. The coder types the next envelope's address code— letter, number, letter, number, letter, number—and the envelope is replaced. The coder types the next envelope's address code—letter, number, letter, number, letter, number—and the envelope is replaced. The coder types the next envelope's address code—letter, number, letter, number, letter, number—and the envelope is replaced. The coder types the next envelope's address code— letter, number, letter, number, letter, number—and the envelope is replaced. The coder types the next envelope's address code—letter, number, letter, number, letter, number—and the envelope is replaced. The coder types the next envelope's address code—letter, number, letter, number, letter, number—and the envelope is replaced. The coder types the next envelope's address code— letter, number, letter, number, letter, number—and the envelope is replaced. The coder types the next envelope's address code—letter, number, letter, number, letter, number—and the envelope is replaced. The coder types the next envelope's address code—letter, number, letter, number, letter, number—and the envelope is replaced. The coder types the next envelope's address code— letter, number, letter, number, letter, number—and the envelope is replaced. The coder types the next envelope's address code—letter, number, letter, number, letter, number—and the envelope is replaced. The coder types the next envelope's address code—letter, number, letter, number, letter, number—and the envelope is replaced. The coder types the next envelope's address code— letter, number, letter, number, letter, number—and the envelope is replaced. The coder types the next envelope's address code—letter, number, letter, number, letter, number—and the envelope is replaced. The coder types the next envelope's address code—letter, number, letter, number, letter, number—and the envelope is replaced.

* * *

If the intelligent reader can scarcely bear to stick with a written description of what a postal coder does in one half-minute because of its emptiness of challenge, how can we expect a postal worker to repeat the operation minute after minute, hour after hour, day after day, *ad nauseam*. The electro-mechanical sortation system that Canada Post workers use is a fine example of

184

human ingenuity, of human creativity; but the roles assigned to postal workers in the sortation process are extreme examples of minimal requirement of human ingenuity and creativity, or as it also might be put, extreme examples of agency-insufficiency. Why is it that the planners of *A Blueprint for Change* who recommended the technological transformation did not assess the agency-sufficiency of prospective jobs and consider the relevance of such assessment for motivation?

Part of the answer is that the reigning paradigm for both management and labour considers motivation in the context of formal means/ends only. For management, person-hours of work are the chief formal means and output is the formal end. Efficiency involves a maximization of the formal end in conjunction with a minimization of the formal means. For labour, person-hours of effort are the formal means and wages are the formal end. To this we might add consideration of complex conditions of work and fringe benefits. Here also what we might call "contractual efficiency" involves a maximization of the formal end (wages) in conjunction with a minimization of the formal means (worker effort). Peter Taylor in "Working in the Post Office" called this "getting more for less." In fact in the later 1960s and in the 1970s the postal worker got a great deal more for a great deal less. But what neither the workers nor management anticipated or understood when it did appear was the radical drop in motivation. "More for less" turned out *not* to be a recipe for a happy workplace: and for a very good reason. The formal motive for working, namely, wages and the satisfaction of the diverse wants which wages make possible, is not as important for a happy workplace as the ulterior motive for working, namely, the challenge of creative encounter.

It is true that in the later 1970s Canada Post management offered the unions a new co-operative approach to the settlement of labour-management problems. This approach, if it had been accepted, might have led to concern by both parties with not only formal matters of pay and working conditions, but the more fundamental matter of the quality of the work life itself. In fact by the mid-1970s the unions (CUPW and LCUC) had become so adversarially minded and the struggle so bitter that the unions (especially CUPW) were in no mood to trust management. Advances made by representatives of management such as John Paré were treated as attempts by management to wring more out of the hard-pressed worker. A literary tear or two were shed by union leadership for the mind-numbing character of postal work, but these tears were not backed by any substantial interest in the "quality of work life" approaches proposed by the Department of Labour.

The inadequacy of want/satisfaction as a comprehensive theory of motivation becomes evident when it is noted that the final outcome of the process of want/satisfaction is *apathy*. If the objective of want/satisfaction is the elimination of want and if there is no satisfaction without want to be satisfied, then the elimination of want involves the elimination of satisfaction. Hence, the fulfillment of want/satisfaction is the achievement of apathy—a state where there is neither the negative experience of want nor the positive experience of satisfaction.

The apathy hypothesis appears to contradict the classical economists' description of the outcome of the process of want/satisfaction as maximizing total utility: *total* utility being maximized at the point where *marginal* utility falls to zero.

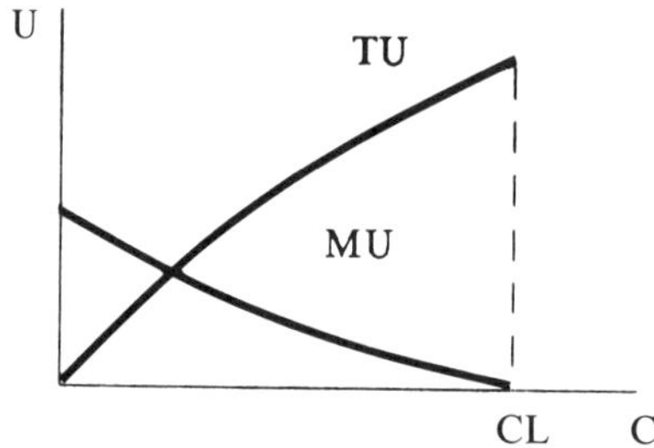

Figure B.1 Total Utility and Marginal Utility

Marginal utility (MU) represents the *increment* in total utility (TU) that accompanies an increase in the *rate* of consumption (C). If, as the rate of consumption increases, total utility increases, but at a declining rate of increase, then at the upper limit of the rate of consumption (CL), that is, at that rate of consumption where total utility stops increasing, marginal utility is zero and total utility is at its maximum (see Figure B.1). Beyond CL total utility will *not* be increased by a further increase in the rate of consumption. Economic analysis has shown that in these terms what is relevant to the determination of exchange values and motivation is not the total utility schedule, but the marginal utility schedule. The classical theory holds that motivation to increase the rate of consumption falls to zero when the *marginal* utility falls to zero; the apathy hypothesis proposes that at this point of zero motivation *total* utility is zero.

Our hypothesis, therefore, appears to contradict the classical theory. It may be shown, however, that the apathy hypothesis is merely a special case of the classical theory. This becomes possible when it is noted (1) that a given marginal utility schedule is compatible with any one of a whole family of total utility schedules and (2) that utility may be conceived in negative as well as positive terms so that positive marginal utility may be derived from a reduction in negative utility as well as from an increment in positive utility. For example let us suppose that total utility curve A (see Figure B.2) is compatible with the marginal utility curve of Figure B.1. If curves B and C are parallel to A, and hence have the same incremental values as A at all levels of C, then curves B and C are also compatible with the marginal utility curve of Figure B.1. Moreover, if we admit negative utility, then curves D, E, and F, which are also parallel to A, are also compatible with the marginal utility curve of Figure B.1. The whole family of total utility curves, A,B,C,D,E,F, and any other curves parallel to them, are compatible with the single marginal utility curve of Figure B.1.

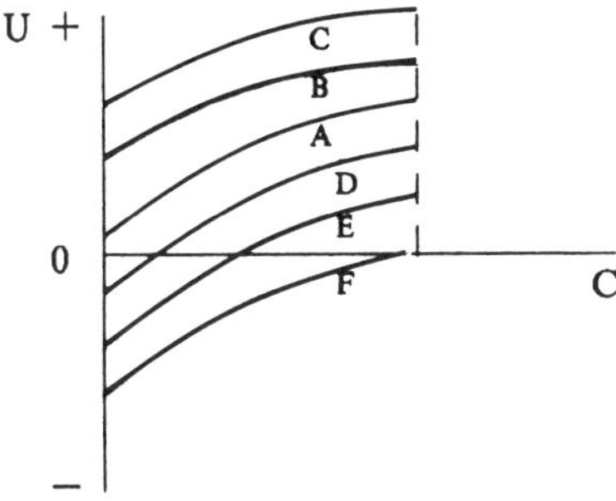

Figure B.2 Total Utility

If it were possible from data on a consumer's preferences to deduce the shape of the marginal utility curve, it would still *not* be possible to deduce from that curve which member of the family of compatible total utility curves would best describe the consumer's subjective experience. For example, would curve A or curve F better depict the subjective experience? The hypothesis of apathy recommends curve F rather than the commonly chosen curve A. Curve A begins at zero rate of consumption with zero utility and rises at the upper limit of the rate of consumption to a high, maximum positive utility. Curve F begins at zero rate of consumption with a high negative utility and rises at the upper limit of consumption to a maximum of zero utility. The hypothesis suggests that subjective experience typically corresponds more closely to curve F in that (1) at zero rate of consumption the subject experiences a high negative utility, that is, a sense of want which the subject is motivated to overcome, and (2) at the upper limit of consumption the subject no longer experiences this want and there is, therefore, no basis for continuing satisfaction of this want, that is, the subject now experiences neither negative nor positive utility. In the case of both curve A and curve F, *marginal* utility is zero at the upper limit of the rate of consumption; but only in the case of curve F is *total* utility also zero at this point. In the case of curve F, as marginal utility *falls* to zero, total utility *rises* to zero. Hence, a rate of consumption that sustains zero marginal utility produces not a state of chronic euphoria, but a state of chronic apathy.

Our conclusion, therefore, is that the ultimate end of want/satisfaction is apathy. This apathy may apply to one good, to a few goods, to many goods, or to perceptual goods in general. In practice, a chronic apathy with respect to a specific want is frequently avoided because it is not possible or convenient to satisfy more than one or two wants at the same time. As wants wait their turn for satisfaction they renew their strength, and hence satisfaction, periodically enjoyed, is other than zero. In practice also, apathy with respect to wants in general is avoided by the discovery of new wants. If in the course of time our usual list of wants is effectively satisfied, we typically find new wants. Freedom from want—in terms of our old list—frees us to discover and pursue new wants.

This then is the positive side of apathy. If we *want* a good, then we are negatively attached to the good by the suffering of want and positively attached to the good by the enjoyment of satisfaction. Apathy is freedom from want— freedom from attachment to goods. Such detachment from goods frees human beings to pursue other, potentially more-enriching challenges.

The procession of wants—the destruction of old wants and the creation of new—adds a dynamic element to human existence. However, it is clear that the dynamic does not arise from want/satisfaction itself: the final outcome of want/ satisfaction is apathy. The dynamic arises from the motivation inherent in human nature, the motivation to engage creatively with challenge. However, if on the contrary want/satisfaction were the only element in human motivation, then the greatest tragedy that could befall a human society would be an exceptional upsurge in productivity bringing in its wake affluence, the fulfillment of want/satisfaction, and the void of apathy.

Acknowledging the primacy of motivation to engage creatively with challenge, we can, nonetheless, imagine a kind of social, cultural environment where the procession of wants and the taking up of new challenges is impeded or frustrated. Let us construct the following strange model of a social, cultural environment.

(1) Through the development of science, technology based on science and industry based on technology, there is a recent, remarkable upsurge in productivity achieving a new affluence and an increasingly strong tendency to apathy. What is needed, therefore, is an acceleration in the procession of wants and a readiness to take up new kinds of challenges.

(2) The development of science, technology, and industry, which made the upsurge in productivity possible, has required human beings to engage in highly specialized bits of a highly complex productive process. For a great many persons their specialized bits of the productive process have offered adequate discretion and made substantial demands upon their creative powers. These persons we may call the *agents* of the system since in a significant sense they are the creators, sustainers, and transformers of the system. For them, therefore, their involvement in the productive process is interesting and sufficiently challenging to be a steady bulwark against apathy. On the other hand, for many, many others the specialized bits of the productive process they touch have offered minimal discretion and made minimal demands on their creative powers. These persons we may call *patients*—for they do or are expected to do whatever little bits the system requires of them. For them, therefore, their involvement in the productive process is not interesting, not challenging, and is no bulwark against apathy.

Let us suppose that in view of the high level of productivity the hours of work are cut back, but work still takes up the major part of the waking day. The problem that emerges is among the patients of the system who are now inclined to apathy, but have no antidote in the challenges of their working day. What is needed, therefore, is either (a) attention to transforming their jobs so as to ugrade radically their agency-sufficiency, or (b) the adoption by workers themselves of new challenges *outside* the formal requirements of the workday.

(3) The society encourages the development of knowledge especially as it concerns science, technology, and industry. Many workers, therefore, in their "free" time pursue learning for itself or as a means to transform themselves from patients into agents of the system. However, a prevailing presupposition of their learning is that perceptual objects persistently conform to limits and are in no respects self-originating. Social studies imitating the sciences presuppose that human beings also are "nothing but" complex perceptual objects persistently conforming to limits. In this society, therefore, the immense weight of the sciences and social sciences falls upon the learners, instructing them that they have been, are, and ever shall be "nothing but" patients. At this point many sensitive persons—like Peter Taylor—find the system in and out of the workplace completely alienating.

This model of a social, cultural environment is indeed a strange one. Our hypothesis, however, is that contemporary Western society conforms in sufficient degree to the main features of this model so that some of the consequences for the model also tend to appear in contemporary Western society.

We turn now to another question: *how* do we move out of a world of imaginal objects that have their being only *within* consciousness into a world of perceptual objects that are experienced as having their being *outside* consciousness? How does consciousness reach out to grasp what is acknowledged to be beyond it? How does consciousness leap beyond itself? The answer that we propose is that consciousness does so by a process of symbolization.

A symbol is something which is accepted as pointing beyond itself to something else. That "something else" we shall call the "symbolandum" (plural, "symbolanda"). A symbol points beyond itself to its symbolandum. Hence, a symbol has two, radically different, kinds of being: its being in itself, what we might call its primary being; and its being for another, i.e., for the symbolandum, what we might call its secondary being. In its secondary being the symbol exists in a kind of symbiosis with its symbolandum. In general the symbiosis is not dependent on likeness. The word *symbol* is derived from the Greek "sym" meaning "together" and "bollo" meaning "to throw." Both alike and unalike can be thrown together and this is the case in symbolization. A flag, for example, is very unlike the being of a nation; yet the former symbolizes the latter.

In perception, sensations that have their being *within* consciousness are accepted as pointing beyond themselves to perceptual objects that have their being *outside* conscousness. A set of sensations symbolizes a perceptual object: the set of sensations is the symbol; the perceptual object is the symbolandum. The symbiosis of symbol and symbolandum in perception is such that typically we are scarcely aware of the sensations *in here* and are fully conscious only of the object *out there*. For example, in visual perception we experience sensations *within us*, let us say of certain colour patches arrayed in a certain pattern, and are immediately conscious not so much of these sensations, but of, say, a chair *out there*. The immediate leap from sensations to chair is not dependent on likeness: a chair is quite different from a set of sensations. Nonetheless, the symbolic leap is made with such immediacy that attention typically falls on the symbolandum only.

Sensations, such as visual sensations, are objects within consciousness that are accepted as symbols of objects beyond consciousness. However, not all objects within consciousness are accepted as symbols of perceptual objects. Why from the totality of objects within consciousness does consciousness select only some to serve as symbols of perceptual reality? Purely imaginal objects conform to limits created by the subject. Our hypothesis is that consciousness selects certain objects within consciousness for symbolization because they are objects that resist conformity to limits determined by the subject. In the imaginal realm, where the subject alone is sovereign, sensations are unruly citizens.

In symbolization consciousness goes beyond the being-within-limits of the symbol. This is a possibility for consciousness since it is constituted by the interplay of being-within-limits and being-beyond-limits. However, the general capacity of consciousness to go beyond the specific being-within-limits of any object does not fully account for what happens in symbolization: consciousness indeed goes *beyond* the specific being-within-limits of the symbol, but it also goes *toward* the specific being-within-limits of the symbolandum. How shall we account for the symbiosis of a specific symbol and a specific symbolandum?

Our hypothesis is that a symbol/symbolandum connection begins with an accidental association that is reinforced and retained as a symbolic connection *if* it assists the self in coping with the challenges of the perceptual world. In this view the symbolic connection is formed and reformed by trial and error. Even though we perceive what we perceive with such apparent immediacy, there is a long history of trial and error behind every act of perception.

It follows that if perceptual existence itself were to change so that the relevance of habitual symbolic connections for coping with perceptual challenges were affected, then these habitual symbolic connections would be reformed. The process of reform would be one of trial and error, with error appearing where it did not show before. The reformed connection would have new symbols for old symbolanda or new symbolanda for old symbols. In the latter case, for example, this would mean that when we experienced a given set of sensations we would now actually perceive something different.

The hypothesis is supported by a simple experiment first performed many years ago. Spectacles devised to turn visual perception upside down were worn by volunteers. Objects on the upward side were now seen as on the downward side and objects on the downward side were now seen as on the upward side. However, after some days, and while still wearing the spectacles, the perception of the volunteers returned to normal. The pattern of sensations had been in some respects reversed, but perception, accommodating to the total context of experience, now saw an object on the upward side as on the upward side and an object on the downward side as on the downward side. We may suppose that the process through which we first learned the symbolic connections that characterize our standard perceptions is lost to memory in the dim recesses of the beginnings of our life (or, perhaps, to some extent as well in the dim recesses of the beginnings of the species).

The arbitrary aspect of the linking of symbol and symbolandum in perception has two consequences: (1) it allows error to arise in perception; and (2) it allows perception to accommodate to the total context of experience and hence to respond to novelty in the total context. The experiment just described illustrates both consequences. The spectacles at first introduced error into perception: the volunteers perceived objects where the total context of experience demonstrated they were not. The later visual experience of the volunteers illustrates the accommodation of perception: in spite of the novelty introduced into the total context, objects were now seen to be where the total context of experience indicated they were.

Symbolization involves a leap from symbol to symbolandum. The leap we have emphasized up to this point is what we might call the vertical leap since the symbolanda have belonged to a higher level of experience than the symbols. However, typically in symbolization there is a complementary horizontal leap. For example, I open the refrigerator door and see an egg—or, rather, I "see" a part of the outside surface of the shell and leap immediately to the "seeing" of a whole egg, i.e., total shell and contents. The leap from part to whole is horizontal in the sense that here the part and whole belong to the same level of experience. We shall use the terms *sign* and *signified* and speak of the process of *signification* when we wish to refer particularly to this horizontal movement. "Part of the outside surface of the shell" is accepted as a *sign* pointing beyond itself to the whole egg (the signified). We could argue that we do not "see" the whole shell, and certainly not the contents, but only *infer* the whole shell and the contents on the basis of probabilities implied by our earlier experience. But in this vein we could argue that we do not "see" anything: we only experience sensations, everything else being inferred. However, perception is this inference-like process experienced as an immediate leap to a symbolandum, a leap that is both vertical and horizontal. When I open the refrigerator door, it is true to my experience to report, "I see an egg," meaning by egg a whole egg, shell and contents.

As we have suggested, "there is a long history of trial and error behind every act of perception." It is clear that from "part of the outside surface of the shell" we could not take the horizontal leap to the whole egg if we had never seen an egg before or examined an egg, e.g., by turning it over and over and by breaking the shell to see the contents. Based on this prior experience we have developed an image of a whole egg—a concept of a whole egg—and it is this image, this concept, that is now immediately signified by the perception of part of the shell. If so, present perception is correlated with prior conception, which is itself based on prior perception. Hence, there is a complementary interplay of perception and conception and the horizontal leap of present perception is based on the long history of this interplay.

Our image of a symbolandum is broad or narrow depending on what has happened in this long history of the interplay of perception and conception. It follows that individuals who have somewhat different "long histories" may have somewhat different images of perceptual objects and, hence, when confronted with certain perceptual objects, may perceive them somewhat differently. For this reason to "seek truth from facts" does not resolve all of our problems: our conceptions affect our perception of facts. We may recall the street vendor in Kabul: by rinsing in the open sewer was the spoon sanitized (as he perceived) or contaminated (as I perceived)?

B.4 Creativity at the Communal Level

In communal experience, imaginal and perceptual factors are still at work; but there is something more as well, and it is this something more that distinguishes the communal sphere. At the perceptual level as at the imaginal level there is *one* subject only. Experience at these levels is *my* experience; I am one without a second. No other imagines with my imagination; no other perceives with my perception. As imagining subject and perceiving self I am radically alone. In communal experience, however, I encounter others like myself—selves that are not only complex perceptual objects like myself, but also subjects like myself. A radically enriched reality confronts the human being. Creativity again is given a new context: in the interplay of self and selves there are not only subjective proposing and objective contraposing, but subjective contraproposing as well. The challenge of creative encounter assumes a higher, communal form.

The dimensionally more-comprehensive reality of the communal sphere is not discovered by perception. A religious text tells us that no one has seen God at any time. We may assert likewise that no self has *perceived* another self at any time. What we perceive is a perceptual object: a self is *more* than a perceptual object, that *more* is essential to a self being a self, and that *more* is *not* perceived by an other self. B. F. Skinner in this respect, therefore, is correct: *if* we legislate that psychology is to be confined to what can be perceived, then no self is to be found within psychology.

Our encounter as selves with other selves involves a leap—a leap beyond perception to communication. Again the leap is effected by a process of symbolization. The principal process of symbolization used to effect communication is language. In language certain patterns of perceptual objects that are amenable to creation by the self (e.g., certain patterns of sounds) are used to symbolize certain aspects of consciousness. Thus selves acknowledging the same symbol/symbolandum connections are able to communicate from one to the other what is otherwise hidden within consciousness. In perception the inwardness of certain sensations is the vehicle of encounter with the outwardness of perceptual objects; in language the outwardness of certain perceptual objects is the vehicle of encounter with the inwardness of other selves. In communication the consciousness of the one self is revealed to an other and a community of consciousness is born. The monological reality of imaginal and perceptual experience is replaced by a dialogical reality.

We speculate again that adoption by a number of selves of the same symbol/ symbolandum connection might initially be accidental. Once common connections are made, however, they will tend to be repeated and continued in use precisely because they enable communication. The adoption of some language symbols by a group facilitates the creation and communication of other symbols until a vocabulary extensive enough for most purposes of communication is established.

The self may respond to the challenge of encounter with other selves in various ways. *First*, we may respond affirmatively by accepting the challenge to leap to a dimensionally enriched existence. The dialogue of community is preferred to the monologue of perceptual existence. The I-You is accepted as dimensionally richer than the I-It. The quest for mutuality is now the highest motivation of the self. If the I-You is accepted as including all selves, the community may be called a genuine non-discriminating community or a classless society. Here, as Marx envisaged, each freely contributes according to ability and receives according to need.

An apparent disadvantage of this affirmative response is that one suffers further loss of control of one's existence. In perceptual existence one loses that sovereign control characteristic of imaginal existence whereby to *propose* something is for that something to *be*. However, if the contraposing of perceptual existence is exercised through the lawful conformity to limits of perceptual objects, then we may discover these limits and in accord with these limits exercise some control over our perceptual existence. In the case of the I-You, however, both the "I" and the "You" must will the relation. If the "I" controls the "You" so that the "You" acts according to the will of the "I," then it is only the will of the "I" that is effective and there is no I-You. In the I-You, therefore, the "I" is dependent not only on its own will, but on the will, the free gift, the grace, we might say, of the "You."

If I ascribe to the will of the "You" the same creative freedom I ascribe to my own will, then I cannot expect of the "You" only "lawful conformity to limits." Here then is that "subject matter which is assumed to move about capriciously" which B. F. Skinner feared would bring his exact science of human behaviour and his hope of controlling human behaviour to nought. In the I-You the proposing of the "I" and the contraproposing of the "You" are complementary. The relation does not come into being without the participation of the will of the "I," but something more is required as well, the participation of the will of the "You." The will of the one participates in, but does not control, the I-You.

Second, therefore, we may respond negatively to the challenge of encounter with other selves rejecting the leap to a dimensionally enriched existence and refusing to recognize other selves as anything more than complex perceptual objects. As we use perceptual objects to make up the deficiencies of our perceptual existence, so we may attempt to control other selves in order to promote our own ends. We refuse to acknowledge the I-You. As Jean-Paul Sartre seems prepared to recommend, I preserve my isolated subjectivity and defend my world from the invasion of any other subject. "Hell is other people!" says Garcia in Sartre's play, *No Exit*.

However, for each and every one of us to seek our own end without acceptance of any restraint is anarchy (from the Greek "an + arko" meaning "no rule"). This is a kind of rulelessness that cannot be sustained. As Thomas Hobbes envisaged in his *Leviathan*, it is a war of all against all in which life is "solitary, poor, nasty, brutish and short."

Third, therefore, we may respond to the challenge of encounter with others by turning from anarchy to the acceptance of some form of "rule," some form of organization, in human relations. However, insofar as human beings conform to "rule," they are conforming to limits and thus assume a form analogous to that of perceptual objects. As there is no way to control perceptual objects unless they "conform to limits," so there is no way to control others in human relations unless they "conform to rule." Accordingly, in providing "conformity to rule" organization makes possible the acquisition of control which some exercise over others. Exercise of control over others tends to lead to treating these others as objects to be manipulated for one's own advantage. The control of perceptual objects or of persons as if they were objects we may call the power principle. Hence, since "conformity to rule" is provided by all organization and since this conformity makes possible an acquisition of control over others, all forms of organization are receptive to the operation of the power principle. Accordingly, organization reflects the operation of diverse principles: the principle of mutuality, for without general acceptance in some form organization breaks down; and, the power principle, because organization provides a context receptive to its operation.

Karl Marx tied the power principle to the "rule" of private property. It is because modern society accepts the private ownership of the means of production that some in society acquire control over others and exploit them to their own advantage. "In this sense," Marx says in the *Communist Manifesto*, "the theory of Communism may be summed up in the single sentence: Abolition of private property." Karl Marx was right: conformity to the "rule" of private property enables some in modern society to acquire control over others and to exploit them for their own advantage. Karl Marx was wrong: the abolition of private property does *not* produce the classless society. Abolition of private property removes "conformity to rule" of one kind, but does not remove "conformity to rule" in general. There are the organization of the Communist Party, the organization of the labour unions, the organization of the "dictatorship of the proletariat"—all of these are based on "conformity to rule" in which private property does not figure. In the historical examples of Marxist parties, unions, and states, the "conformity to rule" demanded has been very strict. In accord with these "conformities to rule" the power principle can flourish—and, indeed, has flourished.

Within an organization power may be distributed among persons in accordance with the principle of mutuality, that is, for the common good. If some are authorized to formulate the "rule" of the organization or to interpret and enforce the "rule," they thereby exercise authority or control over others within the organization. This authority or control is granted for the common good. Nonetheless, the power principle tends to drive out the principle of mutuality. Those who exercise control over others tend to use that control to treat others as objects to be manipulated for their own advantage (whether or not the interests of others are also served thereby).

The power principle is based on the appropriateness at the perceptual level of acquiring power over objects and of using this power for one's own ends. At the perceptual level there is only one self, namely, oneself. It is appropriate, therefore, to use the power that is available in the interest of that one self. If we exercise control over others in human relations, then it is our choice of action and not the choice of action of others that we must be concerned to sustain. Hence, we abstract from (that is, set aside as not relevant for our immediate purpose) the being of these others as self-determining subjects. The others are reduced in effect to perceptual objects. Since the exercise of control involves an abstraction from the being of the others as subjects, the continued exercise of control tends to produce a habitual abstraction from the being of others as subjects. In this abstract context the subject that remains is oneself: it seems appropriate therefore to promote the interests of that one self. Hence, even if the initial intention of control is to give priority to the interests of others, priority frequently tends to be conceded eventually to the interests of the controller.

The power principle operating in the communal context is thus effectively a reversion to the perceptual level. However, to revert to the perceptual level in the face of encounter with others may be offensive to one's own and others' sense of community. The use of control of others to promote one's own interests tends, therefore, to be hidden in the claim that the control is exercised in the interests of others. The claim may be pressed further by reference to an ultimate good: commitment to the ultimate good, it may be contended, involves exercise of this control. Hence, if one group of persons exercises control over other groups, the working of the power principle is camouflaged so that the ruling group is represented as ruling in the interests of all.

The dynamic interplay of the principle of mutuality and the power principle within organization is of great significance to reform. On the one hand, it helps to account for the periodic demand for reform as those who are controlled become conscious that, in accordance with the power principle, they are being used as objects by the controller. Over against this the reformers assert their being as creative subjects in community with each other. On the other hand, insofar as the reformers use organization to effect their purposes, the dynamic interplay of the principle of mutuality and the power principle within the reform organization helps to account for the sad history of reform whereby one discriminating ruling power is merely supplanted by another. Reform, therefore, needs careful scrutiny: (1) with respect to the impact of reform organization on the operation of the established organization; (2) with respect to discerning whose interests are being promoted within the reform organization as it struggles with the old organization; and (3) with respect to discerning whose interests are being promoted if and when the reform organization supplants the old organization.

Whether community is genuinely non-discriminating or is limited in one way or another by organization, community presupposes a measure of trust. For example, language, the primary medium of community, depends not only on members recognizing the same symbol/symbolandum connections, but on members intending to use these commonly understood symbols for disclosure rather than deception. In the symbolization of perception we can be deceived—at least for a time—as the account of the experimental spectacles illustrates. However, we may assume that there is no *intention* on the part of perceptual objects to deceive the perceiver. In the symbolization of communication, on the other hand, if one party in the interchange intends to use the other for its own ends, that party may seek to do so by deception as well as by disclosure and to use language accordingly. Language can create community only if among the participants there is a measure of trust that language will be used for disclosure and not for deception. Trust, in turn, depends on whether the participants as individuals and as groups are trustworthy in their habitual behaviour. If we are to be trusted, then we must be habitually trustworthy. The limits of trust establish the boundaries of community.

B.5 Creativity at the Spiritual Level

In our experience of ultimate good, imaginal, perceptual, and communal factors are still at work; but there is something more as well, and it is this something more that distinguishes the spiritual sphere. At each level of experience we are motivated to seek this, that, and the other good. We seek what we may call "goods." At the imaginal level these goods are images that command our attention. At the perceptual level these goods satisfy perceptual wants and provide contexts with opportunities for creative perceptual encounters. At the communal level these goods provide various forms of mutuality and creative encounter with others. At all levels the goods compete with each other for attention. We may prefer perceptual goods to imaginal goods because they are dimensionally richer; and, for the same reason, we may prefer communal goods to perceptual goods. Nonetheless, among these goods we find none of unconditional worth. Since we cannot have all goods simultaneously, we are continually comparing and choosing among them—continually, we are giving up this or some of this for that or some of that. Goods at the imaginal, perceptual, and communal levels of experience are relative; and whether we choose to seek this or that depends on contextual conditions. At the final level of human experience, however, something more is added: the experience of ultimate good—good with an unconditional dimension as well as conditional dimensions.

The form in which the experience of ultimate good is expressed is typically explicitly religious. In personal or communal worship expression is given to the experience of unconditional worthiness. That which is the ultimate good is experienced as worthy of worship and of unconditional commitment.

However, the experience of ultimate good may be expressed in non-religious, secular terms as well. For example, science may be transformed into an ultimate good by means of an unconditional commitment to its methodology. Science becomes scientism. Some contemporary thinkers commit themselves to modern science not simply as a useful tool for discovering the limits to which perceptual objects conform but, more comprehensively, as the key to truth and reality in general. Accordingly their commitment to scientific methodology is, in effect, unconditional. Since the commitment is *unconditional*, "that to which commitment is made" is accepted as a presupposition to be brought to all experience: all experience is interpreted in its light and not *vice versa*. Hence, B. F. Skinner, who correctly contends that "we cannot apply the methods of science to a subject matter which is assumed to move about capriciously," concludes, less convincingly, that since the self is such a subject matter it may be expunged from psychology. Like the legendary bandit Procrustes, who stretched or cut off his victims to fit his bed, Skinner cuts off all reality that does not fit scientific methodology. Similary, A. J. Ayer in *Language, Truth and Logic* proclaims a like unconditional commitment: "For we shall maintain that no statement which refers to a 'reality' transcending the limits of all possible sense-experience can possibly have any literal significance; from which it must follow that the labours of those who have striven to describe such a reality have all been devoted to the production of nonsense."[6]

An unconditional commitment of a somewhat different kind, but also secular in form, is made by contemporary Marxists. Marxists experience history as a movement toward an ultimate destiny, namely, toward community of co-operative mutuality, and, as such, as having the character of ultimate good. Accordingly, they commit themselves unconditionally to this movement as they, following Marx, comprehend it.

The ultimate good gives ultimate meaning to the existence of human beings unconditionally committed to it. The "goods" that we seek in great variety at the different levels of experience are hedged about by conditions. At the perceptual level, as we have seen, we become more and more apathetic about goods as affluence expands. Here also, depending on conditions, the challenge provided by various perceptual contexts may be much less or, indeed, may be much greater than that which individuals or classes of individuals can creatively bear. In any case, old age, sickness, and death—the three enemies of mankind as the Buddha called them—eventually claim their victim, and however sporting the play may have been, the game is finally lost. At the communal level mutuality is dependent not only on my good will, but the good will of others. Hence, community cannot be made subordinate to my will; and the community in which

---

[6]A. J. Ayer. *Language, Truth and Logic.* New York: Dover Publications, Inc., 1946, p. 34.

I have invested myself may break up leaving me also bruised and broken. If human existence is to have a stable meaning it would seem that an ultimate good is needed. By means of an unconditional commitment to an ultimate good, the meaning of human existence is sustained through the complex play of conditions that otherwise seems to render existence meaningless.

The ultimate meaning brought to human existence by unconditional commitment to an ultimate good also brings in its train extraordinary powers. These are powers that accomplish what in ordinary terms seems impossible. For example, in A.D. 622 Muhammad fled to Madina a fugitive from Mecca. Ten years later when he died, Muhammad was the master of Arabia. Twenty-five years later the followers of Muhammad were masters of the Near East from Egypt to Iran. In one generation nondescript tribesmen from the fringe of the Arabian desert, a people poor, uneducated, and of no account, suddenly exploded into history and became the political, commercial, and cultural giants of the seventh-century world. The one constant factor throughout for Muhammad and his followers was unconditional commitment to the ultimate good, that is, to the will of Allah and his Holy War.

Unconditional commitment with correlated extraordinary powers is not restricted to explicitly religious movements. Lenin was unconditionally committed to a Marxian vision of the march of history and to the class war which that entailed. At the beginning of 1917 Lenin was an outcast from his country with a small band of followers. Seven years later when he died he was the undisputed master of the largest country in the world. The one consistent factor throughout for Lenin and his followers was unconditional commitment to the ultimate good, that is, to the Marxian vision of the march of history, the class war, and the ultimate classless society.

Our experience of the ultimate good is mediated, as is our experience at all the dimensionally more-comprehensive levels, by a process of symbolization. Certain sets of objects from dimensionally less-comprehensive levels are accepted as pointing beyond themselves to something dimensionally more comprehensive. Conditional goods are accepted as pointing beyond themselves to the ultimate good. For example, words from certain writings treasured by a community are accepted as symbols pointing beyond themselves to the ultimate good. Similarly, certain practices are accepted as symbols pointing beyond themselves to the ultimate good.

We may note three important implications of the mediation of the ultimate good by symbolization. First, the symbolandum and only the symbolandum is the ultimate good. The symbols as "what they are in themselves" as distinct from "what they point to" belong to conditional experience. It is important, therefore, that a sharp distinction continue to be made between the symbols and the ultimate good itself. Second, error may enter into the mediation. The transition from symbol to symbolandum is a leap: we may leap to a symbolandum that is not the ultimate good. What is held to be the ultimate good by some may appear not to be so to others. Third, a symbol invites but never compels acceptance of its symbolandum. Hence, there is nothing in the process of symbolization of the ultimate good that compels assent.

It follows that we are free to adopt stands which undercut the reality of the ultimate good. For example, we may contend: (1) that it is an illusion; or (2) that it is whatever we unconditionally will it to be; or (3) that although it is not whatever we unconditionally will it to be, nonetheless, it unconditionally is what we assert it to be. Our hypothesis takes issue with all three of these stands.

That commitment to an ultimate good is commitment to an illusion is held by many and suspected by many more in contemporary culture. We have pointed out that an ultimate good is needed to sustain the meaning of human existence. Sigmund Freud in *The Future of an Illusion* argues that the postulation of an ultimate good is nothing but wishful thinking: the projection in imagination of what is denied by perceptual existence and the treatment of that projection as real. Freud's basic argument takes the following form. *Premise 1:* the ultimate good is not demonstrable in perceptual existence. *Premise 2:* whatever is not demonstrable in perceptual existence is not real. *Conclusion:* the ultimate good is not real. The first premise accords with our hypothesis that something from a dimensionally more-comprehensive level can be symbolized but not demonstrated from a dimensionally less-comprehensive level. The second premise is a dogmatic assertion of scientism whereby reality is cut back to fit the boundaries of science. This, as we have noted, is itself an unconditional position. We are free to conclude that this dogmatic position cuts reality far too small.

The willingness of Freud to deny himself the wished-for ultimate good suggests great moral strength. However, as a scientist Freud very deeply wished for "order" in phenomena, even the phenomena of his patients' dreams. He strove unceasingly, therefore, to find "order" in mental phenomena. Shall we treat that "order" as "nothing but" the product of wishful thinking? If we note further that this "order" was an ultimate good for Freud—that to which he committed himself unconditionally— should we not also begin to suspect that he found "order" precisely because he so deeply wished for it? We contend that neither the deep-set wishes of scientists and ordinary people for "order" nor the deep-set wishes of saints and ordinary people for "ultimate good" is "nothing but" wishful thinking. (This is not to say, of course, that there may not be mere products of wishful thinking associated with them.)

That the ultimate good is whatever we unconditionally will it to be is suggested by the diversity of definitions that have been given the ultimate good in the history of humanity and by the diversity of ways unconditional commitment has been expressed. In this view it is the unconditional commitment which *makes* "that to which commitment is given," whatever it is, the ultimate good. It is not the ultimate good which *persuades* unconditional commitment, but rather the unconditional commitment which *makes* ultimate good. This is the position adopted in essence by Jean-Paul Sartre in ascribing to the human subject an absolute creative freedom. Such a subject cannot be *limited* by any good *beyond* itself. The good and the ultimate good are, therefore, what this subject chooses and what this subject unconditionally chooses. What this does in effect is to make the reality of the imaginal sphere—where the imaginal subject is the sovereign creator of the universe—the ultimate good. However, Sartre is less successful than the mystics of India in casting off perceptual and communal experience. In the frustrations of perceptual/communal existence he is forced to acknowledge that this exaltation of the subject leaves him with an "unhappy consciousness" for which there is no relief.

That we can be creative in our response to the unconditional good accords with human experience of the ultimate good; that we can *create* the ultimate good itself by our commitment does not accord with our experience. The extraordinary power that flows from unconditional commitment to the ultimate good depends on faith in the *priority* of the ultimate good. The power is experienced as flowing *from* the ultimate good that has persuaded us. If Sartre persuades us to the contrary, that the human subject has priority, then the whole collapses and the power ceases to flow. We cannot translate ourselves into gods, suffer frustration in the perceptual/communal world in our self-ordained divine roles, and continue indefinitely to take ourselves and the reality we postulate seriously.

There are many in our contemporary culture who claim that commitment to an ultimate good is an illusion. There are some, but perhaps not so many, who claim that there is ultimate good, but that it is whatever we unconditionally choose to make it. There are many, many more who make a third claim: although they emphatically deny that they have created the ultimate good by their commitment, nonetheless, they claim unconditionally that the ultimate good is what they assert it to be. The claim is that they know inerrably what the ultimate good is and how unconditional commitment to it is to be expressed. This stance flourishes in the dogmatically orthodox wings of both religious and secular groups.

The error here is analogous to the error a scientist would be inviting if he or she claimed unconditionally that the nature of the perceptual world is exactly as he or she conceives it to be. The mature modern scientist, on the contrary, is able to consider the possibility of future conceptual changes: (1) without losing confidence that there is a perceptual reality out there to be investigated; (2) without being so carried away by the significance of conceptualization that he or she claims that the perceptual world is whatever the scientists agree that it is; and (3) without insisting that any deviation from the concept currently asserted is inevitably a distortion of the truth. The mature scientist has sufficient faith in and respect for the perceptually objective world that he or she refuses to fall into any of these ways of derogating its reality.

Symbolization combines with its vertical leap between dimensions a horizontal leap within dimensions. The horizontal leap is from part to whole: we accept the part as standing for the whole. As we pointed out, we accept our perception of part of the outer surface of the shell of an egg as standing for the *whole* egg, shell and contents. We may think of the "filling out of the whole" as taking place with respect to both the symbol and the symbolandum. In any case the symbolandum as accepted is the "filled out whole." The "whole" to which we leap is related to our *concept* of the whole—the concept in turn being related to prior perception. Hence, perception and conception are complementary: changes in the one require correlated changes in the other. Behind every immediate perception, therefore, stands the long history of the interplay of perceiving and conceiving through which they have shaped each other. The danger of declaring at any point that the conception is now identical with the perceptual object is that the process of refining and correcting perception comes to an end. Hence, the claim to inerrancy, if incorrect in any respect, is tantamount to consigning oneself to incorrigible error. Conceptualization, like symbolization as a whole, involves a leap that so long as it is prone to error is open to correction. It is important, therefore, to stand firmly against a final identification of concept and object conceived.

Similarly, at the level of the ultimate good, the claim to an inerrant conception of the ultimate good, if incorrect in any respect, is tantamount to a self-imposed consignment to incorrigible error. It is important, therefore, to stand firmly against a final identification of *conception* of the ultimate good and the *ultimate good* itself.

It might be contended that unconditional commitment to the ultimate good is too exalted a matter to be relevant to the operation of the post office. The matter is indeed exalted in that a dimension is involved that is not to be found in the perceptual/communal sphere itself. However, the dimensionally more-comprehensive level includes the dimensionally less-comprehensive levels. Consequently, whereas events in the perceptual/communal sphere may have no impact whatsoever on unconditional commitment, unconditional commitment may have a very significant impact on events in the perceptual/communal sphere. As we noted, unconditional commitment brings in its train extraordinary powers. These powers may be exercised in the perceptual/communal sphere without being controllable within this sphere. This constitutes the promise or the threat of unconditional commitment. When concern focuses on the perceptual/communal sphere, it is of crucial importance whether the prevailing unconditional commitments tend to have a favourable or unfavourable effect on this sphere. In the case of the post office in its time of troubles what we find is a definite withering away of one kind of unconditional commitment, a commitment with a favourable impact on postal operations (what we termed, following Max Weber, the Protestant ethic), and the emergence of two other kinds of unconditional commitment, the Marxian ethic and the Québécois ethic, with unfavourable impacts on current postal operations.